Equilibration,
Mind,
and
Brain

EQUILIBRATION, MIND, AND BRAIN

Toward an Integrated Psychology

E. J. PARKINS

PRAEGER

New York
Westport, Connecticut
London

Library of Congress Cataloging-in-Publication Data

Parkins, E. J.
Equilibration, mind, and brain : toward an integrated psychology / by E.J. Parkins.
p. cm.
Includes bibliographical references.
ISBN 0-275-93609-0
1. Cognition. 2. Equilibration (Cognition) 3. Neuropsychology. 4. Psychology, Pathological. I. Title.
BF311.P31365 1990
153—dc20 90-32179

Library of Congress Catalog Card Number: 90-32179
ISBN: 0-275-93609-0

First published in 1990

Praeger Publishers, One Madison Avenue, New York, NY 10010
An imprint of Greenwood Publishing Group, Inc.

Printed in the United States of America

∞

The paper used in this book complies with the Permanent Paper Standard issued by the National Information Standards Organization (Z39.48–1984).

10 9 8 7 6 5 4 3 2 1

To the giver of the seed,

with thanks,

is dedicated the fruit

Contents

Figures

Preface

In 1976, while on a post-graduate course at Oxford University, I had a brief encounter with some of the ideas of Piaget. His general ideas on cognitive development seemed to suggest a relationship with neurological development, especially in view of the importance he placed on equilibration. Furthermore, as I had a background in engineering and a knowledge of control processes, I considered that equilibration applied meaningfully to cognition should be described in part in terms of information processing.

This volume is the result of my attempt to address these two points. In the pursuit of a logical and meaningful description, the work soon grew in complexity as it led more widely into various mind/brain-related disciplines and more deeply within each discipline. I hope that in the effort to develop an integrated multidisciplinary description that would be both meaningful and intellgible at a multidisciplinary level, there has not been a detrimental sacrifice of depth. Hopefully, the result is a step toward an integrated psychology.

I would like to express my thanks to those who have helped me in various ways: colleagues for proofreading; Mr. P. Pumphrey and Mr. R. Holden for comments on parts of the work; Mrs. M. Turner for Russian translation; and my parents for being just that. I would like to express thanks to my wife for French translation and typing, and my deepest gratitude for her share in the material sacrifice, for her temporal sacrifice, and, uniquely, for her belief.

Equilibration, Mind, and Brain

1

Introduction

EQUILIBRATION, MIND, AND BRAIN

The cognitive functioning of the human mind as well as its development can both be considered most usefully in terms of biological principles. At the most fundamental biological level, the brain functions as a regulator of basic homeostatic or equilibratory processes. It therefore follows that cognitive functioning can be considered most usefully in terms of the principle of equilibration. As a whole, the neuropsychological system of brain/mind can then be described as one that facilitates survival by maintaining a physiological and psychologically mediated dynamic equilibrium within its environment. In order to do this there are two functions that it must fulfil: first, it must be able to represent and process information about the environment, and second, it must be able to control or modify behavior on the basis of that information processing.

In Part One of this work, the concept of equilibration is considered and elaborated in terms of the representation and processing of information and the control process in order to generate an equilibration model of the mind. This elaboration is carried out systematically on the basis of relevant ideas from psychology, general information-processing theories, cybernetics, mathematical logic, and philosophy. The characteristics of different forms of representation and processing of information are considered in relation to the information requirements for cognitive control. Then, an equilibration model is developed from an innate sub-system to a learning-based control hierarchy that additionally involves, first, a naturomorphic cognitive sub-system, and second, an abstract cognitive sub-system. The elaboration proceeds systematically from a behaviorist description at the learning-based level of stimulus, response, and feedback, to a more complex level that additionally incorporates cognitive concepts. This hierarchical arrangement and the information-representation and -processing characteristics of these two additional cognitive sub-systems are such that the cognitive characteristics of the system as a whole, in a "developmental" sense, correspond to those observed in human cognitive development.

The biological nature of the concept of equilibration clearly implies an integrated relationship between cognitive and neurological development. In Part Two of this work, information concerning the structure, development, and functioning of the brain is considered and then related to the equilibration model of the mind. The relationship is established by correspondence in terms of information representation and processing, and control characteristics. Together, the first two parts of the work present systematically related descriptions of the functioning and development of the mind and brain in terms of a single functional principle: equilibration.

In Part Three of the work, various psychological processes and various aspects of psychological development are considered. First, several current issues in cognitive psychology are characterized as far as is possible in terms of the representation of information and the process of control, and are then related to the system characteristics of the equilibration model. These issues include: consciousness and conscious control; unconsciousness and unconscious control; motivation and emotion; selective attention; imagination and thought; problem solving, induction, and intuition; dreaming; planning; sub-programming; and skill acquisition. Second, information representation and processing in psychological ontogeny are briefly reviewed and then related to development in neurology. On the basis of correspondence between the equilibration model of the mind, the neurological description, and the information from developmental psychology, an integrated description of the development of mind/brain is then presented. Finally, mental health, and factors affecting it, are considered in relation to this integrated description.

In Part Four of the work, a number of "mental illnesses" or disorders of mind/brain are characterized as far as is possible in terms of their information, representation, processing, and control characteristics, and in terms of their neurological characteristics. They are then interpreted in terms of the equilibration model, the neurological description, and the integrated description of the development of mind/brain. Schizophrenia, depression, epilepsy, and Parkinsonian disorders are each considered individually and in relation to one another. Various points are then made concerning the treatment of such disorders.

TOWARD AN INTEGRATED PSYCHOLOGY THROUGH INDUCTIVE EXPLANATION

According to Popper (1959), the primary function of scientific law is prediction. A theory is tested by being used to make a prediction of an observable event: If the event occurs, then the theory is confirmed or corroborated; if the predicted event fails to occur, then the theory is disconfirmed or falsified. However, it has been pointed out that although prediction is important, often what is wanted is not merely prediction but explanation as well (Holland et al., 1986). The dominant view of explanation in philosophy of science is that explanation is essentially a deductive relation (Hempel, 1965). Such deductive explanation necessarily fails to go beyond the information given. Another view of explanation, and one that may be more significant, is that of inductive explanation (Holland et al., 1986). Typically, a theory that explains by induction is one that unifies broad classes of facts. Similarly, it has been suggested that within psychology there may be a need to allow for scientific constructs that are tied, not to a single measure, but to a network of observations that jointly support the construct concerned (Williams et al., 1988).

On the basis of case studies from the history of science, it has been argued by Thagard (1978) that the two main criteria for assessing the worth of competing theories are consilience and simplicity. The principal criterion is consilience: the ability to unify many different classes of facts. The other criterion is simplicity: One theory will be simpler in that it will require fewer special assumptions than its competitors. Elsewhere, it has been suggested in a similar vein that such theories should provide maximum systematicity with minimum assumptions (Pylyshyn, 1984).

Psychology as a whole may be considered to be composed of various component disciplines: for example, behaviorist, cognitive, developmental, neuropsychological, and abnormal. Within these different component disciplines, theories are judged in terms of the selected facts, the interconnecting logic of the theory, and the consistency of these in relation to other established facts within that field. Consistency at these two levels is often considered to be adequate for credibility. However, the different component disciplines of psychology are parts of the whole, so there should also be a systematic interrelationship between the component disciplines, and between the facts and the theories or interpretations within them: The requirement of consistency must logically be extended to a consistency across component disciplines.

The inductive explanation developed in this work integrates observations and theories from a broad range of psychological disciplines including behaviorist, cognitive, developmental, neuropsychological, and abnormal psychology. Furthermore, these are integrated meaningfully and with maximum systematicity; that is, systematically in terms of a single but most fundamental functional principle: equilibration. Finally, I suggest that this work constitutes a significant step toward the development of a relatively detailed integrated psychology.

ONE

AN EQUILIBRATION MODEL OF THE MIND

2

Equilibration

> The point is simply that the functions and the requirements of animate systems include the problem of survival, and that this problem requires a regulatory system of considerable complexity, one in which considerable cognitive power is required.
>
> (Norman, 1981, 274–75)

The cognitive functioning of the human mind, and its development, can most usefully be considered in terms of biological principles (Norman, 1981; Richardson & Brynner, 1984). At the most fundamental biological level, the brain can be regarded as an organ that functions as an elaborate regulator or controller of basic homeostatic processes. It therefore follows that cognitive functioning can most usefully be considered in terms of the principle of homeostasis, or *equilibration* (Norman, 1981; Piaget, 1967, 1975; Richardson & Brynner, 1984). As a whole, the neuropsychological system of brain/mind can be described as one that facilitates survival by maintaining a physiological and psychologically mediated dynamic equilibrium within its environment (Piaget, 1967, 1975; Sayre, 1976; Young, 1964). In order to do this there are two functions that it must fulfil: First, it must be able to represent and process information about the environment, and second, it must be able to control or modify behavior on the basis of the results of the information processing. Seen from this point of view, cognition is essentially the *representation and processing of information* part of an information-driven control mechanism that facilitates adaptive behavior during interaction with the environment (Dretske, 1986; Parkins, 1988; Sternberg, 1984).

PIAGET ON EQUILIBRATION: A BRIEF REVIEW

Piaget was probably the most prolific wrtier on the subject of equilibration (Piaget, 1936, 1958, 1967, 1974, 1975, 1977a). In fact, equilibration is regarded by some as the most fundamental concept in his genetic epistemological theory (Boden, 1982; Voneche & Bovet, 1982). However, it is also regarded as the most controversial concept as well as the one most insufficiently considered (Voneche & Bovet, 1982). Psychologists and philosophers alike have expressed dissatisfaction with the concept, and it has been described as the weakest link in his theory (Boden, 1982; Garfield, 1983; Schvaneveldt, 1980). In view of the controversy, and the fact that equilibration is a concept central to this work, the relevant publications of Piaget will be briefly reviewed before I develop some of the issues further.

Piaget's comments on equilibration extend over at least 40 years. It is from his major publications on the this subject and from a number of short specific articles that the material for this review has been drawn (Piaget, 1936, 1947, 1958, 1967, 1974, 1975, 1977a). From this material it is evident that *equilibration* is used in two ways: (1) to describe the role of cognition; and (2) to describe the process that governs cognitive development. These two usages are quite different, and yet the processes to which they refer are necessarily related.

Equilibration as a Cognitive Process That Is an Extension of Organic Equilibration

Piaget suggests that cognitive processes are an extension of organic autoregulation. This extension may be seen through the continuity from the anatomical and morphological connections to the system of reflexes, then to the recombination of habits, in turn to sensorimotor intelligence, and eventually to verbal or cognitive intelligence. The self-regulating mechanisms concerned with the interaction of organism and environment are seen to be important at every level, and Piaget regards even logico-mathematical operations as facilitating such regulation (Gallagher, 1977). Thus, from this perspective, Piaget argues that what is sought at every level, including cognition, is equilibration within the organism in relation to the environment, and that knowledge is of value primarily in terms of its contribution to adaptive success.

Equilibration as a Cognitive Process That Governs Cognitive Development

Piaget argues that cognitive processes in themselves reflect the autoregulatory mechanisms that are evident at the organic level. His idea is that cognition itself is subject to the principles of self-regulation. At the cognitive level, this process of equilibration manifests as a need for coherence: Most basically, a coherence is required between subject and object or between the subject's schemata and the external stimulus information (Piaget, 1974, 1977a). Thus, for Piaget, the schema in cognition is not just a simple copy of reality but rather is subject to continual evolution, and this continual evolution is to be explained in terms of the principles of self-regulation (Piaget, 1967, 1975). Moreover, Piaget regards lack of cognitive equilibrium (the presence of cognitive "error") as the driving force for cognitive development (Piaget, 1975). As the cognitive structures are equilibrated or corrected for error by active compensations, there is a resultant progressive construction of the schema (Piaget, 1967). From this viewpoint, the two processes of progressive equilibration and progressive construction are inseparable.

"Degrees" of Cognitive Equilibrium. Piaget considered that equilibration was initially based on simple probability but then went on to attain logical necessity. His view on this matter is summarized as follows: "Piaget likes to draw the parallel between probability laws of equilibration and the transition from unpredictable or less predictable and ultimately logically necessary responses of strict implication" (Gallagher, 1977, 26). In relation to this idea, Piaget considered initial equilibratory compensations to be of a coarse nature but eventually to become finer and finally to result in exact reversibility or equilibrium in logico-mathematical operations (Piaget, 1958). Evidently, Piaget envisaged a development of equilibration that initially involves probabilistic determination of coarse compensations and eventually involves certain determination of fine compensations.

Stable or Complete Equilibrium within Equilibration. Piaget's comments regarding the development of cognitive equilibration make it quite clear that he regarded the most highly stabilized or complete equilibration to be found only at the level of logico-mathematical operations (Piaget, 1958, 1967). Moreover, Gallagher (1977) infers from Piaget's work that logical stability is the perfect regulator.

The Primary Function of the Cognitive Process

Although Piaget uses equilibration in the two aforementioned ways, he makes it quite clear that the essential or primary function of the cognitive process, including logico-mathematical operations, is a biological one; that is, to facilitate equilibrium between the organism and the external environment by setting up a system of control (Piaget, 1958, 1967, 1975). In order to facilitate this there must also be correspondence between cognitive schema and the environment, and this requires equilibration within cognitive development. Thus, equilibration within cognition subserves cognition as an extension of organic equilibration. More recently, from the cognitive science perspective, a similar view has been expressed by Norman (1981):

> The point is simply that the functions and the requirements of animate systems include the problem of survival, and that this problem requires a regulatory system of considerable complexity, one in which considerable cognitive power is required. And so, *the cognitive system is apt to be the servant of the regulatory system, not the other way round.* (pp. 274–75, emphasis added)

DEVELOPMENT OF PIAGET'S CONCEPT OF EQUILIBRATION

In a detailed critique of Piaget's account of equilibration, Boden (1982) inquired whether there are other ideas that address the problem more satisfactorily and, if so, whether such ideas are so consonant with Piaget's approach that they may be seen as filling out his own account of equilibration. According to Voneche and Bovet (1982), Piaget strongly believed that developments in systems theory and cybernetics were relevant to an understanding of a growing, self-regulating adaptive system. Similarly, Boden (1982) considered it reasonable to use cybernetic or information-processing ideas to clarify and, where necessary, elaborate Piaget's views on equilibration. One objective in this work will therefore be to develop the concept of equilibration in terms of the representation and processing of information and the process of control, in order to generate an equilibration model of the mind.

The biological nature of the concept of equilibration clearly implies an integrated relationship between cognitive and neurological development. As Piaget was fully aware, this implied the need for an interdisciplinary development in psychology (Boden, 1983). A further objective of this work will therefore be to relate the developmental model of the mind to the development of the structure and functioning of the brain. It should be possible to establish this relationship on the basis of the characteristics required of the representation and processing of information in homeostatic control. The establishment of such a relationship in terms of the unifying functional principle of equilibration should in turn generate a meaningfully integrated model of mind/brain.

3

Representation and Processing of Information

BASIC REQUIREMENTS FOR THE REPRESENTATION AND PROCESSING OF INFORMATION

In order to process information about the environment, the mind/brain must first have access to an internal representation of it. This internal representation, which is "re-presented" from within memory, may be a regeneration of the neural electrical activity correspondent to that produced by the original stimulus from which the memory was formed (Pribram, 1971). At a most rudimentary level, the representation, in its re-presented form, should have a similar structural organization to the aspect of the environment that it represents (Ashby, 1956a). Arguments have been put forward against the notion of psychoneural isomorphism (Sperry, 1952)—the concept that neural representations resemble in form the corresponding external objects. However, such arguments can only validly be applied to the form of the storage of the information within memory. In fact, the form of the storage of information within memory, from which the representation is evoked within the brain, need not itself be structurally similar to the original percept; rather, what is represented from the memory is what needs to have a similar structural organization.

The environment exists in a "continuous" form and as a whole, within which the four dimensions of space-time are merely implicit (Bohm, 1980; Sloman, 1971); only as a secondary development out of this whole do space and time become explicitly differentiated. Similarly, the environment is manifest through amodal or polymodal energy, and so it should be perceived through all the senses (visual, auditory, etc.) organized together, rather than one sense at a time (Powers, 1974; Sloman, 1971). The primary level of representation should reflect these continuous or holistic characteristics.

To represent the environment in terms of its variable nature, the primary-level representation must allow one structure to develop out of another by means of continual metamorphosis (Bohm, 1980). In particular, it should allow for the spontaneous internal evolution of features or patterns in accordance with their environmental occurrence (Mackay, 1956a, 1958).

In order to facilitate processing of information concerning the organism and environment in terms of their interaction, the representation should embody the changing information from the external world and the corresponding changing information concerning the organism's response, including its internal conditions (Arbib, 1972; Pribram, 1971). This will provide an indication of whether the organism's actions are beneficial or detrimental to itself in terms of equilibration.

The facilities for learning and for learning-based control should develop together. This is necessarily true, for without learning there is no basis for additional control above the innate level, and similarly, without the facility for additional control, the learning (recorded experience) cannot be applied to action. At a rudimentary level, the cognitive process associated with learned behavior should therefore be intimately linked with the sensory and motor functions that are involved in obtaining information from the environment and in the expression of action on the environment. The intimate relation between sensory and motor processes is explicit in the psychological concepts of ideomotor action (Dunlap, 1914), enactive representation (Bruner, 1964, 1973), and sensorimotor intelligence (Piaget, 1936, 1947). From the perspective of developmental psychology, these sensorimotor processes are not only inseparable from mental processes but actually provide a foundation for them (Bruner, 1964, 1973; Piaget 1936, 1947).

On the basis of the recorded experience, the organism should be able to make anticipatory responses—responses that take into account the anticipated consequences (Bandura, 1977). First of all, this requires the recognition of a stimulus as one that matches a recorded perception, which in turn notionally requires that the present perception (stimulus-generated neural electrical activity) be compared with the neural representation (regenerated neural electrical activity) of past perceptions by superimposition (Lashley, 1954; Uttley, 1956c). During the recognition process the organism must be able to recognize situations that merely resemble or are "roughly the same" as those of the past (Raaheim, 1965). This detection of a rough sameness between two or more experiences that are perceived and recorded whole requires the detection of common features or patterns (Raaheim, 1965). Once the stimulus has been recognized, it must then be evaluated further on the basis of relevant past experience. The stimulus must, therefore, somehow evoke all the relevant associated past experience from memory. For this to be possible, the neural representations must be stored in an associative manner. This requires temporal contiguity (in a spatial sense) between associated items (Postman, 1968); that is, it requires a spatially atemporal form of storage (a spatially atemporal form of storage is one in which the temporal values are not indicated by spatial position; it is a form that would, coincidentally, provide an undifferentiated space-time representation). Further evaluation should then take into account the probable consequences of the relevant responses available and reveal the action or sequence of actions most likely to produce the most beneficial outcome in the given stimulus situation. As the determined action must then be applied to the situation in a manner that anticipates the consequences, the primary-level representational system must also facilitate temporal induction.

FORMS OF INFORMATION REPRESENTATION AND PROCESSING

Information may be represented in different forms, and within fundamentally different representational forms information will be organized and processed in fundamentally different ways (Bobrow, 1975; Kosslyn & Pomerantz, 1977; Paivio, 1977). Once information from the environment has been transformed during storage into a particular representational form, that form will therefore determine the manner in which the external world can be evaluated, the basic kind of knowledge that can subsequently be derived, and the kind of action that can be taken on the basis thereof (De Bono, 1969; Mackay, 1949).

Different representational forms may be best suited to performing different functions (Bobrow, 1975; Klahr & Wallace, 1976; Waterman & Hayes-Roth, 1978a). However, by utilizing more than one form of representation, it may be possible to combine the advantages of the different representational forms. Thus, for maximum efficiency, the cognitive system as a whole would utilize more than one form of representation and processing (Bobrow, 1975; Sternberg, 1983). The different forms of representation and processing that are used should have different powers of resolution or abstraction (Klahr & Wallace, 1976; Waterman & Hayes-Roth, 1978a; Zucker, 1978).

On the basis of empirical data, it would appear that, most simply, there are two classes or representational form (Bobrow & Norman, 1975; Hunt, 1973; Kosslyn, 1975). One class is characterized by a relatively lower discriminatory power and contains the representational forms referred to as imagistic, analogical, holistic, or parallel-distributed. The other class is characterized by a relatively higher discriminatory power and contains the representational forms referred to as abstract, digital, logical (deductive), analytical, or in-series. These two classes of representational forms will in future be referred to respectively as naturomorphic and abstract.

A naturomorphic representation is, essentially, one that has a perceptible form that in itself directly communicates the perceptual characteristics of the thing that it represents; for example, the thing *apple* may in some respects be externally represented in a naturomorphic manner by a picture or colored plastic model of an apple. Ideally, a naturomorphic representation should represent the thing in every respect, as would be made possible in an experiential sense by a regeneration of neural electrical activity. A neurally generated naturomorphic representation could be a reevocation of the total neural excitation correspondent with that produced in the brain during the original perception of the referent. Cognitively, this representation could be imagistic and have analog characteristics without necessarily assuming that there are underlying analog synaptic characteristics (Kosslyn, 1981; Shephard, 1984).

In contrast, an abstract representation is of an entirely arbitrary form in that it does not necessarily have a structure that corresponds in any respect to the thing that it represents—it is nonisomorphic (Sloman 1971). For example, the thing *apple* may be abstractly represented by the printed word *Apple* or by a letter *x*, neither of which are, in their perceptible form, morphologially characteristic of the thing *apple*.

The information-representation and -processing characteristics of these two classes of representational form, naturomorphic and abstract, need to be considered in more detail in relation to the requirements of primary representation. Within the naturomorphic class, imagistic, analogical, and parallel-distributed forms of information representation and processing will each be considered, while within the abstract class, formal language, formal logic, mathematical logic, and, where relevant, digital information-processing techniques, will be considered.

NATUROMORPHIC CLASS OF INFORMATION REPRESENTATION AND PROCESSING (IMAGISTIC, ANALOGICAL, IN-PARALLEL)

Imagistic Representation and Processing

Within the mind/brain, representation of the environment may be in the form of an image (Bruner, 1964; Piaget & Inhelder, 1971; Pribram, 1971). A neural image may be considered a representation that has initially been formed directly from sensory information during the perceptual process (Bugelski, 1970; Neisser, 1972). Concerning its form, an image is thought to have a relational likeness or similar structural organization to the environmental percept that it represents or imitates (Dretske, 1986; Kosslyn, 1980; Paivio, 1986). The relational likeness may be such that the image depicts not only whole organizations but also, implicitly, the relationship between parts within the whole (Herriott, 1974; Horowitz, 1975). Images in themselves directly represent what they "mean."

Neural images may be formed from information obtained through any sensory modality, and so they may be visual, auditory, or somatosensory (including motor actions). Moreover, they may be polymodal or amodal, as they may be formed from information from more than one modality. Neural images may simultaneously represent information from both the external and internal environment. For temporally changing conditions, the images may consequently provide a representation of the changes in the external environment, the corresponding changes in the internal environment, and the relationship between them; that is, the dynamic interactional relationship between the organism and its environment (Horowitz, 1975; Paivio, 1975).

Images such as these could provide a record of experiences that could be used by simple comparison to evaluate a present experience and facilitate anticipatory response (Inhelder, 1965). However, it has been theorized that the stored images may not simply be a collection of numerous discrete images or image sequences

(G. Allport, 1924). Such distinct and context-specific images would inevitably lead to strictly stereotyped responses that would subsequently only be applicable to strictly identical situations. Rather, it is thought that through superimposition there may be a cumulative influence of a number of images or image sequences such that from within a given class of images there may emerge the most salient features of that class (G. Allport, 1924). Processing a number of images in the manner proposed (a spatially atemporal form of storage/processing) would allow for the emergence of common patterns. The emergence of the most characteristic pattern from a number of images within a given class of images may be regarded as a generalization process, and a generalized image so derived could be applicable to a range of nonidentical but similar situations.

Images are thought to facilitate resemblance detection, associative memory, and speed of thought (Bower, 1972; Paivio, 1969; Yukawa, 1973). They are thought to be involved in "intuitive" thought, creative thought, discovery, and problem solving (Beveridge & Parkins, 1987; Kaufman, 1984; Yukawa, 1973).

There are a number of characteristics of imagistic representation and processing that for some purposes may be considered disadvantageous. First, imagistic processing would appear to suffer from a lack of fine discrimination, as a result of which it does not facilitate distinction between images that are roughly the same but finely not the same (Arieti, 1966). Second, although an image may implicitly represent a large amount of information simultaneously in a holistic manner (Hilgard & Bower, 1975; Paivio, 1975), that information cannot be apprehended simultaneously or as a whole in detail; it can only be apprehended in detail if the information is represented or analyzed bit by bit in a sequential, logical manner (Matte Blanco, 1975; Pribram, 1971). Likewise, the determination of the interactional relationship between pairs of related items requires the sequential or logical analysis of the "whole" (Hamlyn, 1970; Piaget, 1927).

Imagistic representation and processing of information is considered to correspond to analogical processing (Cooper & Shephard, 1973; Paivio, 1974), and to simultaneous or parallel processing (Hilgard & Bower, 1975; Horowitz, 1972a, 1972b; Paivio, 1975).

Analogical Representation and Processing

According to William James (1890), the faculty of noting resemblances or of perceiving analogies is one of the ultimate foundation pillars of intellectual life. This view of analogical reasoning as a centrally important part of human intelligence has been reiterated over recent years (Goldman, 1986; Holyoak, 1984; Sternberg, 1983), and the development of a theory of analogical thinking is regarded as a major focus of cognitive science (Holyoak, 1984).

An important issue within the study of analogical reasoning concerns analogical representation within memory, and in particular, the structural properties of analogical representations (Dawis & Siojo, 1972; Kintsch, 1974). A definitive feature of analogical representation is the structural correspondence between the representation of a referent and the referent that is so represented (Sloman, 1978). Ideally, the correspondence should apply in every respect; that is, for the whole structure, the parts of the structure, and the relationship between parts in terms of their organization within the whole of that structure (Beveridge & Parkins, 1987; Sloman, 1978). Moreover, if the representation is to be a dynamic one, the correspondence must also apply to the dynamic interactional organization of the parts within the whole of that structure (Sloman, 1978). Essentially, therefore, an analogical representation should be fully isomorphically related to its referent (T. Evans, 1968; Gallagher, 1978). Analogical representations are basically holistic and continuous in form (Chafe, 1975; Palmer, 1975; Sloman, 1978).

It is thought that analogical processing of analogical representations facilitates the holistic comparison of two or more whole information structures (Boden, 1977; Dreistadt, 1968). It is also thought that analogical reasoning involves the detection of similarity between two or more information structures (Getner, 1982; Hofstadter, 1981). The *strength* of an analogical relationship between two or more structures may be considered in terms of the degree of similarity of structure or form (Beveridge & Parkins, 1987). The detection of a structural similarity between similar but nonidentical structures involves ignoring the details that constitute differences. In particular, it involves ignoring detailed and insignificant differences or mismatching details between otherwise correspondent structures (Gick & Holyoak, 1983). Alternatively expressed, the *ignoring* may be a *failure to discriminate* the detailed and insignificant differences; this could be facilitated by a representation and processing system of low discriminatory power.

Analogical representation and processing of information involves the processing of information in the form of patterns; for example, in pattern recognition or pattern matching (Hayes-Roth, 1978; Mulholland et al., 1980). These recognized or matched patterns may of course merely be sufficiently similar to one another rather than strictly identical (Boden, 1977; Hofstadter, 1981).

It is believed that in general analogical reasoning involves the application of past experience to new but similar experience (Holyoak, 1984; Sternberg, 1977; Winston, 1978). It has been suggested that analogical representation and processing may naturally or most efficiently facilitate sensorimotor thought (Attneave, 1972; Kintsch, 1974; Sloman, 1971). Mental images are considered to be analogical representations or to possess analogical properties (Arieti, 1970; Chafe, 1975), and reciprocally, analogical representation and processing is also considered to facilitate imagistic thought (D. Beck, 1978; Kosslyn & Pomerantz, 1977). From an information-processing point of view, analogical reasoning processes are thought to involve the *superimpositional* processing of whole patterns, or *in-parallel* processing (Hunt, 1973; Reitman, 1965).

In-Parallel Representation and Processing

Within an in-parallel system of representation and processing, information is stored in a superimposed fashion (McClelland & Rumelhart, 1986). In-parallel processing of information has certain characteristics that are *statistical* and that, in effect, facilitate the determination of patterns or features. These patterns or features may be determined partly, but not solely, on the basis of the relative frequency with which they occur. Therefore, the characteristics of in-parallel processing partly facilitate the statistical revelation and statistical evaluation of features that are to varying extents common to a number of experiences (Salmon, 1970; Thorndyke & Hayes-Roth, 1979). Within some in-parallel processing systems, what is stored in memory is a set of statistically determined connection strengths which, when activated, have the implicit ability to generate states that correspond to the schemata or representations (Rumelhart, 1986).

Parallel information processing allows for the integration of diffuse inputs and should allow for the blending of information from different sensory modalities, as would be required for the formation of a polymodal representation. Furthermore, within such a system, information from different events will be stored in a spatially atemporal manner. Parallel processing has the facility to allow the information from each experience to organize itself within memory in terms of its content and the content of all the previously stored information from earlier events, thereby allowing for a continuous development in memory (Mackay, 1958; Norman, 1986), and its occurrence in a manner that is not necessarily bound by the strict order in which the events are experienced (De Bono, 1969). The schemata formed within such a representational system will be flexible configurations continually undergoing modification to reflect the current regularities of experience on the basis of past and present circumstances (Norman, 1986). The system will therefore embody a representation that, on a cumulative statistical basis, reflects the environment as it is sensed (Mackay, 1956b; Norman, 1986). As a result of this cumulative type of memory, the total stimulus configuration of any present event may be evaluated *statistically* on the basis of all previous experience (Estes, 1964; Spinelli, 1970; Uttley, 1956a). Since the information from each event is allowed to organize itself within memory in terms of its content and the content of all the previously stored information from other events, the representational system may be described as *passive* or *imitative* (Mackay, 1956a; Richardson, 1972).

The system's inability to distinguish between finely different configurations may be regarded as a facility for recognizing or evaluating as the same as number of configurations or patterns that are "roughly the same" but "finely not the same," or different (Rosenblatt, 1958). This characteristic may loosely be described either as an ability to recognize and evaluate a number of wholes or items that resemble one another (Uttley, 1956a) rather than only those that are identical, or as an inability to distinguish between a number of similar but nonidentical wholes or items (Rosenblatt, 1958; Uttley, 1956c). This characteristic may also be considered to facilitate *generalization* of response (Uttley, 1956c; Whyte, 1954)—generalization being defined as the establishment of a single response corresponding to the dominant features of a series of similar but not identical stimuli (Whyte, 1954).

A particularly important feature of in-parallel processing is that of pattern completion (Uttley, 1956c). When a significantly large part of a frequently occurring pattern is received as an input, the system will tend to recognize that part as though it was the whole; moreover, it will therefore respond as if the whole pattern had been indicated, thus, in effect, completing the "expected" pattern. Alternatively expressed, a cue that corresponds to a fragment of the originally perceived information will serve to elicit automatic retrieval of all the correspondent information from within memory (McClelland & Rumelhart, 1986). This phenomenon may occur for an individual spatial structure, and as such may be considered spatial pattern completion. It may also occur for a temporal pattern; that is, when part of a familiar sequence is received as an input, the system will respond so as to complete the expected temporal pattern (Uttley, 1956c). The latter phenomenon, temporal pattern completion, may be considered a kind of predictive or temporally inductive mechanism that in effect facilitates an anticipatory response (Reichenbach, 1956; Uttley, 1956c). Thus, on the basis of the record of past experience, the system may, upon the receipt of a particular input, respond with the action sequence most likely to produce a favorable outcome.

Finally, it will be possible to represent a causal relationship between two events by statistical means. An event may be considered causally relevant to a later event if the probability of the later given the former is greater than the probability of the later event alone (Reichenbach, 1956).

Naturomorphic Representation and Processing: Overview

The naturomorphic class of cognition may now be characterized more fully on the basis of the preceding information concerning imagistic, analogical, and in-parallel information representation and processing.

General Characteristics in Relation to Primary-Level Processing. A neural naturomorphic system could provide a continuous, holistic polymodal representation, and could therefore represent, in these respects, the environment as it is perceived at a primary level. This form of representation could facilitate superimpositional or cumulative storage of continuous, holistic polymodal information. The superimpositional storage would be a form of spatially atemporal storage. The naturomorphic system could allow for a continuous development of information organization within memory. The received information could organize itself in terms of the information's own organization and the content of all the previously stored information, and could embody representations that on a cumulative statistical basis reflect or *imitate* the environment.

Recognition and Associative Recall. The recognition of a stimulus may, in effect, be considered to be an instantaneous automatic retrieval of a record of the past stimulus from memory cued by a new stimulus that corresponds either to the whole or a fragment of the past stimulus information (McClelland & Rumelhart, 1986). Naturomorphic processing would have a limited and fairly low power of resolution (relative to abstract representation and processing). It would therefore fail to discriminate between items that are generally similar but nonidentical "in detail." This may be considered an advantage in that it would facilitate resemblance detection. The naturomorphic system would therefore be able to recognize not just identical wholes or fragments, but also similar ones. The superimpositional storage of information within in-parallel processing facilitates associative storage of information. As a result of associative storage, the recognition process could also result in a virtually simultaneous recall of associated information (J. Van Heerden, 1970)—with the associated information being recalled on the basis of its significance in terms of the present stimulus input.

Consequential Meaning and Anticipatory Responses. The naturomorphic system could represent continuous sequences and contain statistical information about the sequential relationships between parts of the sequence—sensory, motor, and autonomic. The information could also include the magnitude of beneficial or detrimental consequences. It could therefore contain information about the consequential significance or consequential meaning of a given stimulus pattern. As a result of the cumulative memory, the total stimulus configuration of any present input could be evaluated on the basis of all previous experience. Such a system would therefore facilitate an anticipatory response that on a statistical basis would most probably produce the most beneficial outcome.

Elaboration of Naturomorphic Response Sequences. Within the superimpositional storage, the temporal value of a given part of a sequence would be indicated not by its spatial value but by its statistical value in terms of its probability of occurring before or after another given part. A consequence of representing temporal relationships in this manner is that the parts of a sequence are not themselves totally bound by the temporal order in which they occurred in any single actually experienced sequence. Furthermore, a particular recorded sequence or event will, once recorded, cease to have its individual identity in space-time; rather, it will coexist with all the other recorded information. Its individual identity may be retained by the relationship within its particular set of significance values, but only implicitly. If it has anything in common, in this respect, with the data already recorded, or with data subsequently recorded, its particular set of significance values will be altered (because of the cumulative nature of the memory), and it will no longer even implicitly have its original identity. Consequently, the individual parts of different but associated sequences would be interchangeable and could be expressed in a variety of orders (Lashley, 1954). However, this very characteristic will inevitably make it difficult for the naturomorphic sub-system, in itself, to determine the temporal relationship between strongly associated items, and so there may be confusion in attempting to recall the order in which strongly associated events have taken place. A major limitation of the system arising for its atemporal characteristics is, therefore, the fact that it is limited in its ability to deal with sequential information of *individual* experiences.

As a result of pattern completion, a recorded temporal pattern or sequence may be evoked by only a part of the information represented in that sequence. Within such a recalled sequence, each fragment may be evoked by its predecessor, or an associated predecessor. Thus for a given initial external input I.1, a fragment of a past sequence Fa1 may be evoked as the first fragment of the present response sequence F1 according to its significance with respect to that input I.1. The fragment Fa1 may then serve to evoke the next fragment of the present sequence. This next fragment of the present response sequence may either be the next fragment of the original past sequence to which Fa1 belonged, that is, Fa2; or it may be a fragment of another sequence with which Fa2 is associated, that is, it may be Fbn. Which of Fa2 or Fbn follows on from Fa1 will depend on the fragments' significances in terms of the previous fragment Fa1 and the corresponding next fragment of the external stimulus information I.2. Thus, the external sequence I.1 → I.2 could recall a response sequence Fa1 → Fa2 (the old sequence), or Fa1 → Fbn (a new sequence). It is therefore possible that a whole response sequence could be formed by fragments from associated sequences that are run together in a new, continuously executed sequence according to their statistical significance as determined in part by the external sequence of events. For a novel sequence of environmental conditions, such a sequence may, as a whole, be itself novel. New sequences may therefore be passively evoked according to the demands of the environment—a kind of passive creativity.

Long-established or habitual response sequences, because of their frequent use, will have high statistical significance values connecting the fragments of the sequence. The sequence will therefore be less *fluid*—that is, less susceptible to fragmentary incorporation within a novel response—than will newly acquired or nonhabitual temporal patterns in which the fragments of the whole pattern are connected by relatively low statistical significance values. Habitual response sequences will, in effect, be released as a statistically predetermined whole, with less effect being produced by any variation of input conditions between the start and finish of the response.

Similarly, within whole sequences there may be certain sub-sequences (or subroutines) that prove to be more successful than others. The more successful sub-sequences are more likely to be used again under similar circumstances. If they continue to be successful, these sub-sequences, through their frequent usage, will develop high statistical significance values connecting the fragments within them, and thus will be likely to be recalled in effect as a *whole*.

Processing of Information as a Whole. A naturomorphic system would allow for the gradual emergence of the most frequently occurring or otherwise most significant configurations, patterns, or features contained within a number of wholes (spatial or temporal). Features that so emerged could be in the form of relatively large patterns or smaller ones, although the larger patterns would emerge more quickly. The emergence of configurations or patterns according to their statistical significance may, in effect, be considered a form of statistical separation or "abstraction" in that the most significant features of a number of wholes would possess significance values that separated them, in terms of their significance values, from the features of lesser significance. This process of abstraction would be abstraction in effect rather than abstraction in deed: the "abstracted" information would not actually be taken away from its background context, it would merely appear to be more significant. Moreover, the difference between the significance values of parts within the whole would not be fixed but would be liable to change as a result of further experience, and so some emerged features could later remerge with their background while other once-insignificant features could subsequently emerge from it. The content of significant parts within this system would therefore be subject to continual change during further experience. Within a naturomorphic system, information would both be represented and processed as a whole, and so no information available to the organism would be lost.

Discrimination in the Naturomorphic System. Naturomorphic processing would have a limited and fairly low power of resolution (relative to abstract representation and processing). It would not be able to process relatively detailed information, and would therefore fail to discriminate between similar but nonidentical data. This may be considered to be an advantage in that it would facilitate resemblance detection. It may, however, also be considered to be a disadvantage in that there could be failure to distinguish between importantly different data at a detailed level, and therefore, under such circumstances, inappropriate responses might occur.

Passive Learning within the Naturomorphic System. As the system is in passive receipt of information, and as the development of the statistical significance values depend on the frequency with which the information naturally occurs in the environment, then the speed at which a significant feature emerges will depend entirely on the environment. It could possibly take years for the feature to emerge—during which time inappropriate responses may occur (these inappropriate responses may not be glaringly detrimental; they may just be time-consuming irrelevancies such as superstitious behaviors).

Inappropriate Pattern Completion. Naturomorphic representation and processing of information would facilitate both spatial and temporal induction or pattern completion: A significantly large part of an often experienced or otherwise important spatial or temporal pattern would be treated as if it were the whole pattern. In a small number of (low-probability) circumstances, this pattern completion would, however, be inappropriate. For example, a largely familiar cue could evoke a habitual response (motor or mental) which, upon its completion, would be inappropriate because of the small but nonetheless important difference between the actual total stimulus and the inductively perceived total pattern.

Pattern completion, be it spatial or temporal, operates inductively on a statistical basis. Because part of a pattern in, say 99 percent of experienced events is accompanied by the remainder of that pattern, on a subsequent presentation of that a part of the pattern it will be statistically inferred that the remainder of the pattern will also occur. However, in 1 percent of events, this inference will probably be invalid. Thus, for low-probability situations or unlikely occurrences, the high-probability pattern completion will be inappropriate; for example, a familiar cue evoking a habitual response which, on its completion, turns out to be totally inappropriate.

The occurrence of low-probability events and low-probability inappropriate responses may increase initially if the system moves into a new and different environment. However, the increase in occurrence of such events will automatically cause an increase in the relevant statistical values, and so the frequency of inappropriate responses will eventually be returned to a low level.

Duration of Memory. The cumulative growth of memory means that long-established patterns or patterns with high probability values (for example habitual response patterns or habitual perceptual sets or ways of looking at things) may take a long time to change, or, more specifically, may require the occurrence of many new responses in order to accumulate a probability value in excess of that of the old response pattern. However, clearly the process will also depend on the consequences of the habitual response. If the consequence suddenly became very detrimental, there may be more rapid modification.

Cumulative growth in memory would mean that a long-established perceptual set or sequence of responses may take a long time to *change*. That is, considerable repetition of the new response sequence may be needed in order for it to accumulate a significance value equal to or greater than that of the old response sequence, and so to be equally or more likely to be evoked. Old habits would not, therefore, simply be eradicated from memory: They would have to be gradually replaced (on a probability-of-occurrence basis) by the newer, more appropriate habits.

Summary. From the previously described characteristics it is evident that a neural naturomorphic system would be able to fulfil the requirements for the representation and processing of information at a primary level, but with certain limitations.

ABSTRACT CLASS OF INFORMATION REPRESENTATION AND PROCESSING

Abstract representation and processing of information is exemplified in those forms of thought commonly referred to as logical, rational, or discursive. This form of thought is, as a process, analytical or deductive. It is often considered to be the *higher* intellectual process, and its use is exemplified in symbolic logic or in formal propositional language.

Abstract Representation and Processing

Abstract representation is of a form that is symbolic and discrete or discontinuous. Abstract representations do not in themselves directly indicate what they represent or mean, they do so only indirectly through reference (Reichenbach, 1947; Sloman, 1968). An abstract representation is, characteristically, nonisomorphic with its referent (Sloman, 1971). This characteristic allows abstract representations and processes to be used equally well for different sets of information—the same *x* can be used in different operations to represent a profit value, an apple, or a quantity of heat. This form of representation and processing is therefore very versatile.

During the formation of abstract representations, information from the environment is converted from a continuous into a discrete form. The process of abstraction includes separate processing of information from different sensory modes; thus, an abstract system handles unimodal rather than polymodal or amodal information. Because abstract processing handles discrete data, it is capable of virtually unlimited discrimination and accuracy. In the process of forming abstract representations, insignificant information is discarded: Consequently, the information retained within the abstract representation is merely a filtrate of what is available—the retained information is abstracted *in deed.* Information so abstracted may then be processed completely apart from its background context or its original contextual meaning. In the latter respect it may be considered to be an *active* form of representation and processing. As a result of these features it is possible to extract information and determine relationships between items of information much more quickly than could the *passive* parallel statistical system.

The serial representation of information enables abstract processing to make explicit what is implicit within an organized structure, whether that structure is an image, picture, or intuitive hypothesis. However, the abstract system cannot itself completely represent organized structures, and so the abstracted bits and the abstract processing of them must be given a structure, and organization, or a context by some nonabstract system.

Abstract representations are absolutely defined, in that they do not in themselves vary in accordance with the natural variation of the real-world objects that they represent (the same *x* may be used to represent any apple). Their structure is therefore independent of statistical variability.

Logical Processing of Abstractly Represented Information

Logical processing of information is concerned with the sequential expression, description, or analysis of the relationship between two discrete bits of information; for example, between two items in an organized structure, two items causally related, observation and inference, or premise/hypothesis and conclusion. In these instances the logical processing can only elaborate, clarify, or make explicit what is already implicit to the structure, causal relationship, observation, or premise/hypothesis (Theobald, 1968). These initial items upon which the logical process operates—the structure, causal relationship, observation, or premise/hypothesis—cannot themselves be obtained logically; necessarily, they are of prelogical origin. It is considered that the initial empirical observation (or structure or causal relationship) is obtained directly from perceptual experience (B. Russell, 1950), and that in this respect the logical process is necessarily secondary to and dependent on such perceptual experience (Lunzer, 1965). Likewise, there must also be a nonlogical process that provides the logical process with the premise/hypothesis that is to be logically expressed or analyzed. It has been suggested that the nonlogical process responsible for the provision of the premise or hypothesis is what is referred to as *intuition* (Tarski, 1969; Yukawa, 1973).

Logic is not only incapable of providing hypotheses; similarly, it is incapable of providing creative solutions or making inferences (Mackay, 1958; Popper, 1959; Yukawa, 1973). Concerning the logical description of any organized structure, it is important to note that a description of a relationship between two items abstracted from that organized structure may, because it is based on abstracted data, be logically consistent in itself without necessarily involving a description that is consistent in terms of the organized structure as a whole (Sloman, 1971): It may be internally consistent but inconsistent in terms of the context to which it naturally belongs. More generally, relationships or arguments may be logically consistent in themselves without being consistent in terms of their original context or *reality*.

It is thought that the system of abstract representation and processing cannot fully represent reality as it is directly perceived or experienced because it handles abstract and discrete information rather than holistic or continuous information. As noted, abstract representations are rigidly defined and are in themselves independent of statistical variability, and so do not allow for a continual evolution or metamorphosis of representations.

Because information is represented in a discrete and rigidly defined manner, the system of abstract representation and processing does not naturally facilitate associative storage or resemblance detection; moreover, because of its discrete and serial characteristics, it does not allow for the development of patterns. The abstract representation and processing system does not facilitate induction and, strictly speaking, it has no predictive value (B. Russell, 1950); it cannot, therefore, provide the basis for an anticipatory response. Another serious objection to abstract or digital processing being the sole system is that its representation and processing speed together will often be unable to meet real-time real-space requirements (Jacobowitz, 1963; Pylyshyn, 1974–75).

Verbal Propositional Representation

A formal or an abstract language such as the spoken or written word does not necessarily in its perceptible form directly communicate any information about what it refers to; that is, it is nonisomorphic with its referent (Sloman, 1971). Accordingly, such a language is in itself devoid of empirical or real-world meaning (Ayer, 1946; B. Russell, 1950). In order to obtain the meaning of a linguistic representation such as a word or a sentence, it is necessary to *interpret* the representation by relating it to or translating it into its referent (Reichenbach, 1947; Sloman, 1968). The referent may be an externally observable object, relationship, or event in the external world; that is, a concretely represented referent (Traill, 1976). Alternatively, it may be another form of mental representation which is to some extent isomorphic with the real-world referent; for example, it may be a mental image (Paivio, 1971; Reichenbach, 1947; Traill, 1976). The referent may, however, be a concept that in itself may not be amenable to direct observation, but that may be understood in terms of other words for which the referents are available. Ultimately, a verbal propositional representational system would have to be connected to, or mapped onto, a perceptually based representational system in order to obtain its meaning (Gregg, 1974; Hunt, 1973; Kintsch,

1974). Language could not, therefore, be learned in any meaningful sense unless the learner either had developed an understanding of the word's referent before hearing the word, or could determine the word's meaning directly from its context at the time of usage (Brown & Desforges, 1979). This view is supported by the work of Moeser and Bregman (1972, 1973) on miniature artificial languages. Their work indicated that initially the early learning of the miniature artificial language must be mediated through an understanding of a concrete or pictorial reference field, but that later learning may be built around the existing syntactic framework. The theoretical description of the referential nature of language and the work of Paivio (1971, 1977) and Moeser and Bregman (1973) together indicate that there may naturally be a sequence of referential dependency such that linguistic representation depends for its meaning on imagistic (mental or *external*) referents, or on concrete referents, and that imagistic representation (mental), in inverse proportion to its degree of isomorphism, depends for its meaning on concrete referents. This relationship may be summarized as follows:

linguistic ⟶ imagistic ⟶ concrete

and that the relationship for a maximum degree of *mental freedom* from the real world as:

linguistic ⟶ imagistic ⟶ concrete

This latter sequence of referential dependency necessarily implies a development relationship in the reverse direction such that the normal evolution of forms of representation and information processing would be:

concrete ⟶ imagistic ⟶ linguistic

Summary

It is evident from the previously described characteristics that a neural abstract representation and processing system would not be able to fulfil the requirements for representation and processing of information at a primary level. Furthermore, both formal logic and verbal propositional representation are clearly dependent to some extent on a nonabstract form of representation and processing, for example, imagery.

RELATIONSHIP BETWEEN NATUROMORPHIC AND ABSTRACT REPRESENTATION AND PROCESSING

Developmental Relationship

From the preceding section it is evident that both formal logic and verbal propositional representation are to some extent dependent on a nonabstract form of representation and processing. In terms of the information-representation and -processing requirements, it is generally considered that imagistic, analogical, and parallel forms of representation or cognition would be at a developmental level that precedes, and that in part provides a basis for, verbal propositional, deductive, analytical, or logical thought (D. Beck, 1978; Gregg, 1974; Hunt, 1973; Narismhan, 1970; Palmer, 1975).

Complementary Relationship

It would appear that the characteristics of these two classes of representation and processing are mutually exclusive (Hofstadter, 1981; Polanyi, 1962), but that for overall maximum efficiency each of the two classes requires the other (Bobrow, 1975). Accordingly, the two classes of representation and processing may be considered complementary (Bruner, 1986; Inhelder, 1965; Mackay, 1949).

SUMMARY

The basic requirements for a form of representation and processing of information that would enable an organism to successfully interact with its environment are: (1) the facility for the formation of a continuous amodal (polymodal), four-dimensional, whole representation of the external environment, which has a structural organization determined by and similar to that environment; (2) a similarly structured representation of the organism's corresponding actions and internal conditions; and (3) the storage of all this information in a continuous, cumulative, associative manner so that the total input of an environmental stimulus will automatically evoke relevant information from past experience and enable the organism to make an anticipatory response that will most probably produce the most favorable outcome in terms of the organism's homeostatic needs.

There are two basic categories of representation and processing: naturomorphic and abstract. The characteristics of naturomorphic representation and processing are such that it would fulfil the basic requirements for enabling the organism to successfully interact with the environment—but with a limited power of discrimination. The characteristics of the abstract representation and processing would not, in themselves, enable the organism to successfully interact with the environment—but they would facilitate a much higher power of discrimination. In relation to one another: (1) the naturomorphic form would be required before the abstract form; and (2) the two forms would, in terms of their characteristics of representation and processing, be complementary and mutually exclusive.

4

Learning-Based Control

LEARNING-BASED EXTENSION OF ORGANIC EQUILIBRATION

In order to consider the learning-based extension of organic equilibrium, it is first necessary to describe the fundamentals of homeostatic control or equilibration at a most basic level.

Basic Features of Control at the Innate Level

Homeostasis is a biological process of maintaining equilibrium in correspondence with the environment, and is directed to ensuring survival. As it involves the maintenance of a certain condition, it may be viewed as a process of control. The basic features of a homeostatic circuit are: (1) a reference standard that indicates the required value of the variable to be controlled; (2) a sensor to detect the actual value of that variable from the stimulus; (3) a comparator to compare the required value with the actual value and to thus detect the error; (4) a corrective action signal generator or *response information* generator which, on receipt of the error signal, will provide the appropriate corrective action signal or response information; (5) an action implementor or effector with the ability to implement this action as the response of the system; and (6) feedback indicating the result of the action on the environment—this will be as a subsequent input providing a new actual value. These features may be organized in a circuit or feedback loop as shown in Figure 1.

At the lowest evolutionary level, the homeostatic process would be completely automatic. For a particular variable the reference standard would be innate and in itself fixed, albeit within certain limits (Bize, 1976). Any deviation of the actual value of the variable from the innate reference standard would evoke an

Figure 1
Basic Homeostatic Circuit

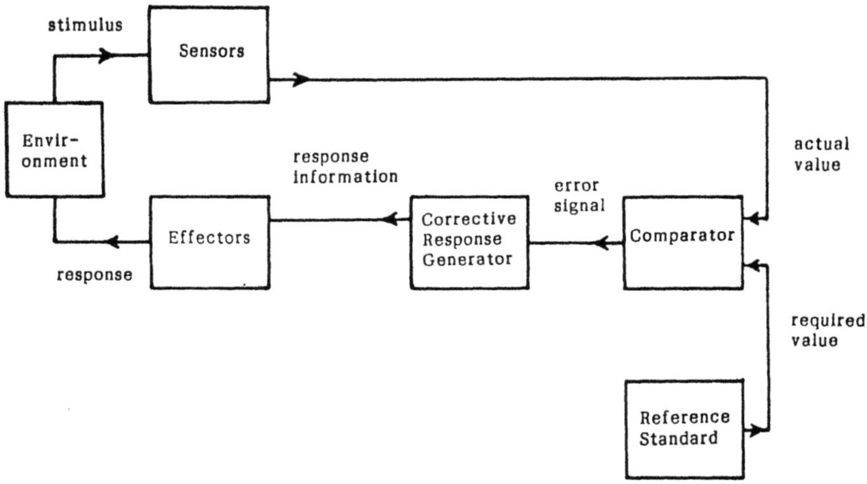

immediate and innately prescribed, automatic corrective response from the organism. The innate response would be the most generalized in form and in range of application for all types of responses (Herrick, 1956).

Basic Features of Control Involving Learning

At higher evolutionary levels, the newly evolved neural structures would facilitate learning during interaction with the environment (Young, 1964). Functionally, the newly evolved neural structures would be hierarchically above the older ones and would be able to exert control over them or their output (Arbib, 1972; Miller et al., 1960). The facility would therefore exist for cognitively based refinement and elaboration of the innate homeostatic responses.

When an organism with the newly evolved facilities acted, it would do so at first on the basis of the innate reference standards. However, it could record within its memory the information from the external environment; the information from the internal environment, including the organism's actions; and the information concerning the result of the organism's response—whether it was beneficial or detrimental. This recorded information would provide the basis on which the learned reference standards could be formed (Bize, 1976). The recorded information would also provide a basis for the learned corrective action signal or learned response. Once the organism had recorded this information, it could then act on the basis of the learned reference standards rather than on the basis of the innate standards (Pribram, 1967; Traill, 1976). Within the brain the recorded information would be embodied by a secondary sub-system placed, in a functional sense, hierarchically above the innate sub-system (Pribram, 1967; Traill, 1976). This more complex homeostatic circuit may therefore be viewed as a composite of two sub-systems, one of which embodies learned reference standards. The two sub-systems could be hierarchically arranged as shown in Figure 2. (In Figure 2 the location and connections of the memory are meant to show only its involvement.)

In this arrangement a sample of the innate response information provides an input to the comparator of the second (learning) sub-system. Thus, information concerning the innate response, as it is released throughout the response, would be fed to the learning sub-system, enabling it to monitor this together with the internal and external environmental conditions via the sensors, and to refine or modify the response on the basis of the learned reference standards. The learned reference standard LRS1, which was based on the organism's first experience, could subsequently be modified to LRS2 on the basis of further experience. Furthermore, this further experience may result from a response based on the learned reference standard LRS1 rather than from a response based directly on an innate reference standard (Luria, 1973; Popper & Eccles, 1977).

Within the human brain, information processing seems to operate in a hierarchical manner (Arbib, 1972; Mackay, 1965). The lowest level of processing within the neuropsychological system should be of fairly low discrimination (Klahr & Wallace, 1976; Mackay, 1965). It should handle a range of information from that which is whole and continuous in form to that which is of simple whole features or patterns. Finer discrimination than this would have to be made by a second sub-system with greater discrimination and analytical capability (Klahr & Wallace, 1976; Uttley, 1956c). Within a hierarchy, therefore, the lower-level cognitive sub-system should be naturomorphic, whereas the higher-level sub-system should be abstract (Arbib, 1972). This conforms to the developmental relationship between the naturomorphic and abstract representation noted in Chapter 3.

NATUROMORPHIC LEARNING-BASED CONTROL

As noted earlier, the processing characteristics of the naturomorphic sub-system are such that it would allow a recognized stimulus to automatically evoke the relevant information concerning the response that would most probably produce the most beneficial result for a given set of internal and external conditions (Uttley, 1956c). The evoked information could be in the form of an anticipatory action sequence, and would constitute a corrective action signal (Arbib, 1972; Mackay, 1949). A simplified version of the more complex circuit involving an innate sub-system and a naturomorphic learning-based sub-system is shown in Figure 3.

A More Detailed Account of Naturomorphic Learning and Its Relationship to Control

It is assumed that schemata develop as a consequence of an individual's repeated participation in behavioral episodes, and that the schemata reflect the regularities

Figure 2
More Complex Homeostatic Circuit Involving a Learning-Based Sub-System

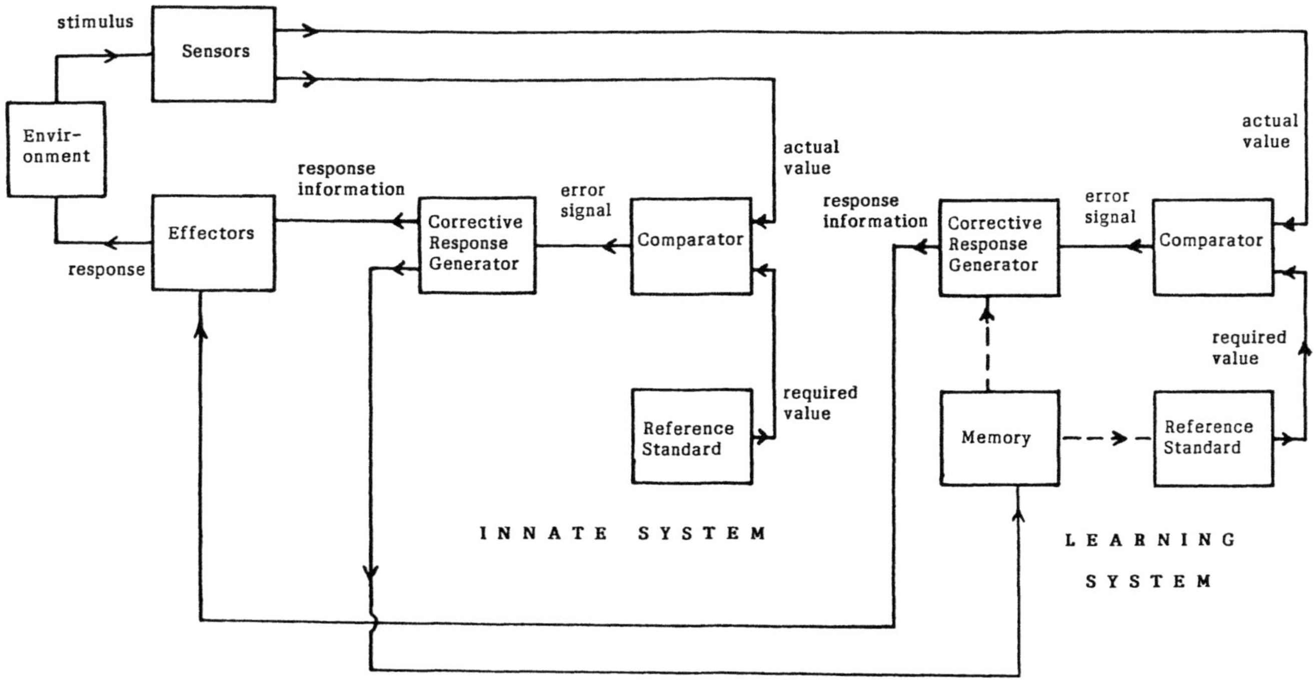

Figure 3
Simplified Homeostatic Circuit Involving Innate and Naturomorphic Sub-Systems

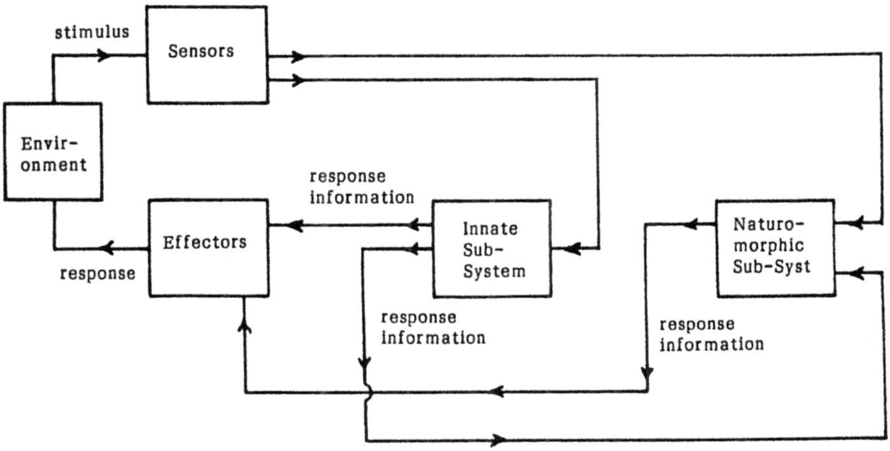

and invariants of these episodes (Landau & Godfried, 1981). This process of schemata development now needs to be considered in more detail in order to relate it systematically to the control process in homeostasis.

When the organism first responds, it will do so entirely on the basis of innate data. The naturomorphic sub-system will, however, facilitate for the whole of this response a continuous recording of:

1. the innate response sequence (r1) that has been initiated—this will involve a continuous record of the resultant conditions within the motor system and all that is entailed in the response including the autonomic component. This information will be transmitted from the appropriate internal sensors to the naturomorphic sub-system; and
2. the external context (c1) in which the response takes place—this will involve a continuous record of all the external information to which the system is sensitive. This information will be transmitted from the appropriate external sensors to the naturomorphic sub-system.

The complete record of the resultant innate response (r1) and external context (c1) from the beginning of the response (i) to the end of the response (f) will, in effect, serve as the first learned naturomorphic reference standard (nrs1). (For the sake of simplicity in the following argument, the context and response will be treated as separate components in the naturomorphic memory, although as noted earlier they would not in reality be separate.)
Thus:

$$\text{nrs1} = (\text{r1i} \longrightarrow \text{r1f}) + (\text{c1i} \longrightarrow \text{c1f})$$

It may reasonably be assumed that, in a natural environment, the naturally evolved homeostatic circuit and reference standards embodied therein will more often than not operate in the organism's favor—otherwise they would not have evolved. It may therefore be assumed that as an ultimate result of the innate response, the error in the innate circuit will be effectively reduced; that is, equilibrium will be restored.

When the organism subsequently responds to remove the same type of error within the innate circuit, if the external context as a whole is judged to be "roughly the same" as it was in the past (c1), the organism may utilize its past experience by responding, not directly in terms of the innate reference standard and the error signal within the innate circuit, but by controlling the implementation of the innate response in terms of the learned naturomorphic reference standard (nrs1) and the error within the naturomorphic sub-system. The error signal in the naturomorphic sub-system (Ne) will be indicated by a comparison of the initial information concerning the same innate response or corrective action sequence for the second event (r2i) and the externally sensed initial information concerning the "roughly the same" context for the second event (c2i) with the learned naturomorphic reference standard based on the first event (nrs1). Thus, Ne will be equivalent to the difference between nrs1 and the sum (r2i + c2i).

Using # to denote "the difference between the preceding and succeeding information," then:

$$\text{Ne} = \text{nrs1} \ \# \ \text{r2i} + \text{c2i}$$

or

$$\text{Ne} = (\text{r1i} \longrightarrow \text{r1f}) + (\text{c1i} \longrightarrow \text{c1f}) \ \# \ \text{r2i} + \text{c2i}$$

Now, for the "roughly the same" context:

$$\text{c2i} = \text{c1i}$$

and, for the "roughly the same" initial response state:

$$\text{r2i} = \text{r1i}$$

so,

$$\text{Ne} = (\text{r1i} \longrightarrow \text{r1f}) + (\text{c1i} \longrightarrow \text{c1f}) \ \# \ \text{r2i} + \text{c1i}$$

To remove the error signal within the naturomorphic sub-system, the learned response sequence (r1i ⟶ r1f) must be completed, which, in the first instance, would be equivalent to the unmodified completion of the innate response; in addition, the external context must, in effect, be made the same as it was at the completion of the first event (c1i ⟶ c1f). The removal of the error signal in the naturomorphic sub-system should then automatically result in removal of error from the innate circuit.

It is important to note that the record that acts as the naturomorphic reference standard, when compared with the input to the comparator, yields an error signal that contains information about the appropriate corrective action or response. This corrective action signal may, in a sense, be considered an indication of how things should be (Powers, 1974). The response component of this information has been referred to variously elsewhere as "image of achievement" (Pribram, 1971), or "anticipatory schemata" (Piaget, 1936, 1947); and, with respect to the contextual component, as a "search image" (Hinde, 1970).

Because of the properties of the naturomorphic sub-system, the initial condition (r1i + c1i), as the input, will automatically serve to evoke, or *cue*, the remaining parts of the sequence (r1i ⟶ r1f) + (c1i ⟶ c1f). Thus, within the naturomorphic sub-system, the functions of memory, comparator, and response sequence generator may all be *embodied* within one functional unit rather than in three separate units as shown in Figure 2.

Modification of Naturomorphic Reference Standards

It is possible that the naturomorphic sub-system will only be able to control the innate sub-system output on the basis of recorded data that has reached a certain level of significance (through frequency of occurrence, severity of consequence, or a combination of the two). However, it may be assumed that the corrective response evoked from the naturomorphic sub-system in the very first instance of its operation would be basically the innate response. In the first instance this response will be evoked from the naturomorphic sub-system by a stimulus which is "roughly the same" in the most general level possible. The evaluation of "roughly the same" will, furthermore, only apply to the initial context; that is, the context at the start of the response. The actual context during the response may not actually be so similar. The differences that do exist may have to be taken into account in the execution of the actual movements required during the response. As a consequence, the general form of the innate response may have to be modified in its expression at a detailed level (detailed relative to the innate system). This modification will have to be carried out by the naturomorphic sub-system, which will be able to influence the effectors as necessary on the basis of the internal and external information received from the sensors during the response. Thus, in the second event, the response sequence (r2i ⟶ r2f) may, within the response, be different in detail from the first innate response (r1i ⟶ r1f). In like manner, the context sequence (c2i ⟶ c2f) may, within the response, be different in detail from that of the first response (c1i ⟶ c1f). These slight differences in the response and context may result in a different reduction of the error signal in the innate sub-system. The reduction may be more efficient, less efficient, or the same. Information regarding this relative error reduction will be provided by a comparison of the recorded changes in the organism's internal state during the response r1 with the actual changes in the organism's internal state during the response r2. This information will provide the naturomorphically controlled response with a value of *beneficial* or *detrimental* in terms of the relative efficiency with which it reduces the error signal in the innate sub-system (Hagbarth & Finer, 1961). It should thereby serve as a reinforcement signal.

As in the first event, the conditions of the second event may be recorded, only this time the record will be $(r2i \longrightarrow r2f)$ and $(c2i \longrightarrow c2f)$. On the basis of this new record, in statistical combination with the first, the naturomorphic sub-system reference standard nrs1 may be modified to nrs2. So,

$$nrs2 = (ri \longrightarrow rf) + (ci \longrightarrow cf) \text{ averaged on events 1 to 2}$$

Now, when the organism responds for the third time to remove the same error signal within the innate sub-system in roughly the same context judged as a whole on the basis of its past experience, the organism may again utilize its past experience. However, its experience now involves a record of two events, and the error signal within the naturomorphic sub-system will be determined by comparison with the modified, learned naturomorphic reference standard nrs2.

Thus,

$$Ne = nrs2 \;\#\; r3i + c3i$$

or,

$$Ne = (ri \longrightarrow rf) + (ci \longrightarrow cf) \text{ averaged on events 1 to 2} \;\#\; r3i + c3i$$

Now, for the "roughly the same" context:

$$c3i = ci \text{ averaged on events 1 to 2 } c1i$$

and, for "roughly the same" initial response state,

$$r3i = ri \text{ averaged on events 1 to 2}$$

so,

$$Ne = (ri \longrightarrow rf) + (ci \longrightarrow cf) \text{ averaged on events 1 to 2} \;\#\; ri + ci \text{ averaged on events 1 to 2}$$

Thus, to remove the error signal within the naturomorphic sub-system, the learned response sequence $(ri \longrightarrow rf)$, averaged on events 1 to 2, must be completed (which in this instance, is the naturomorphically determined average of the innate response from event 1 and the first detailed modification of the innate response from event 2); and the external context must, in effect, be made the same as (ci ⟶ cf); averaged on events 1 to 2. The removal of the error signal in the naturomorphic sub-system should then automatically result in the removal of error from the innate circuit. The efficiency with which this takes place will be indicated as noted earlier, and a record of this indication will give value to the recorded sequence (and to naturomorphically distinguishable parts or sub-sequences within the whole response sequence). An important difference between the response in the second event and the response in the third event is that the latter response will have been based not just on innate information but also on the learned refinement of the innate response as provided by the data (r2i ⟶ r2f).

Clearly, this process may be repeated a large number of times; this will gradually develop a learned naturomorphic reference standard based on a large number of responses and a large number of contexts (within the same context class). As a result of these many experiences, there may have emerged within the naturomorphic sub-system:

1. statistically significant features within the whole contexts;
2. statistically significant response pattern variations or sub-sequence variations within the whole response sequence; and
3. statistically significant relationships between contextual features and response patterns

The point would now have been reached where the context may be evaluated as a whole, but in terms of significant features within the whole. Furthermore, the evoked corrective action signal, or response, may be the particular response variation most suited (or most significantly related) to those significant features. To facilitate the release of the most significant response sequence rather than a sequence of lower significance would simply require that the activation threshold be inversely proportional to the significance value (John, 1967).

If a particular context, or contextual feature, arises often enough preceding the direct evocation of an error signal within the innate sub-system, then that context may evoke directly from the naturomorphic sub-system the appropriate anticipatory response. In this mode of operation, the naturomorphic sub-system may be considered to be operating in an evaluative role (Pribram, 1963) in that the environmental context may be responded to on the assumption that a certain type of event will probably follow. Clearly, such anticipatory responses will only continue to be elicited directly from the naturomorphic sub-system for as long as they are accompanied by positive consequences. Thus, the evaluative function will only continue to operate for as long as it proves to be justified in terms of the innate sub-system. However, a "positive" consequence may in some contexts be no more than the absence of an expected detrimental consequence. Avoidance behavior may therefore continue to be elicited when it is no longer necessary—provided that it does not indirectly have an adverse effect on the innate system requirements.

Imitative/Vicarious Learning within the Naturomorphic Sub-System

The learning characteristics of the naturomorphic sub-system considered so far have been described only in terms of an environment, without explicit reference to "other people." Obviously, other people and their behavior in relation to achieving goals that satisfy human needs will be part of the environment and the observation of their actions may facilitate learning (Bandura, 1977; A. Ellis, 1979). According to Bandura (1977,12) "observation enables people to acquire large integrated patterns of behavior without having to form them gradually by tedious trial and error. . . . One forms a cognitive image of how certain behaviours are performed [and] . . . this coded information serves as a guide." There will therefore be the possibility of vicarious learning. The naturomorphic sub-system may record as image sequences its observation of other people carrying out action sequences. The initial *value* of other people's actions will be assigned in terms of how well the action sequences appear to achieve desirable goals, and on any observed beneficial or detrimental consequences for the observed person, as judged by the observer. This initial observational evaluation may be considered to constitute vicarious reinforcement. The record of the observed action and its consequential meaning may thereafter function as guides for behavior in much the same way as the learned reference standards described earlier. There will be virtually simultaneous associative recall of the vicariously learned response sequences on the basis of statistical significance in terms of the present stimulus input. One major difference, however, will be in terms of the physical response information. This is unlikely to have been "incidentally" recorded sufficiently well for the observer to carry out the actions as effectively as the observed person or to experience the physiological consequences. The observer will therefore have "some idea" or a "limited information" image of what he or she can do, but would actually need to do it for him- or herself in order to obtain further information. As the learning within the naturomorphic sub-system is of a statistical nature, the frequency of observed actions will be of importance. Thus, the people with whom one regularly interacts, either by preference or imposition, will strongly "weight" the behavior that will be observed and vicariously learned (Bandura, 1977).

Limitations of Naturomorphic Sub-System Control

The naturomorphic sub-system would have a number of disadvantages. In particular, there could be detailed information that could be of importance and that could not be handled by the naturomorphic sub-system because of its limited power of discrimination. Consequently, there could be failure to respond to important but naturomorphically indistinguishable detail, or there could be response to insignificant information *wholes*. Under these circumstances the organism would need an additional processing sub-system that could make finer discriminations and could overrule the less discriminate sub-system (Uttley, 1956c).

ABSTRACT LEARNING-BASED CONTROL

An abstract representation and processing sub-system would have a relatively much greater power of discrimination and be able to exert much more refined control that the naturomorphic sub-system. The abstract sub-system would have to act in parallel with, but hierarchically above, the naturomorphic sub-system in order to control it. So arranged, with the appropriate feedback loops, the higher sub-system could perceive and reorganize the operations of the lower one on the basis of its greater discriminating power (Mackay, 1966; Zucker, 1978).

The innate-naturomorphic circuit could therefore be improved by the functionally hierarchical and in-parallel addition of an abstract sub-system. The abstract sub-system, like the naturomorphic sub-system, would be equipped with a memory in which to record its input. The input to the abstract sub-system would consist of three components: (1) information direct from the internal and external environment via the sensors; (2) a sample of the innate sub-system's response information; and (3) a sample of the naturomorphic sub-system's response information. On the basis of this information, the abstract sub-system would be able to develop its own set of reference standards. These abstractly derived reference standards would then provide an additional cognitive basis for control of the organism's behavior (Bize, 1976). Whereas the naturomorphic sub-system's first learned response would be derived from an innate response, the abstract sub-system's first learned response would normally be based on a naturomorphic response. As a result of the relatively greater power of discrimination and the ability to determine the interactional relationship between the individual items by sequential analysis, the abstract sub-system could perceive and determine a greater number of features and relationships within the input and exert more refined control. This control could be exerted in two ways (Arbib, 1972): as a bias control directly on the naturomorphic sub-system, inhibiting unwanted components of the naturomorphic response sequence; or as control directly on the effectors. The hierarchical in-parallel arrangement of the innate, naturomorphic, and abstract sub-systems is shown in a simplified version in Figure 4. In this circuit there is a switch that enables the controlling output of the abstract sub-system to be directed either to the naturomorphic sub-system or to the effectors.

The Process of Abstraction

It is thought that an organism will expend as little of its information-processing capacity on a given task as is compatible with its successful execution (Sayre, 1976). To do this the organism must, wherever possible, take advantage of redundancy of information (Mackay, 1955; Marr, 1970); that is, it must abstract and process only the information significant to the task in hand while discarding the insignificant (redundant) information.

The process of abstraction takes place in part during the formation of abstract representations within the abstract sub-system. As was noted in Chapter 2, abstract

Figure 4
Simplified Homeostatic Circuit Involving Innate, Naturomorphic, and Abstract Sub-Systems

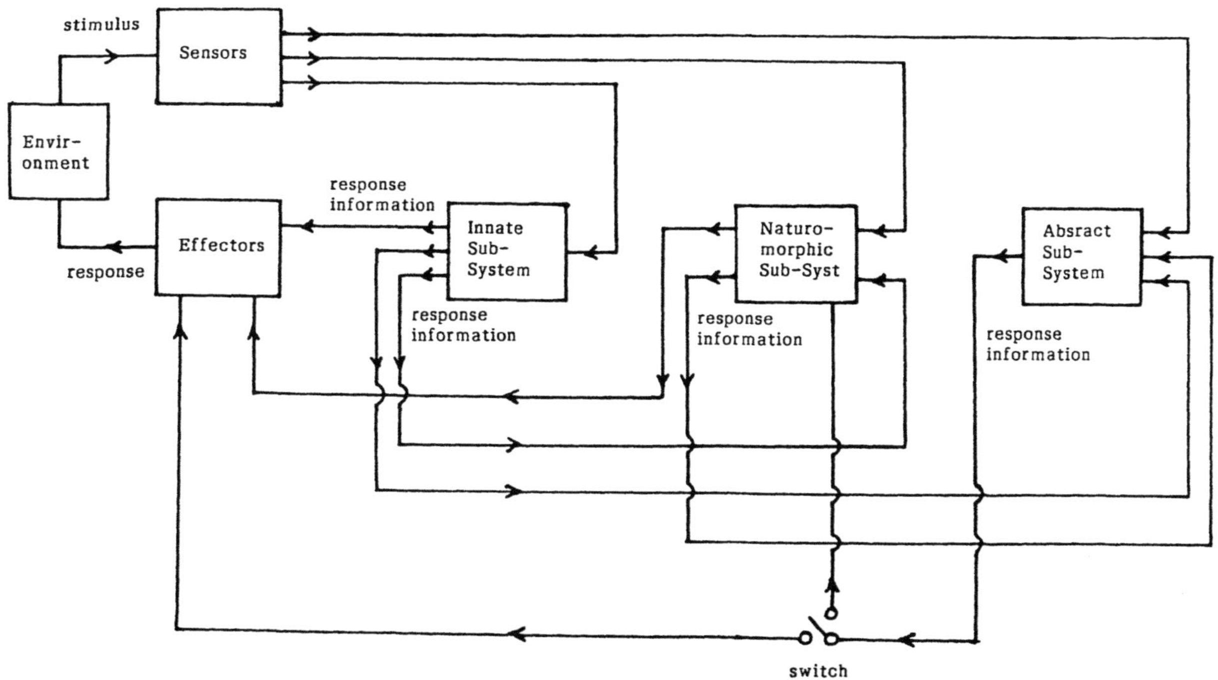

representation and processing involves the selection and representation of certain important or key features that are deemed to be representative of the thing to be represented. This selection of certain important features necessarily entails disregarding other features. During the process of forming abstract representations, insignificant information is therefore discarded, and the information retained within the abstract representation will be merely a filtrate of that available. The process of abstraction may, however, begin at an earlier stage by selective attending to, or filtering of, the information that is received by the abstract subsystem. By selectively attending only to the significant information within the whole of what is available, the load on the perceptual system in receipt of the selected information will be reduced (Broadbent, 1958; Norman, 1981). Therefore, the organism may first of all abstract a certain amount of information at a peripheral level prior to the arrival of information at the abstract system. It may then extract further within the abstract system during the formation of abstract representations or concepts.

Abstraction, the Development of Abstract Reference Standards, and the Process of Control

The capability of a controlling system is limited by the information it receives (Ashby, 1956a; Shannon & Weaver, 1949). The abstract system will necessarily receive and process only a limited amount of the total information available (Broadbent, 1958); that is, the information attended to. It will, therefore, at best be restricted to controlling in terms of the attentively received information. Evidence indicates that the process of attending to selected information is controlled by the organism itself (Noback & Demarest, 1975). The abstract system, as the highest level controller, would be able to control the information that it receives in that it would only attend to information that it determined to be important. More specifically, a particular schema (or abstract reference standard) could be used in the directing of movements and exploratory activities that make more information available, on the basis of which the schema will be further modified (Neisser, 1976). Consequently, a particular abstract reference standard ARSn could determine the information that is attended to and subsequently used in the modification of ARSn to ARSn+1.

The modification of ARSn to ARSn+1 will involve two levels of abstraction: first, the abstraction entailed in the filtering of the information available to the abstract system—out of the whole of the information available only a fraction would be received by the abstract system; second, of the fraction received, only a further fraction may be embodied in the abstract representation that constitutes the abstract reference standard ARSn+1. In turn, ARSn+1, based on but a fraction of the information available to the organism during the response based on ARSn, will provide a basis on which will be determined future responses—including the attention to information during those responses. On the basis of the information attended to, as determined by ARSn+1, ARSn+1 may be modified to ARSn+2, and so on. Clearly, within a cumulative process such as this which may go on indefinitely, there is little room for error in the determination of what is significant and what is not.

Unfortunately, it is only possible to evaluate information as significant or insignificant in terms of present and past events: Evaluation of the significance of information cannot be made with certainty in terms of the future. Thus, the information selectively attended to is what is considered to be significant at that time as determined on the basis of the information available up to that time. Assumptions made at one time regarding what is significant may, in the long term, prove unjustifiable (Bohm, 1980; Grey-Walter, 1954). Consequently, information that may be valuable in the long term could be irretrievably lost to the abstract system during the filtering process (Beurle, 1962; Grey-Walter, 1954; Marr, 1970; Sloman, 1978). An abstract reference standard may therefore be formed on the basis of a certain amount of information and may thereafter influence behavior—including the process of attention—and yet, in the long term, it may be an erroneous reference standard. Moreover, the erroneous aspect of the reference standard may be such that it automatically precludes correction by the abstract system because it causes a discarding of the very information that could serve to correct it. Thus, as a result of focussing on only select aspects of the full range of data available in the perceptual field, there may develop a *distorted* conception of reality (Bernard & Joyce, 1984).

This selective process may also apply at a very general level, for although the abstract sub-system may derive its abstract reference standards or concepts from the information it receives from the external world either directly or from the naturomorphic sub-system, it may also receive information indirectly through language; that is, through teaching from others (A. Ellis, 1979; Pugh, 1978). For example, this may occur in the form of laws, rules, proverbs, conventions, ideas, and theories. Clearly, the reception of this type of information may also be subject to the process of selective attention. This problem of information loss during selective attention or representation formation, and the resultant distorted conception of reality, will clearly be detrimental to the process of control (Mackay, 1956a; Pugh, 1978), and must be compensated for by somehow updating the abstract sub-system. Under normal circumstances the abstract system is the uppermost controller in the homeostatic circuit, and so the efficiency of the whole equilibration process will depend on this updating. In turn, the efficiency of the updating process will depend partly on how often it occurs (Pugh, 1978).

NATUROMORPHIC AND ABSTRACT LEARNING-BASED CONTROL

Independent Operation of the Naturomorphic Sub-System

While the higher sub-system may control the motor output directly or may bias the low-level sub-system (Arbib, 1972), it is possible that the low-level sub-system may be allowed to operate on its own without interference from above (Arbib,

1972; Hilgard, 1977; Legge & Barber, 1976; Pugh, 1978). This may be because the higher-level sub-system is busy "attending to other things" and so "not attending to" what the lower-level sub-system is doing. Also, if an immediate response is required, there may not be time to use the planning facility of the abstract sub-system, and so the naturomorphic sub-system will act on behalf of the whole system.

Simultaneous Independent Operation of the Naturomorphic and Abstract Sub-Systems

The two learning-based sub-systems may operate independently (Hilgard, 1977; Legge & Barber, 1976; Pugh, 1978), either with each dealing with different problems (Pugh, 1978) or with each dealing with the same problem in their respectively different ways (Legge & Barber, 1976).

In the first instance, the higher level sub-system may deal with a behavior that requires attention, or with nonroutine processing, while the lower-level sub-system may carry out a routine operation. For example, the low-level sub-system may be involved in driving a car along a familiar route or making a cup of tea, while the higher-level sub-system is working out the day's work schedule or solving a chess problem.

In the second instance, it is not impossible that the two sub-systems may arrive at conflicting "conclusions" with regard to some problem with which they are simultaneously dealing. Ideally, in the event of such a conflict, the abstract sub-system would consider both possibilities before the whole system responded. However, time may not permit the delay entailed in such further consideration. Also, it may be that the motivational component of the naturomorphic sub-system is so strong that the response cannot be fully inhibited by the abstract sub-system, and so the naturomorphic sub-system response is executed even though the abstract sub-system "disagrees" with it in terms of logic.

AN ESSENTIAL RELATIONSHIP BETWEEN NATUROMORPHIC AND ABSTRACT LEARNING-BASED SUB-SYSTEMS

Sources of Error in Cognitive Control

It was noted earlier that the naturomorphic form of representation was liable to error primarily because of its limited power of discrimination. The system of abstract representation and processing also has a number of disadvantages: First, there is the problem of information loss during selective attention or representation formation; second, abstract representations are in a form totally dissociated from their meaningful content and, as noted earlier, their meaning is referential. Partly for this reason and partly because of the entirely deductive nature of logic or formal language, it is possible to produce perfectly logical and internally consistent expressions, statements, or propositions that are nonsense in that they do not describe or correspond to anything that exists in the real world (Reichenbach, 1947; B. Russell, 1950; Sloman, 1978). Although logical representations may be perfectly equilibrated within the system of logic, as Piaget has suggested, they may not necessarily, according to the above, correspond to the real world. Taken together, these deficiencies indicate that the abstract representation and processing sub-system is itself liable to error. The abstract representation and processing sub-system does not necessarily facilitate complete equilibration either in itself or in the entire organism, in terms of its correspondence with the environment.

The sources of error outlined above will clearly be detrimental to the homeostatic process (Mackay, 1956a; Pugh, 1978), and must somehow be compensated for. The erroneous information or schemata must be corrected, and outdated schemata updated in terms of new experience and past data relevant to new experience, in order to maintain correspondence with the environment. This correction or progressive updating of schemata is considered to be a most important process (Arbib, 1972; Minsky, 1958; Sloman, 1978).

Checking for Error and Updating: Theoretical Requirements for a Self-Correcting Learning-Based Homeostatic System

Simple Hierarchical Arrangement of Sub-Systems in Homeostatic Control. It has been shown that a system of representation and processing, for example, mathematical logic or formal language, can produce theorems or statements that cannot be proven or disproven by using the system that produced them (Godel, 1931; Tarski, 1951). Thus, a system of representation and processing cannot check itself for error and correct itself. To prove the consistency of the object language (a given language or system of representation and processing), it is necessary to describe it in terms of another language (or system) called a meta-language (Carnap, 1958; Reichenbach, 1947; Tarski, 1969). The structure of the meta-language must be different from that of the object language in such a way that it is "richer" or "stronger" with respect to the particular aspect of the object language that it is to describe or evaluate (Godel, 1931; Mendelson, 1964; B. Russell, 1961; Tarski, 1969). However, this first meta-language would also be subject to an inability to check itself for error, and so a second meta-language to describe or check the first would be needed. Accordingly, it has been suggested that there would necessarily develop a hierarchy of languages (or cognitive sub-systems) extending indefinitely toward increasing levels of formalization (B. Russell, 1950). In theory, this would lead to an infinite regress of the ultimate evaluator (Reichenbach, 1947).

It would be possible to have one sub-system (naturomorphic) equivalent to the object language and a second sub-system (abstract) equivalent to the meta-language, and to have the second sub-system describe or evaluate and correct the first. However, it would then be necessary to check the second sub-system (abstract) for error, as, for example, in the updating process. This would require a third sub-system which would also be liable to error, with an infinite regress of the ultimate controller (Young, 1964). The problem of infinite regress would seem to be inherent to a strictly hierarchical arrangement.

A Reciprocal Arrangement of Sub-Systems in Homeostatic Control. It is thought that for a homeostatic circuit composed of a number of sub-systems, optimum control may be achieved by interconnecting the sub-systems such that each biases the other (Ashby, 1956a, 1960); that is, they should be interconnected so that their relationship to one another is reciprocal rather than hierarchical. Such a relationship may be applied to the process of evaluation and correction. Reciprocal evaluation should operate successfully provided that the type of errors made by the two reciprocally related sub-systems are mutually exclusive; that is, the type of error inherent to one sub-system should not be inherent to the other, and vice versa. If this requirement is fulfilled, each of the two sub-systems should be able to check and correct the other despite its own errors.

From their characteristics it is evident that the naturomorphic form is of a relatively lower, power of discrimination than the abstract form. The characteristics of these two forms of representation and processing are considered to be mutually exclusive (Hofstadter, 1981; Polanyi, 1962), but for overall maximum efficiency, each of the two forms is considered to require the other (Bobrow, 1975). Accordingly, the two forms of representation and processing are considered to be complementary (Bruner, 1986; Inhelder, 1965; Mackay, 1949). The mutually exclusive–complementary nature of the naturomorphic and abstract forms of representation and processing is of fundamental importance in relation to cognitive control, as it would suggest that their basic types of error would be complementary or mutually exclusive. It ought to be possible, therefore, for the naturomorphic and abstract sub-systems to reciprocally evaluate and correct each other. However, as this point is of crucial importance, it will be considered in more detail.

In order to evaluate the naturomorphic sub-system, the abstract sub-system should be relatively stronger in terms of that aspect of the naturomorphic sub-system that is responsible for error. The inadequacies or sources of error within the naturomorphic sub-system are most basically a result of its limited power of discrimination. Relative to the naturomorphic sub-system, the abstract sub-system has a much greater, if not unlimited, power of discrimination. As it is stronger in this respect, the abstract sub-system should provide a meta-language by means of which the reference standards, responses, or schemata of the naturomorphic sub-system could be checked for error.

In order to evaluate the abstract sub-system, the naturomorphic sub-system should be relatively stronger in terms of the aspect of the abstract sub-system that is responsible for error. The inadequacies or sources of error within the abstract sub-system are most basically a result of its loss of information during the process of abstraction. Relative to the abstract sub-system, the naturomorphic sub-system represents and processes information in a holistic manner, and no information available to the organism is discarded in naturomorphic representation and processing. As it is stronger in this respect, the naturomorphic sub-system should serve as a meta-language by means of which the reference standards, responses, or *conclusions* of the abstract sub-system could be checked for error.

I therefore propose that the naturomorphic sub-system and abstract sub-system would be able to evaluate one another, and that the naturomorphic sub-system could update the abstract sub-system provided that the two sub-systems are, in a functional sense, related reciprocally.

This theoretical proposal that the naturomorphic and abstract sub-systems will be able to evaluate one another on the basis of their complementary information-representation and -processing characteristics is in conformity with, and therefore to some extent supported by, empirical work and theoretical arguments in mathematics and philosophy. For example, concerning the abstract sub-system correction of the naturomorphic sub-system, it is considered that analogically or intuitively derived judgements may be checked for validity by a finer logical analysis (Reichenbach, 1947; Salmon, 1963). As concerns naturomorphic sub-system correction of the abstract sub-system, an abstract logical language may be checked for consistency by using a language that relies as directly as possible on perceptual data (Reichenbach, 1947) or pictorial representation (Wittgenstein, 1961); abstract propositions may be validated by presenting them in a form that is geometrical (Sloman, 1968) or effectively continuous (using transfinite induction; Mendelson, 1964).

A point that must be stressed is that in order for the reciprocal relationship between the two cognitive sub-systems to be effective, they must interact specifically in terms of their complementary abilities. Although the naturomorphic sub-system may represent and process information holistically; that is, without losing information, the detail within the holistic information can only be represented and processed in a bit-by-bit sequential manner (Pribram, 1971). Thus, although the naturomorphic sub-system does not lose any information, it is limited in terms of what detail it can itself deal with from within the whole. If the significant detail is too small for the naturomorphic sub-system, and if as a result the naturomorphic sub-system response is erroneous, then the abstract sub-system will be able to employ its greater power of discrimination to locate the significant detail and correct the response.

Turning now to the naturomorphic sub-system correction of the abstract sub-system errors, if the naturomorphic information concerning some past event or class of past events is fed from the naturomorphic sub-system to the abstract sub-system, then the abstract sub-system can treat that information as though it were directly perceiving it and so process it abstractly according to its current (not past) criterion for the selection of important detail; that is, according to its current needs. This naturomorphic information should incorporate the most significant or *representative* pattern of features common to a particular class of experience, rather than a single feature or characteristic. The abstract sub-system may then obtain the relevant data that it may not have selected or attended to itself when the (now relevant) past events took place. In providing the abstract sub-system with this information, the naturomorphic sub-system can facilitate the correction of abstract sub-system deficiencies.

The most important point in the preceding section may be summarized as follows: Interaction of the two sub-systems specifically in terms of their complementary information-representation and -processing characteristics is of crucial importance for effective equilibration.

Normally, the naturomorphic sub-system would be involved in responding to the environment and, while doing so, would be unable to specifically output updating information to the abstract sub-system. Furthermore, during normal interaction with the environment, the hierarchically dominant abstract sub-system may have to, or may choose to, focus its attention on information input from the environment, and therefore may only allow minimal input from the naturomorphic sub-system. Under these circumstances, uninhibited transmission of information from the naturomorphic sub-system to the abstract sub-system could not be guaranteed. It is therefore proposed that there must exist the facility for periodic naturomorphic sub-system dominance over the abstract sub-system, during which time the abstract sub-system cannot inhibit input from the naturomorphic sub-system. This periodic dominance should occur selectively during those times when neither the naturomorphic sub-system nor the abstract sub-system are interacting with the environment, and it should occur often enough for the updating process to be efficient. The reciprocal relationship between the naturomorphic and abstract sub-systems therefore requires a periodically alternating dominance rather than total abstract sub-system dominance. Such an arrangement should then provide the basis for a self-correcting homeostatic system.

ELABORATION OF THE LEARNING-BASED SUB-SYSTEMS

An Additional Naturomorphic Sub-System for Sub-Programming

It is thought that within a naturomorphic sub-system type of memory, it would be desirable to have two separate storage spaces: one where all the information from past experience is pooled together, and another where different items or sequences are kept separate to ensure more clearly defined recall (P. Van Heerden, 1963). Such a division could maximize the advantages of sub-programming without the detrimental effects: one naturomorphic sub-system could be sub-programmed—the high connective statistical significance values of the sub-programmed routines would "in effect" separate them within this memory; a second naturomorphic sub-system could be independent of abstract sub-system bias and so retain a naturomorphic correspondence with the environment and a greater possibility of nonhabitual or novel responses. In relation to the updating process, it is the unbiased naturomorphic sub-system that must provide the abstract sub-system with the relevant past data—although both naturomorphic sub-systems may be involved to some extent.

An Additional Abstract Sub-System for Translatory Representation

Representational form has so far been described most simply as either naturomorphic or abstract. However, it is thought that there may be an intermediate form of representation that may be described in terms of abstracted (unimodal) images or symbolic images (Bruner, 1964; Piaget & Inhelder, 1973). Such an intermediate form of representation could fulfill a translatory role and facilitate interaction between the naturomorphic and abstract sub-systems. This intermediate form would require its own memory and processing space. The abstract sub-system may therefore be considered to be made up of two sub-systems: one involving low-level abstraction as exemplified by pictograms and *concrete* words, and a second sub-system involving high-level abstraction as exemplified by nonisomorphic symbols and abstract words. It may be expected that the smallest naturomorphically detectable polymodal feature will correspond to the largest unimodal feature handled by the low-level abstract sub-system, and that the smallest low-level abstracted feature will correspond to the largest feature that is represented by the high-level abstract sub-system.

Elaborated Circuit for Homeostasis Involving Naturomorphic and Abstract Sub-Systems

The simplified circuit of Figure 4 has been elaborated to accommodate the additional features of selective attention, sub-programming, and translation. This elaborated circuit is shown in Figure 5.

Concerning this elaborated circuit, it must be noted that: (1) the main output from the abstract sub-system goes via the higher-level part, and (2) the abstract sub-system's bias is on only one of the naturomorphic sub-systems.

SUMMARY OF MAIN POINTS FROM THE EQUILIBRATION MODEL

In order for the mind/brain to be of use in terms of interaction with the environment, it should be able to represent and process information, and upon the basis of this to control behavior. There are two basic forms of representation and processing: naturomorphic and abstract. Of these, the naturomorphic form would be necessary, and should develop before the abstract form. Initially, equilibration would be facilitated by an innate sub-system. This innate level of control could be refined by the addition of learning-based control sub-systems: by the addition of a naturomorphic sub-system and then later by the further addition of an abstract sub-system. Error in learning-based equilibration would arise

Figure 5
Homeostatic Circuit Involving Innate, Naturomorphic and Abstract Sub-Systems, Elaborated to Facilitate Attention, Sub-Programming, and Intermediate Representation and Processing

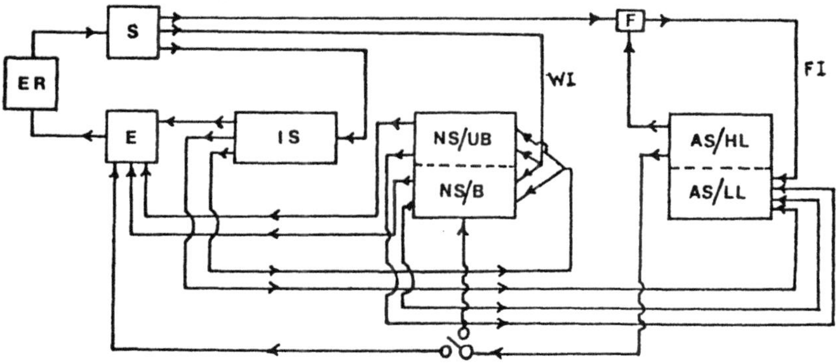

E = Effectors
S = Sensors
F = Filter
ER = Environment
FI = Filtered Information
WI = Whole Information
IS = Innate Sub-System
NS/UB = Naturomorphic Sub-System, Unbiased
NS/B = Naturomorphic Sub-System, Biased
AS/HL = Abstract Sub-System, High-Level
AS/LL = Abstract Sub-System, Low-Level

when the abstract reference standards became outdated. To compensate for this it would be necessary to periodically update the abstract sub-system reference standards or schemata. This updating process could be facilitated by periodically forwarding the appropriate information from the naturomorphic sub-system to the abstract sub-system during those times when the abstract sub-system did not have to attend to information from the external environment. The continued efficiency of learning-based equilibration would depend on the frequency with which the updating process took place.

TWO

THE BRAIN AND EQUILIBRATION

5

The Brain: Structure, Development, and Function

BRAIN STRUCTURE AND DEVELOPMENT IN RELATION TO THE REPRESENTATION AND PROCESSING OF INFORMATION

It has been suggested that the structure of the brain may be related to the form of representation and processing involved in thought (Young, 1964). Forms of representation and processing that are fundamentally different, for instance, naturomorphic versus abstract, would require different neuroanatomical regions with appropriately different neural structures (Hunt, 1973; Mackay, 1966). Consequently, it should be possible to attribute different forms of representation and processing, or cognitive sub-systems, to neuroanatomically distinct sub-systems according to the neural characteristics of those regions or sub-systems.

The form of information representation within the brain will be determined partly by the content of the input information and partly by the form or structure imposed on that information during its assimilation and storage (Mackay, 1949). Of these, the content of information input to particular regions of the brain will be determined by processes occurring during transmission to those regions, such as filtering, whereas the form of the structure imposed on the information during assimilation and storage will depend on the structure of the particular region in receipt of the information, for example on the type of, and interactional connections between, the information receivers within the reception area (Marr, 1970).

A naturomorphic sub-system would have to receive unfiltered information in a polymodal (amodal) form. The latter requirement would be fulfilled by a polymodal primary reception area; that is, one where there is a homogeneous distribution of information from the different sensory modes or within which there are polymodal neurons. An abstract sub-system would need to be able to filter its input. Also, in order for the abstract sub-system to be able to discriminate between information of different modalities, it would have to receive the information from those different modalities separately (Schroder et al., 1967). Its primary reception areas should therefore be unimodal.

The naturomorphic sub-system would, in theory, be present before the abstract sub-system. Thus, the region that corresponds to the naturomorphic sub-system should develop, in phylogeny and ontogeny, before the region that corresponds to the abstract sub-system.

It should be possible, therefore, to attribute naturomorphic and abstract forms of representation and processing to neuroanatomically distinct regions or sub-systems. These neuroanatomic regions or sub-systems should be identifiable in terms of their neurostructural and processing characteristics, and in terms of their relationship to one another in phylogeny and ontogeny.

THE BASIC STRUCTURE AND FUNCTION OF THE BRAIN

An Outline of the Structure of the Brain

Simple diagrams outlining the basic structure of the human central nervous system, composed of the spinal cord and brain, are presented in Figures 6 and 7. The three externally most discernible features of the brain are the brain stem, the cerebellum (with two hemispheres), and the cerebrum (with two hemispheres).

The brain stem is sometimes considered to refer to the parts of the brain between the spinal cord and the cerebellum and cerebrum. It is thought to include the medulla oblongata, the pontine brain stem, and the midbrain. Anatomically, as can be seen from Figure 7, the thalamencephalon appears to be enclosed, from above, within the cerebrum. From a developmental perspective, however, the thalamencephalon is considered to be part of the brain stem (Barr, 1979; Yeo, 1979). For the purpose of interpreting the function of the brain in terms of the development of information-processing and control systems, a developmental classification of the thalamencephalon would seem to be the most appropriate. In this work, therefore, the thalamencephalon is considered part of the brain stem. The four primary subdivisions of the brain stem—the medulla oblongata, midbrain, pons, and thalamencephalon—are shown in Figure 7. Also within the brain stem, and extending throughout its length, is the reticular formation, which is a complex network of nuclei and interconnecting fibers. The two most anatomically distinct structures appended to the brain stem are the cerebrum and cerebellum; these are the two largest single structures of the mammalian brain.

An Outline of the Function of the Brain

At the lowest evolutionary level, the homeostatic process is completely automatic and is facilitated by the spinal cord and brain stem (Brazier, 1963). With regard to motor function at least, the nervous system above reflex level is considered to be divided into two major sub-systems: the cerebellum and the cerebrum. Both

Figure 6
Simple Diagram of the Human Central Nervous System Showing the Spinal Cord, Brain Stem, Cerebellum, and Cerebrum

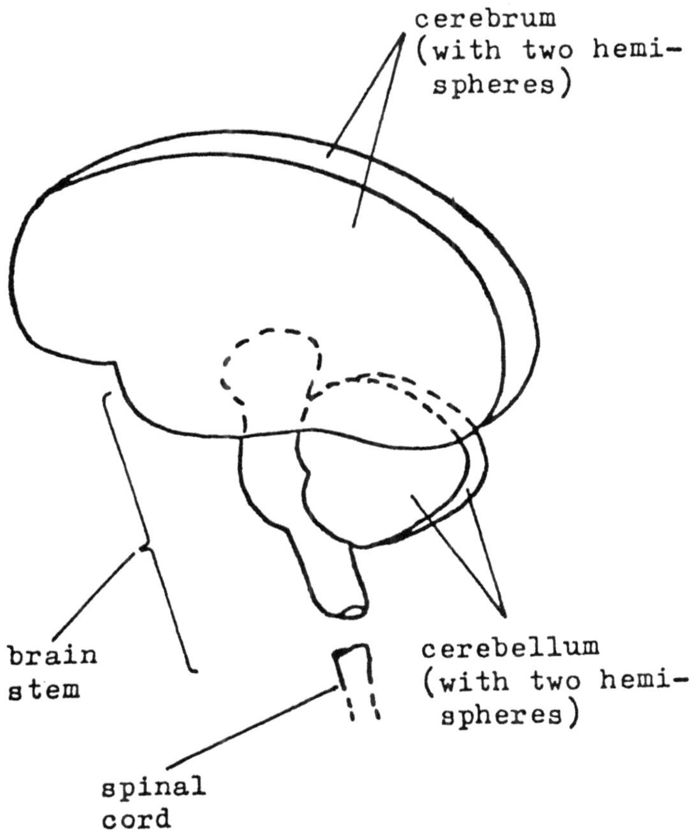

the cerebellum and the cerebrum are considered to be involved in the learning-based elaboration of basic homeostatic processes (Herrick, 1956).

DEVELOPMENT OF THE BRAIN STEM, CEREBELLUM, AND CEREBRUM

Phylogenetic Development

During vertebrate phylogeny, the structure and function of the brain has become elaborated, and control of the organism's behavior seems to have shifted to higher (newer) levels within the brain (Sarnat & Netsky, 1974). Although the structure and function have become elaborated, the older parts of the brain have remained, and retain their basic connections, operating principles, and functions (Barr, 1979;

Figure 7
Simple Diagram of the Human Central Nervous System (Saggital Section)

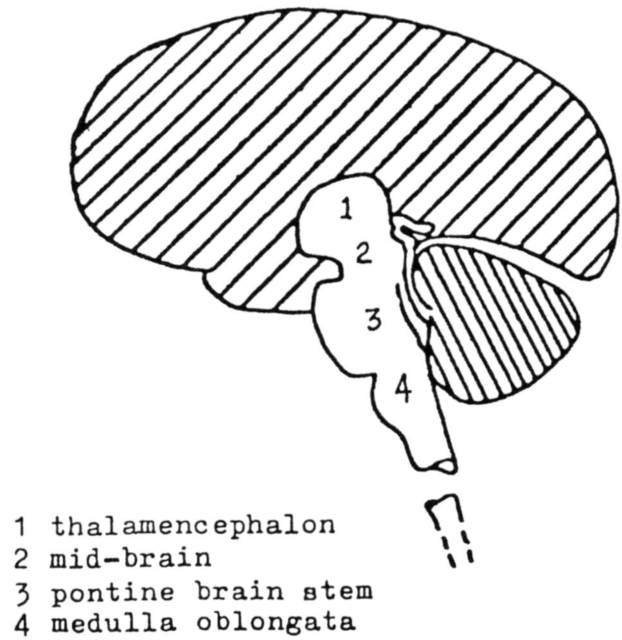

Sarnat & Netsky 1974; Yeo, 1979). Thus, the more recently evolved parts do not replace or take over the intrinsic function of the older parts, but rather control or elaborate upon them by functional superimposition (McCleary & Moore, 1965; Yeo, 1979). However, it is thought that to some extent the newer evolutionary levels are dependent on the lower, older levels, (Herrick, 1956; MacLean, 1973).

In the most primitive vertebrates, homeostatic functioning is controlled by brain stem structures (Romer, 1971; Stahl, 1977). At the phylogenetic level of the fish, however, the cerebellum (vermis and flocculonodular lobes, which correspond to the mammalian archi-cerebellum) has become involved with the elaboration of reflexes (Karamjan, 1962). Although fish generally have a well developed cerebellum, they have only a poorly developed cerebrum, which does not contain any cortical tissue and is almost exclusively concerned with olfactory sensation (Diamond & Hall, 1969; McCleary & Moore, 1965). In birds there is considerable development of the cerebellum (Romer, 1971; Yeo, 1979). It is in some reptiles that true cerebro-neocortex is first in evidence (Barr, 1979; Yeo, 1979). Then, within the mammalian brain, the cerebral cortex becomes much enlarged (Diamond & Hall, 1969; Romer, 1971). Accompanying the mammalian enlargement of the cerebrum is a commensurable enlargement of the cerebellar hemispheres (Abbie, 1941; Dow, 1942). This lateral enlargement of the cerebellum is thought to be a superimposition of a cerebrally influenced neo-cerebellar system upon the archi-cerebellar system (Abbie, 1941).

Phylogenetic data therefore indicates that, structurally and functionally, the brain basically develops in the order of brain stem, cerebellum, and cerebrum.

Ontogenetic Development

It is thought that there is a general correspondence between the order in which the nervous system becomes differentiated and elaborated during phylogeny and the order in which these changes occur in ontogeny (Llinas & Hillman, 1969; Yeo, 1979). Just as the organism's behavior appears to shift to newer (higher) levels through phylogeny, so it also appears to do so through ontogeny (Bronson, 1965). A variety of studies show that during ontogeny, in terms of structure and function, at a general level the brain develops in the order of brain stem, cerebellum, and cerebrum (McCaman & Aprison, 1964; Rorke & Riggs, 1969; Scheibel & Scheibel, 1971).

Ontogeny of the Human Cerebellum. There is evidence that at birth or even a month or so before the regions of the archi-cerebellum are well developed (Langworthy, 1933); there are from the cerebellum well-myelinated descending projections, and ascending projections to the midbrain and thalamic levels (Langworthy, 1933; Yakolev & Lecours, 1967); and the cerebellum can exert supra-spinal control (Langworthy, 1933). Although the inferior peduncle and superior cerebellar peduncle (including the brachium conjunctivum) are both well developed at birth and fully myelinated at about 4 and 9 months of age respectively (Langworthy, 1933; Yakolev & Lecours, 1967), the middle peduncle shows no corticopontine myelin at birth and is not fully myelinated until about 3-4 years of age (Rorke & Riggs, 1969; Yakolev & Lecours, 1967). The facility for ascending input to the cerebrum from the cerebellum is therefore probably fully developed by 9 months of age, whereas the facility for descending input to the cerebellum from the cerebral cortex is probably not fully developed until around 3-4 years of age.

In terms of its mass, the human cerebellum grows most rapidly over the first 6 months of age, reaches nearly two-thirds of its adult mass by 1 year of age, and reaches about four-fifths of its adult mass by about 18 months to 2 years of age (R. Ellis, 1920; Lewin, 1974). Full growth of the cerebellum, however, may not be complete until 15 years of age or more (R. Ellis, 1920).

Ontogeny of the Human Cerebrum. At birth and for about the first month or so thereafter, the cerebral neocortex is basically immature (Conel, 1963; Prichard, 1964): there is little or no dendritic growth or myelination (Laidlaw & Richens, 1976; Rorke & Riggs, 1969), and it is thought to be largely nonfunctional (Peiper, 1961; Prichard, 1964). Over the first two years of age there is continual development of the cerebral cortex; however, its overall growth during this period is slower than that of the cerebellum (Marshall, 1968): It is beyond 2 years of age that the cerebral neocortex grows most. Although by 4 years of age the neuronal growth of the brain as a whole appears to be almost completed, there is a slower but continued increase up to about 6-7 years (Hurlock, 1950; Young, 1971). Between 4 and 7 years of age, the cerebral frontal and prefrontal lobes complete their maturation (Luria, 1973). Also between 4 and 7 years of age the corpus callosum largely matures (Witelson, 1977)—although its complete maturation is protracted to about 10 years of age (Yakolev & Lecours, 1967).

Ontogeny of the Human EEG. It is thought that EEG (electroencephalogram) changes during ontogeny may validly be related to structural and functional development within the brain (Grey-Walter, 1953; Lindsley, 1964). The ontogenetic evolution of the EEG pattern is not gradual but rather is characterized by relatively sudden changes that may be the result of phylogenetically and ontogenetically more recent structures maturing and modifying the activity of the older, already mature structures (Himwich, 1964).

EEG studies indicate that electrical activity can be recorded from the brain at birth and even for a month or so before (Gibbs & Knott, 1949; Laidlaw & Richens, 1976). Because at this age the cerebral cortex is largely immature, it is thought that the electrical activity recorded through the cerebral cortex is not actually generated therein but elsewhere in sub-cerebrocortical regions (Laidlaw & Richens, 1976; Martin, 1971). The EEG activity has, for example, been related to projections from the brain stem including the thalamus and reticular formation (Himwich, 1964; Laidlaw & Richens, 1976; Scheibel & Scheibel, 1964).

Over the first year of age there is a rapid increase in the frequency and amplitude of the electrical activity recorded from the cerebral cortex, and this continues to increase, but less rapidly, up to 1-1/2–2 years of age (Hill, 1955; Lindsley, 1939, 1964). From about 1-1/2–2 years of age to around 4 years of age the delta rhythm becomes less predominant until it is absent in the awake 4-year-old's EEG (Grey-Walter, 1950, 1953). A corresponding change in the EEG at around 4 years of age has also been noted in other studies (Lindsley, 1939, 1964). At 4 years of age the predominant frequency in the EEG is the theta rhythm, although the alpha rhythm is also clearly evident at this age (Grey-Walter, 1950, 1953). By 5-6 years of age the alpha rhythm appears to peak and to be as predominant in the occipital areas as is the theta rhythm in the central areas (Gibbs & Knott, 1949; Hill, 1955). From 6-7 years of age onwards, the alpha rhythm begins to be consistently blocked by the beta rhythm when the child attends to visual stimuli (Grey-Walter, 1953). The complete adult EEG record begins to be produced between 8-14 years of age, most often around 10-12 years of age (Gibbs & Knott, 1949; Grey-Walter, 1953; Hill, 1955; Lindsley, 1964). In summary, the results of a number of independent studies all indicate that significant changes in the EEG take place particularly around 2 years of age, 6-7 years of age, and 10-11 years of age, and possibly around 4 years of age.

DETAILED STRUCTURE AND FUNCTION OF THE BRAIN STEM, CEREBELLUM, AND CEREBRUM

The Brain Stem

Basic Functions of the Brain Stem. One function of the brain stem is to facilitate innate homeostatic processing. Another function is to provide a transmission system between the cerebellum and the environment, between the cerebrum and the environment, and between the cerebellum and the cerebrum. Within the brain stem, the reticular formation and the monoamine neurotransmitter systems both appear to be particularly involved with the function of transmission of information through the brain stem.

Functions of the Brain Stem Reticular Formation. The reticular formation has been described as a ''universal connector'' (Milechnin, 1967) or a ''transactional link'' (Livingstone et al., 1954) for all parts of the brain. In addition to connecting the cerebellum and the cerebrum to the environment, the reticular formation may facilitate interaction of the cerebellum and the cerebrum (Schoolman & Delgado, 1958).

Through the ascending reticular formation, the cerebral cortex receives a nonspecific or polymodal input (Rossi & Zanchetti, 1957; Yoshii & Ogura, 1960), the content of which is thought to be based on experience (J. French, 1957) and related to the contextual significance of the stimuli (Smythies, 1970), and to provide the equivalent of a ''psychological set'' (Rioch, 1954) that may serve as a background for subsequent cerebrocortical processing.

The cerebral EEG may be influenced by input through the reticular formation (Brodal, 1957; Rossi & Zanchetti, 1957)—this may be a synchronizing or a desynchronizing influence. Evidence indicates that the reticular formation is involved in cerebral arousal or alerting, and in the process of attention (Brodal, 1957; Bronson, 1965; French, 1957; Rossi & Zanchetti, 1957). Reticular formation involvement in the process of attention may be twofold: A *psychological set* or data concerning the contextual significance of stimuli may be forwarded through the reticular formation to the cerebrum; and, second, on the basis of this information, the cerebral cortex may selectively attend to, or filter, subsequent ascending information by means of its influence on the reticular system through cerebro-reticular projections (Scheibel & Scheibel, 1958; Smythies, 1970). It is also thought that the reticular formation may be involved in what is referred to as *introspection* (J. French, 1957).

The Brain Stem Monoamine Systems. The monoamines norepinephrine (NE), dopamine (DA), and 5-hydroxytryptamine (5HT) appear to be particularly concentrated within, or released from, a collection of cells located mainly within and around the reticular formation (Ellison, 1979; Fuxe, 1971; Reis, 1974): NE neurons are found mainly in the medullary and pontine brain stem regions (Fuxe, 1971; Reis, 1974) and, in part, involve the locus coeruleus (Fuxe et al., 1968; Reis, 1974); DA neurons are distributed mainly in the nigro-striatal system and the mesolimbic system (Ellison, 1979; Thierry et al., 1976); and 5HT neurons are distributed mainly within the raphe complex (Fuxe, 1971; Trulson & Jacobs, 1975).

These three monoamine systems appear to be intimately related to one another. There are reciprocal connections between the main NE system of the locus coeruleus and the main 5HT system of the raphe complex (Morgane, 1972; Fuxe, 1971). Evidence indicates that the NE and 5HT systems may play antagonistic or complementary roles (Fuxe, 1971). As DA is a precursor of NE, it may, through this relationship, be antagonistically related to the 5HT system.

All three monoamine systems appear to be involved with the *gating* or control of information transmission through the brain stem (Ellison, 1979; Ljungberg & Ungerstedt, 1976). It is thought that the NE/5HT systems may regulate the appearance (activation or preponderant emergence) of neural circuits or subsystems within the brain (Ellison, 1979).

In particular, the NE/5HT systems are thought to be involved with the process of activation or arousal of the cerebral cortex (Ellison, 1979; Ungerstedt & Arbuthnott, 1970), and with the process of attention (Ljungberg & Ungerstedt, 1976).

The Cerebellum

Historical View of the Function of the Cerebellum. For a long time the cerebellum was regarded as an organ primarily if not exclusively concerned with motor control. This may be traced back to Sherrington's tremendously influential work, *Integrative action of the nervous system* (1906), wherein he almost definitively described the cerebellum as the ''head ganglion of the proprioceptive system'' (p. 347) and the cerebrum as the ''ganglion of the distance receptors'' (p. 349). Indeed, his concluding remark that ''It is then around the cerebrum, its physiological and psychological attributes, that the main interest of biology must ultimately turn'' (p. 393) may have condemned the cerebellum to obscurity. However, this may not have been quite his intention, for in the same publication he remarked that ''knowledge is not yet ripe for an adequate definition of the function of the cerebellum'' (p. 348).

Several articles published before Sherrington's work indicated that the cerebellum was in receipt of a range of sensory information and that it seemed to be involved in more than just motor processes (Bechterew, 1905; Ferrier, 1876; Pagano, 1902, 1905; J. Russell, 1894). Since then, considerable exploratory work on *non-motor* aspects of cerebellar function has been carried out, in particular the extensive work carried out by R. Snider (of which only a fraction is directly referred to in the bibliography).

The Functional Connections of the Cerebellum. Fiber tracts leading to and from the cerebellum connect it directly with all major subdivisions of the central nervous system (Larsell & Jansen, 1972; Palay and Chan-Palay, 1973).

There is anatomical and physiological evidence that the cerebellum is connected to all levels of the brain stem, including the inferior and superior colliculi, the sub-thalamus, the hypothalamus, and the specific, intrinsic, and association groups of nuclei within the thalamus, including the pulvinar and both geniculate nuclei.

There is anatomical and physiological evidence that the cerebellum is connected to the reticular formation at every level within the brain stem including the thalamic level. These connections include projections to the descending reticular formation and extensive projections to the ascending reticular formation. Many of these ascending cerebellar projections are of archi/paleo-cerebellar origin, and leave the cerebellum from the fastigial nucleus. In particular, the cerebellum projects to the nucleus reticularis pontis oralis (nrpo), the nucleus reticularis pontis caudalis (nrpc), and the nucleus sub coeruleus. It also projects to and receives projections from both the locus coeruleus and the raphe system. Physiological data indicates that the cerebellum may activate or be a driving force for neurons within the reticular formation. It may influence ongoing activity within the reticular formation, possibly interacting with ascending impulses (Livingston, 1958), and possibly exerting some kind of discriminatory control (Von Baumgartem & Mollica, 1954).

It is thought that the norepinephrine projections from the locus coeruleus to the reticular formation, hippocampus, and cerebral cortex may be influenced by the cerebellum (Nakamura & Iwama, 1975; R. Snider, 1975); and similarly that the activity of the 5-hydroxytryptamine projections from the raphe complex may be influenced by the cerebellum (Morrison & Bowker, 1975).

There is anatomical and physiological evidence of reciprocal connections between the cerebellum and the cerebrum including the amygdala, corpus striatum, hippocampus, septum, and all four lobes of the cerebral hemispheres. The cerebellum may contribute to, or influence the electrical activity of, all four cerebral lobes, including cerebral responses to external stimuli. Conversely, electrical activity of the cerebellum may be influenced or evoked from the cerebrum, including the occipital and temporal lobes. Cerebellar contribution to, or influence on, cerebrocortical activity (including the EEG) may be exerted in part through the ascending reticular activating system, and may involve the hippocampus as there is a marked parallelism between, or coincidence of, the electrical activity within the cerebellar cortex, hippocampus, and cerebral neocortex (Green & Arduini, 1954; Heath, 1975; Matsumo, 1961).

The Functions of the Cerebellum. It is thought that the basic circuitry within the cerebellar cortex is the same in all vertebrates (Llinas, 1969a), that connections such as the tecto-cerebellar tracts evident in fish may also persist in humans (Abbie, 1941), and that the functions of the cerebellum may be fundamentally the same from fish to humans (Pearson & Pearson, 1976). Given this assumption, some information regarding the function of the cerebellum may be obtained from observations throughout vertebrate phylogeny.

There is a variety of evidence that the cerebellum is involved in the learning of a wide range of conditioned reflexes in fish, amphibians, and mammals, without necessarily involving the cerebrum (Buchtel, 1970; Karamjan et al., 1969; Riklan et al., 1978). In particular, the cerebellum can, without cerebral mediation, learn to produce discriminatory responses to visual and auditory stimuli (Brogden & Gantt, 1937, 1942; Sjoquist & Weinstein, 1942): This indicates quite clearly that the cerebellum must be capable of recording visual and auditory information together with motor information, of evaluating visual and auditory information on the basis of recorded information, and of producing an appropriate motor response on the basis of that evaluation. It has also been shown that the cerebellum is involved in the production of hallucinatory-like behavior (McDonald, 1953); that is, upon stimulation of the cerebellum without spread of the stimulating current to extra-cerebellar regions (McDonald, 1953), there have been observed responses as if to external visual or auditory stimuli when in fact no such external stimuli existed.

The cerebral activation pattern evoked by cerebellar stimulation has been likened to that produced during attention (Heath, 1976). In fact, EEG data and observations of behavioral responses to external stimuli both indicate that the cerebellum is involved with the process of attention (Chambers & Sprague, 1955; Morrison & Bowker, 1975; Peters & Monjan, 1971). It is considered that cerebellar involvement with the process of attention may be through its connections with the ascending reticular formation (McMaster & Russell, 1958). This involvement may be as a direct influence on information travelling through the ascending reticular formation from the periphery to the cerebrum (Dow et al., 1962), or as an influence on the cerbral cortex which, on the basis of this influence, in turn selectively controls the information it subsequently receives from the periphery (Dow et al., 1962; Mizuno & Snider, 1961).

A number of articles, including extensive reviews, indicate that the cerebellum is involved with the reception, storage, correlation, and processing of the full range of sensory information (Adams, 1969; Bloedel, 1973; Fadiga & Pupilli, 1964; Leaton & Supple, 1986; Llinas, 1969a; Mortimer, 1975; Skelton, 1988; R. Snider, 1967; R. Snider & Mitra, 1970; Thompson et al., 1984; Yeo et al., 1985). Furthermore, several presentations clearly suggest that the cerebellum is involved with both affective and cognitive processes (Berntson & Torello, 1982; Frick, 1982; Gellman & Miles, 1985; Haines et al., 1984; Leiner et al., 1986; Levinson, 1980; Parkins, 1986; Thompson, et al., 1984; Watson, 1978). The most notable of these is the recent review by Leiner et al. (1986), who conclude that "there seems to be no theoretical reason why [the cerebellum] should not contribute both to motor and to mental functions" (p. 450).

Within the field of psychiatry, the traditional concept of the cerebellum as a simple regulator of motor functions now appears to be changing as a result of the increased use of computerized axial tomography (CAT scan) in the investigation of functional psychiatric disorders. Numerous articles, including several on the basis of CAT scans and postmortem confirmation studies, have now indicated that cerebellar dysfunction is correlated with affective disorders and with the psychotic aspects of schizophrenia (Courchesne et al., 1987; Dewan et al., 1983; Diaz-Infante et al., 1982; Freedman, 1977; Gutzmann & Kuhl, 1987; Hamilton et al., 1983; Heath et al., 1979; Kish et al., 1988; Kutty & Prendes, 1981; Lippman et al., 1982; Luchins et al., 1981; Reider et al., 1983; Weinberger et al., 1980; Yadalam et al., 1985). These studies, like those referred to in the preceding paragraph, indicate that the cerebellum is involved with certain aspects of mental function.

Form of Representation and Processing of Information within the Cerebellum. On a gross anatomical level, and at a neuronal level, information from the various peripheral sensory receptors appears to be received and represented largely, though not exclusively, in a polymodal or amodal manner (Fadiga & Pupilli, 1964; Freeman, 1970). Cerebellar microstructural and functional characteristics indicate that the form of cerebellar representation and processing is analogical or in-parallel (Albus, 1971; Freeman, 1970; Sabah, 1972). While it is believed that the cerebellum must be able to record temporal information, such information may be stored in a probabilistic manner rather than spatially (Freeman, 1970). The cerebellum should therefore be able to process space and time as an undifferentiated whole. It is thought that the cerebellum does not allow for the erasure of recorded information (Gilbert, 1974). The only way that information can *in effect* be forgotten is by functionally overlaying the *to be forgotten* information with the *to be remembered in preference* information (Gilbert, 1974). Thus, the cerebellum appears to have a permanent memory. As the information is recorded in a probabilistic manner, the ease of recall will be related to the statistical significance of the information.

The form of representation and processing is thought to facilitate associative storage of information within the cerebellum (Marr, 1970), but at the same time to limit its power of discrimination (Marr, 1969). It is considered that the cerebellum can recognize and generate patterns (Albus, 1971; Eccles, 1973; Marr, 1969). The generated patterns may be motor patterns of behavior (Berntson et al., 1973), or they may be *sensory* patterns (necessary for pattern recognition). Motor patterns generated by the cerebellum appear to be released in an all-or-none fashion (Blomfield & Marr, 1970); that is, as wholes. Evidence indicates that the cerebellum is involved in the anticipatory use of cues (Leiner et al., 1986), and it has been suggested that interaction between the cerebellum and the cerebral association cortex may facilitate the skillful manipulation of ideas (Leiner et al., 1986). There is some evidence that the cerebellum is involved in the utilization of mental images (Sasaki, 1985).

Concerning motor function, it is considered that the cerebellum does not operate at the level of normal consciousness but rather, relative to the cerebrum, at an unconscious level (Brain, 1963; Eccles, 1977; Noback & Demarest, 1975). Similarly, it is considered that its sensory processing operates not at a conscious level (Fadiga & Pupilli, 1964; R. Snider, 1950) but rather as an ''unconscious mind's eye'' (Bullock, 1969).

In summary, the cerebellum receives and represents information in an amodal/polymodal manner, and stores information in a spatially atemporal manner; it processes information in-parallel on a probability basis, in an analogical manner; it facilitates associative storage and pattern recognition; information is processed in a holistic form, possibly as images; it is considered to be a low-resolution processor relative to the cerebrum; and it is considered to operate at a level of consciousness below that of the cerebrum.

The Cerebrum

The Function of the Cerebrum. It is generally considered that the cerebrum has reciprocal anatomical and physiological connections with most parts of the brain stem, including the reticular formation and most, but not all, parts of the cerebellum.

Under normal circumstances, the cerebrum is the highest controller of motor actions and the elaborator of the innate homeostatic processes (Eccles, 1977).

The discriminatory power of the cerebrum is considered to be greater than that of the cerebellum (Marr, 1969). This is clearly related to the functioning of the cerebrum, for it appears to be particularly involved with discrete movements and precisely refined movement, and with the discrimination or abstraction of fine detail (Bishop, 1959; Diamond & Hall, 1969; Ingle, 1973; Richards, 1971; Travis, 1955).

The cerebrum may also function as a controller and elaborator of cerebellar processing (Barr, 1979; Freeman, 1970; R. Snider, 1950). The cerebrum may "teach" the cerebellum or program it with the action sequences that are habitually used (Blomfield & Marr, 1970; Eccles, 1977; R. Snider, 1970). Such action sequences may thereafter be switched on by the cerebrum and then released automatically from the cerebellum without further involving the cerebrum (Eccles, 1977). Alternatively, the cerebral input to the cerebellum may modify the cerebellar output to the motor system, for example, during detailed cerebral modification of cerebellar automatic sequences. This latter form of control may be considered as a cerebral bias of cerebellar output. Other functions that are considered to depend mainly on the cerebrum are: *active* interaction with the environment (Adrian, 1943); delayed application of solutions to problems (Pribram, 1971); and volitional action (Luria, 1973; Romer, 1971).

Form of Representation and Processing of Information within the Cerebrum. The primary information reception areas within the cerebral neocortex are unimodal. There is no direct interaction between the different primary reception areas (motor, somatosensory, visual, and auditory), and so, even together, the primary reception areas do not in themselves provide for polysensory integration (Luria, 1973; Popper & Eccles, 1977). The cerebral cortex can selectively control its own input via the thalamus (Luria, 1973), and most of this control is inhibitory; that is, of a filtering kind.

Through its ability to abstract information (facilitated partly by input filtering and partly by unimodal primary representation) the cerebral cortex is thought to provide the brain with a system for high-level discrimination and for the analytical and abstract processing that is characteristic of logical thought (Jerison, 1973; Luria, 1973: Marr, 1969).

A More Detailed Account of Processing by the Cerebrum

The Association Areas. In addition to the primary areas within the four main cerebral lobes, there are large areas of association cortex. Within these areas, complex processing appears to be carried out. For example, association areas within the temporal lobe, particularly the inferotemporal region, are thought to be involved in emotional processes (Kluver & Bucy, 1939), imagination (Weiskrantz, 1974), the "integration" of consciousness (Brain, 1958), experiential memory (Barr, 1979), and comparison of present percepts with recalled memories for the purpose of recognition and interpretation (Niell et al., 1972; Penfield & Jasper, 1954). Concerning the experiential memory, it appears that the temporal lobe is involved in the experience of the hallucinatory-like replay of past experiences that are automatically released as episodes or continuous sequences in an all-or-nothing manner (Penfield, 1975a).

Transmission of information from the primary sensory areas through association fibers to subsequent areas, zones, or layers, have been outlined in a number of schemes. These various schemes each indicate projections from the primary area to a second area, and then to a third and perhaps a fourth area, and that during this cascade of information from each primary area to the subsequent areas, there is the representation of increasingly complex and polymodal information (Luria, 1973; Popper & Eccles, 1977). Within these subsequent association areas—for example, the infero-temporal cortex—there appears to be a synthesis of information and a representation of patterns or wholes (Gross et al., 1974; Mountcastle, 1975).

The primary reception areas may not be the sole source of input to the association areas. There is evidence that when the primary reception areas are either ablated or transcortically disconnected from their association areas, evoked responses may still be recorded from within those association areas (Albe-Fessard & Rougeul, 1955, 1958; Buser & Borenstein, 1956). It is considered that the association areas cannot be entirely dependent on the primary areas either for the information they receive or for their functioning (Albe-Fessard & Fessard, 1961; Diamond & Hall, 1969), but rather that they must to some extent depend upon sub-cerebrocortical sources for their input of information (Pribram, 1969; Trevarthen & Sperry, 1973). For example, it is considered that the temporal lobe may not be the location of the experiential memory record (Adey, 1965; Penfield & Jasper, 1954), but rather that this information may be transmitted to the temporal lobe from sub-cerebral areas (Penfield, 1966, 1969).

The Hippocampus. The hippocampus is involved with a variety of functions including memory and attention (Douglas, 1967; Milner, 1972; Penfield & Mathieson, 1974). Concerning its involvement with memory, it is considered that the hippocampus is not the site of storage for memories (Horel, 1978; Milner, 1970; Penfield, 1975a) but that it acts more as a "key of access" to the "experiential record" (Penfield & Mathieson, 1974); that is, it enables, or is involved with, the mechanism that enables information to be consciously recalled from the memory bank containing all the information from past experience. Concerning its involvement with attention, the hippocampus can, through its reticular connections, influence the input to the cerebrum (Douglas & Pribram, 1966; Smythies, 1970), and possibly control the filtering of information (Gray, 1970; Luria, 1973). The control of the filtering, or the direction of attention, by the hippocampus may be on the basis of a comparison between the present stimuli from the environment and relevant information recalled from the experiential record (Douglas, 1967; Penfield, 1965). Clearly, the roles of the hippocampus in memory and attention are related, and possibly the same.

Concerning the transmission of information through the brain stem to the cerebrum, the activity of the hippocampus is influenced by the NE and 5HT monoaminergic systems (Grant & Jarrard, 1968; Torda, 1968). This influence may be a direct biochemical influence or an indirect influence via the effect of the neurotransmitters on the transmission process.

Reciprocal interaction between the cerebral neocortex and the cerebellar cortex may involve, or in part be mediated by, the hippocampus (Fox et al., 1967). It is therefore possible that hippocampal involvement with memory and the process of attention may be partly explained in terms of its involvement in the control of interaction between the cerebrum and the cerebellum.

Input to the Cerebral Cortex. Sensory information is transmitted to the cerebrum by a direct lemniscal pathway. The lemniscal pathway involves short latency transmission of information (Rose, 1971) via the specific thalamic nuclei to the primary reception areas. These primary reception areas are unimodal and are considered to be involved with the localization, discrimination, and abstraction of fine detail (Barr, 1979; Diamond & Hall, 1969; Ingle, 1973).

Sensory information may also be transmitted to the cerebrum by a number of extra-lemniscal, less direct, pathways. One extra-lemniscal pathway is through the tectum (Cracco & Cracco, 1976; Starr & Achor, 1975). The tectal route involves long latency transmission of information via the nonspecific thalamic nuclei to the polymodal association areas; for example, the transmission of polymodal information from the tectum via the pulvinar to the inferotemporal cortex (Mathers, 1971; Mishkin, 1972; Riss et al., 1972). Information transmitted by this route is involved with pattern perception (Chalupa et al., 1976; Diamond & Hall, 1969) and the process of attention (Chalupa et al., 1976; Ingle, 1973)—especially shifts of attention (Ingle, 1973). Another extra-lemniscal pathway is through the ascending reticular formation. The reticular route involves long latency transmission of information via the intrinsic thalamic nuclei diffusely to the cerebral cortex (Brain, 1958; Jasper, 1958).

Under normal circumstances, perceptual processing appears to involve both short- and long-latency components (Lindsley, 1964; Sprague et al., 1961). Of these, the extra-lemniscal long-latency component is considered to provide the psychological set or contextual background for subsequent processing (Rioch, 1954); that is, for subsequent processing involving the lemniscal system input.

The main nonperipheral source of extra-lemniscal input to the cerebral cortex is the cerebellum. From the cerebellum there are projections to the tectum, to all three groups of thalamic nuclei including the pulvinar, and to the ascending reticular formation. Physiological data indicates that the cerebellar contribution to the extra-lemniscal input is of relatively long latency (Cracco & Cracco, 1976; R. Snider, 1970; Wiederholt & Iragui-Madoz, 1977).

A BASIC MODEL OF THE BRAIN IN TERMS OF THE BRAIN STEM, CEREBELLUM, AND CEREBRUM

On the basis of the neurological information considered in this chapter, a fairly detailed representation of the brain has been constructed and is presented in

Figure 8. This model indicates the connections between the brain stem (BS), cerebellum (CL) and cerebrum (C). All input to the brain stem from the peripheral stimuli (S), whether somatosensory, vestibular, auditory, or visual, is shown, for simplicity, to ascend from the base of the brain stem. Similarly, all output from the brain stem to the effectors (E) is shown to descend to the base of the brain stem. For a given transmission route between two regions, only a single pathway is indicated. The diagram only depicts the functional connections between regions: It does not depict the spatial arrangements of these connections within the brain.

Within the brain stem, only the main nuclei or groups of nuclei are shown: the vestibular nuclei (V), the olivary nuclei (O), the tectal nuclei (T), the pontine nuclei (P), the red nucleus (R), the substantia nigra (S), the thalamic nuclei (TH), and the reticular formation (RF), which, for simplicity, is also used to include the brain stem monoamine systems.

The cerebellum is subdivided into the cerebellar nuclei (CLN) and cerebellar cortex (CLX), and the cerebrum is similarly subdivided into the cerebral nuclei (CN) and cerebral cortex (CX).

Relationship of the Neurological Data to the Innate, Naturomorphic, and Abstract Sub-Systems of the Equilibration Model

Neurological data indicates that the innate homeostatic sub-system involves the spinal cord and brain stem. Appended to the brain stem and connected through it are the cerebellum and the cerebrum. Both these additional structures are involved in learning-based cognitive control of the innate-level processes. On the basis of neurostructural and processing characteristics, and phylogenetic and ontogenetic data, it is proposed that, fundamentally, the cerebellum may be considered as a naturomorphic sub-system, whereas the cerebrum as a whole may be considered an abstract sub-system. The correspondence between the brain stem, cerebellum, and cerebrum, and the innate, naturomorphic, and abstract sub-systems may be considered in more detail by systematic comparison of the basic model presented in Figure 8 with the control system represented earlier in Figure 4. This comparison should prove to be particularly useful for interpreting the function of the brain stem transmission system. For ease of comparison with the detailed representation of the brain, the homeostatic circuit shown in Figure 4 has been redrawn, retaining exactly the same functional circuitry, and is presented in Figure 9.

Comparison of Figures 8 and 9 shows that the brain stem/innate sub-system would receive a direct input from the sensors. Its output would be direct to the effectors and, as a sample of the response information, to the cerebellum/naturomorphic and cerebrum/abstract sub-systems. The cerebellum/naturomorphic sub-system would receive direct input from the sensors, a sample of the innate sub-system response information, and a bias signal from the cerebrum/abstract

Figure 8
Relatively Simple Model of the Brain in Terms of the Brain Stem, Cerebellum, and Cerebrum

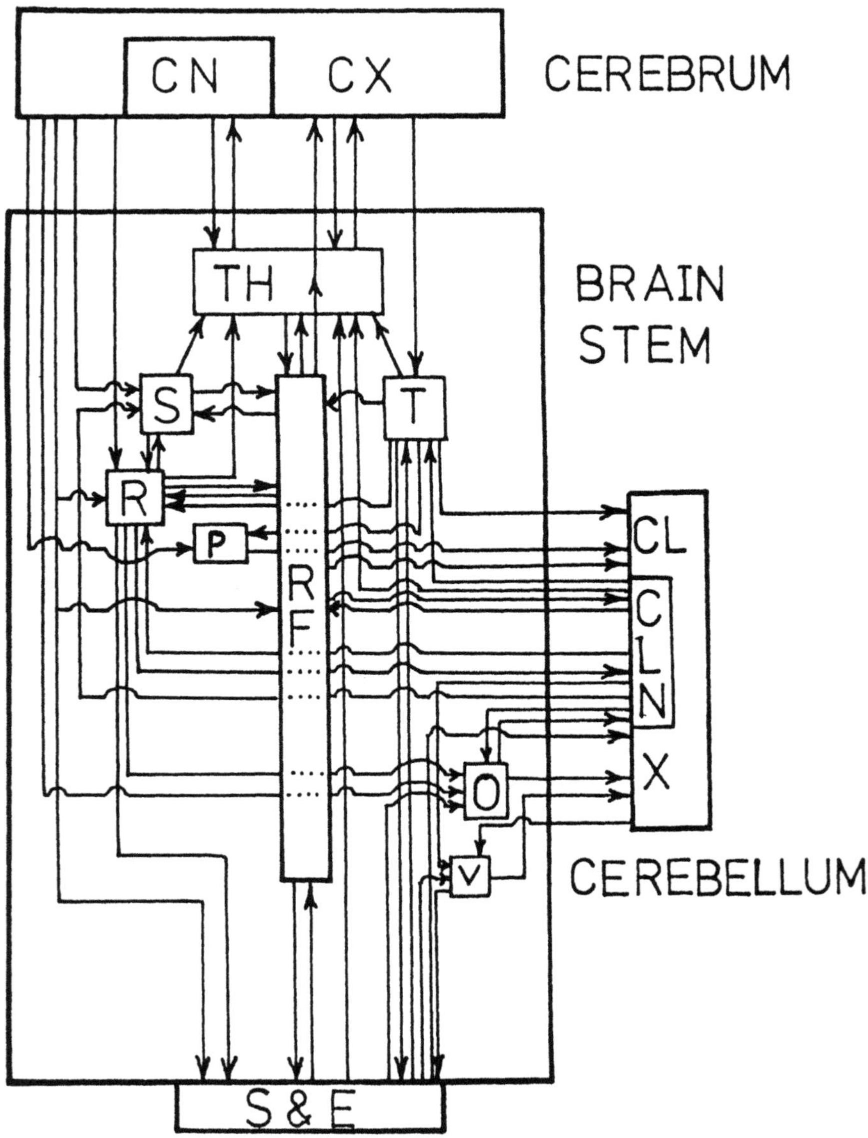

sub-system via projections including the cerebrocortico tracts (pontine and olivary). Its control to the effectors could partly be through its rubral and vestibular projections. A sample of its response information would be transmitted to the cerebrum/abstract sub-system through one or more of the various cerebellar

Figure 9
Simplified Homeostatic Circuit Involving Innate, Naturomorphic, and Abstract Sub-Systems Redrawn in an Arrangement Comparable with That of the Relatively Simple Model of the Brain

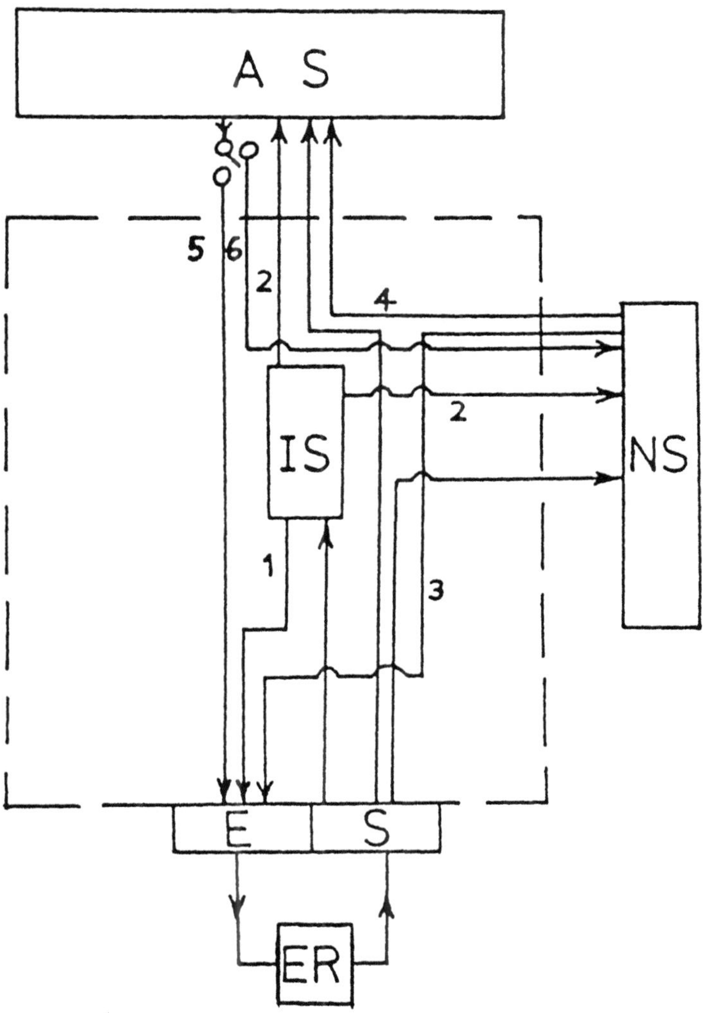

E = Effectors
S = Sensors
ER = Environment
IS = Innate Sub-System
NS = Naturomorphic Sub-System
AS = Abstract Sub-System

1 = Innate sub-system response information
2 = Sample of innate sub-system repsonse information
3 = Naturomorphic sub-system response information
4 = Sample of naturomorphic sub-system response informatior.
5 = Abstract sub-system response information
6 = Sample of abstract sub-system response information

ascending projections within the extra lemniscal system, for example, via the tectum and thalamus to the association areas including the inferotemporal lobe, or through the ascending reticular formation. These transmission routes could facilitate cerebellar contribution to the manipulation of ideas suggested by Leiner et al. (1986).

The cerebellum/naturomorphic sub-system would receive a direct unimodal input from the sensors via the lemniscal pathways. It could also receive a sample of the brain stem/innate sub-system response information and a sample of the polymodal cerebellum/naturomorphic sub-system response information via the various extra-lemniscal pathways. The switch arrangement for descending cerebrum/abstract sub-system control to the effectors and to the cerebellum/naturomorphic sub-system would be correspondent to, or involve, its pyramidal and extra-pyramidal projections. Although only the transmission pathways have been considered in the above description, it is proposed that the action of the monoamine neurotransmitters within the brain may be partly understood in terms of activation or inhibition of these pathways.

Suggested Function of the Brain in Relation to the Process of Attention

The region most strongly involved in the process of attention seems to be the reticular formation. Through the ascending reticular formation, information is transmitted to the cerebrum. This information may be polymodal, and its content may be based on experience. This experience determines the contextual significance of the stimuli. On the basis of this information, the cerebrum may then, by filtering, selectively attend to subsequent information by means of its influence on the reticular formation. The transmission of information through the reticular formation to the cerebrum seems to be related to, or controlled by, the brain stem monoamine systems in part and in part by the hippocampus. Another brain stem transmission route that seems to be involved with attention, especially shifts of attention, is that through the tectum and pulvinar to the inferotemporal lobe.

From the cerebellum, information is transmitted to the cerebrum partly through the reticular formation. Both the hippocampus and the brain stem monoamine systems seem to be involved with the regulation of this transmission pathway for interaction between the cerebellum and the cerebrum. The cerebellum also projects to the tectum, the pulvinar, and the temporal lobe. Anatomical data therefore indicates that the cerebellum could contribute to the information that is transmitted to the cerebrum and that provides the basis for cerebrally directed attention. Physiological data indicates that the cerebellum can influence the cerebral EEG via the reticular formation, and that it can exert a discriminating influence on the activity of, or information transmitted through, the reticular formation. The cerebellum may produce a desynchronization of the cerebral EEG similar to that produced during attention. Behavior-based observations also indicate that the cerebellum is involved in the process of attention. The cerebellum could, moreover, provide polymodal information, the content of which could be based on experience and could be related to the contextual significance of the environmental stimulus.

It is therefore proposed that the cerebellum makes a major contribution to the information transmitted to the cerebrum during the process of attention. This contribution may be through the reticular formation and through the tectal-pulvinar route. The information transmitted from the cerebellum to the cerebrum could, in part, contain the most significant naturomorphically determined features of a given stimulus. Initially, this information would be received by an association area—most probably the inferotemporal cortex. As the association areas receive a synthesized input by cascade from the primary areas and an input from the cerebellum, they would facilitate interaction of the results of cerebral primary processing and cerebellar processing. In part, this interaction could enable a cerebellar context to be given to the cerebral processing, and in part it could enable the cerebellar information to be cerebrally evaluated by comparison. Upon receipt of the information from the cerebellum, the cerebral cortex could therefore determine whether the cerebellum's naturomorphically determined significant features were of importance in terms of the abstract processing of the cerebrum. It could then either ignore the information or selectively attend to the most important part of it. Meanwhile, the cerebellum could continue to receive and record all the available input. The selective attention of the cerebrum could be facilitated through hippocampal-reticular interaction or through thalamically mediated control.

Suggested Function of the Brain in Relation to the Process of Imagination and Intuition

The region most often implicated in the process of imagination is the inferotemporal cortex: Stimulation of this region results in an all-or-nothing hallucinatory or dream-like replay of events from past experience. It is considered that the temporal lobe is not the site of storage for these memories, but that the information is transmitted from some sub-cerebrocortical region and involves the reticular formation. Data also indicates that both the hippocampus and the brain stem monoamine systems may be involved in controlling the transmission of this information.

The cerebellum transmits information through the reticular formation to the cerebral cortex, including the temporal lobe. Behavior-based observations indicate that the cerebellum may be involved in the production of hallucinatory-like behavior, and there is considerable evidence that the cerebellum is involved in the production of dreams (see Chapter 6). It is considered that the cerebellum releases its information in an all-or-nothing manner. The cerebellum could therefore be responsible for the provision of the information that constitutes the hallucinatory-like replay of past events and that, in a less extreme form, constitutes the imagination.

Information transmitted from the cerebellum to the cerebrum could be in the form of an all-or-nothing polymodal image sequence. The source of the image sequence may be primarily from the archi-cerebellar region or from the paleo-neocerebellar regions. Those image sequences released from the archi-cortex would be from that area of the cerebellum not under direct cerebral control, and so would be the most correspondent with environmentally determined experience; the most spontaneous in that they would not be amenable to cerebral initiation or cerebral bias during their release; and the most dream-like or hallucinatory-like images. Those image sequences released from the newer regions of the cerebellum that the cerebrum could directly bias may be evoked directly by the cerebrum and biased by the cerebrum during their release. These cerebrally evoked images could have their *topic* content determined by the cerebrum. The cerebrally evoked image sequences from within the cerebellum would be autonomous in their unfoldment with regard to content but would be subject to bias from the cerebrum in the form of inhibition. During imagination, the images released from the cerebellar neocortex need not be accompanied by an overt expression of the motor component: This may be because the minimum intensity of excitation necessary for an ascending cerebellar output is less than that necessary for descending cerebellar output, or because expression of the motor component is inhibited by the cerebrum via its bias connection to the cerebellum.

There is evidence that during vivid imagination there is inhibition of the cerebrocortical response to external stimuli (Schatzman, 1980). This may be facilitated by cerebral control of the ascending sensory stimuli via the reticular formation.

Relative to the cerebrum, cerebellar processing is unconscious. The cerebrum would therefore receive the results of cerebellar processing, or the cerebellar *solution* to a problem, without itself having any information as to how the solution was arrived at by the cerebellum and without necessarily having had anything to do with the production of the solution: Cerebral receipt of the cerebellar-generated solution would therefore be experienced as *intuition*.

Sub-Programming of the Cerebellar/Naturomorphic Sub-System by the Cerebrum/Abstract Sub-System

It is generally accepted that the neocerebellum can be sub-programmed by, or can learn from, the cerebrum.

An Intermediate Translatory Representational Form of Information

The earliest development of cerebral neocortex occurs in reptiles as a multimodal area that is in receipt of information through the tectum and the pulvinar. This area is considered to be correspondent to the area that forms the rudimentary (ontogenetically earliest) association cortex in mammals (Bishop, 1959). As the rudimentary association cortex is the first part of the cerebral cortex to develop, it is the part to which the earliest cerebellar projections will travel. It is therefore proposed that the most rudimentary cerebral/abstract representations—the most basic intermediate translatory form—will be processed within the rudimentary association cortex. These areas are known to be involved in the processing of patterns and *whole* features or *whole* parts.

LATERALIZATION OF FUNCTION WITHIN THE BRAIN

Anatomically, most of the brain stem, cerebellum, and cerebrum are bilaterally structured. Although there are both ipsilateral and contralateral connections between the brain stem, cerebellum, and cerebrum, the cerebrum is predominantly connected to the brain stem and to the cerebellum by contralateral projections.

Lateralization of Function within the Cerebral Hemispheres

Lateralization of function within the cerebral cortex is well documented. The two cerebral hemispheres appear to represent and process information in different ways. The type of representation and processing evidenced by, or through, the minor (most often right-side) cerebral hemisphere has been described variously as naturalistic, imagistic, pictorial, simultaneous, in-parallel, analog, Gestalt, global, polysensory, and holistic, while that evidenced by, or through, the dominant (most often left-side) hemisphere has been described as abstract, analytical, digital, sequential, serial, and logical (Carmon, 1971; Galin, 1974; Gott, 1973; Levy, 1974; Sperry, 1974; Tzeng et al., 1979; Young, 1962). Of the two cerebral hemispheres, the dominant one is considered to be involved with consciousness (Popper & Eccles, 1977; Serafetinedes et al., 1965; Sperry, 1966; Zangwill, 1974), especially self-consciousness (Dimond, 1979; Popper & Eccles, 1977).

It has been proposed that normal development of lateral specialization of language occurs when the verbally predisposed hemisphere callosally "inhibits" the nondominant partner, preventing it from developing all but the most rudimentary of language abilities and, more important, from duplicating the functions of the dominant hemisphere (Birchwood et al., 1988). Another reason given for hemispheric specialization within the cerebral cortex is that it occurs in order to allow the coexistence of two incompatible modes of information processing (Levy, 1969; Witelson, 1977). Yet another suggestion is that cerebral hemisphere specialization is of value with respect to capacity limitations and selective attention: There is evidence that each hemisphere can selectively attend to input of the type that it is best suited to process (Friedman & Polson, 1981).

Anatomical, electrophysiological, and behavioral data indicate that hemispheric functional differences are present in rudimentary form at birth (Molfese, 1977; Wada et al., 1975) and possibly even before (Wada, 1977). Anatomical and physiological data indicate that the corpus callosum and other forebrain commissures on which cerebrocortical lateralization of function is thought to depend are at birth both unmyelinated and not fully functional (Leussenhop et al., 1970; Rorke & Riggs, 1969; Sechzer et al., 1977; Yakolev & Lecours, 1967). It is therefore probable that the rudimentary lateralization of function evident at birth is of subcerebrocortical origin.

Although there are rudimentary functions lateralized at birth, it appears that, over the first 2 years at least, speech is completely bilateral (Basser, 1962; Lennenberg, 1967). The study of interhemispheric transmission time in young children suggests that callosal maturation, in terms of the myelination of specific fibers, continues at least until 5 years of age (Salamy, 1978). The emergence of a stable right-ear (left-brain) advantage on a verbal dichotic listening task appears to correlate temporally with increased efficiency of callosal transmission: A relatively stable significant ear advantage only develops in children beyond the age of 5 years (Geffan, 1976). This correlates well with the decrease in interhemispheric conduction time (Salamy, 1978) and improvement on intermanual tasks (O'Leary, 1980). Not surprisingly, therefore, the period around age 4-5 years appears to be of crucial importance for the hemispheric specialization of more sophisticated functions (Kimura, 1967; Lennenberg, 1967; Zaidel, 1976). By this period speech has become hemispherically specialized (Kimura, 1967; Lennenberg, 1967).

The myelogenetic cycle of interhemispheric fibers appears to continue up to between 10-15 years of age (Randall, 1983; Yakolev & Lecours, 1967). Correspondingly, hemispheric specialization may continue to increase up to 11-12 years (Lennenberg, 1967; Zaidel, 1976).

The forms of representation and processing of information exhibited by the minor and dominant cerebral hemispheres are in many respects correspondent to naturomorphic and abstract forms respectively. However, it is suggested that theoretically neither the left nor the right cerebral hemisphere can in itself be the anatomical substrate for naturomorphic representation and processing of information in its basic form because both have fundamentally the same cytoarchitecture (Barr, 1979), both have unimodal primary reception areas, and both receive filtered input. Much of the currently available information points to differences between the cerebral hemispheres that are merely relative or quantitative rather than qualitative (Corballis, 1983; Perecman, 1983; Zaidel, 1985). Furthermore, there is evidence that when the entire dominant or minor cerebral hemisphere is removed in adults, the remaining brain as a whole (that is, including the cerebellum) will essentially "subsume" the functions of the removed hemisphere (Dennis & Whitaker, 1976; Gott, 1973; McFie, 1961; Smith, 1966): this would not be possible if either of the two cerebral hemispheres were *the* naturomorphic processor. It is therefore proposed that the two cerebral hemispheres are each fundamentally abstract processors but that the dominant hemisphere further develops to represent and process information at a much higher and relatively incompatible level of abstraction than that of the minor hemisphere. In turn, the unimodal areas of the dominant and minor cerebral hemispheres would each facilitate a higher level of abstract representation and processing than the association areas. Within the cerebral cortex as a whole there would therefore be a number of increasingly abstract levels of representation and processing in the order of minor-hemisphere association cortex, dominant-hemisphere association cortex, minor-hemisphere primary areas, and dominant-hemisphere primary areas.

Lateralization of Function within the Brain Stem and Cerebellum

In addition to the well-known lateralization of function within the cerebral cortex, there is evidence of lateralization of motor and sensory processes within the brain stem, for example, in the thalamus, the superior colliculus, the substantia nigra, and the ascending reticular formation (Glick et al., 1977; Kirvel et al., 1974; Ojeman, 1977; Watson et al., 1974). There is also anatomical and physiological evidence of lateralization within the cerebellum (Fischer-Williams, 1961, Riklan et al., 1974; Upton & Cooper, 1976). The brain stem monoamine systems also evidence lateralization. A number of lateralized behavioral effects may be induced or mediated by dopamine, norepinephrine, and 5-hydroxytryptamine. These may be motor effects such as unilateral rotation, or sensory effects such as unilateral inattention (Ljunberg & Ungerstedt, 1976). As the monoamine systems within the brain stem are thought to be involved partly with the transmission of information through the brain stem (Ellison, 1979; Ljunberg & Ungerstedt, 1976), the lateralized effects may be related to the lateralized transmission of information through the brain stem. Concerning this, the lateralized effects mediated by the brain stem monoamine systems may be influenced in a lateralized manner by the cerebrum (Glick et al., 1977) and by the cerebellum (Hoffer et al., 1973; Nieoullon et al., 1978; Siggins et al., 1971; Ungerstedt, 1971). Altogether the evidence indicates that lateralization of neurotransmitter activity involves, intimately related with one another, the cerebrum, the brain stem (including the substantia nigra, raphe system, and locus coeruleus), and the cerebellum.

Reciprocal Control between the Lateralized Brain Stem Transmission Systems

It has been reported that there are reciprocal changes in the excitability of the two cerebral hemispheres and that this may be related to arousal from the subcortical regions (Koella & Ferry, 1963). There is evidence of a reciprocal relationship between the two lateralized sides of the monoamine systems, for example the nigro-striatal dopamine system, such that increased activity in one side is accompanied by decreased activity or inhibition in the other side (Nieoullon et al, 1978). Moreover, unilaterally presented sensory stimuli may evoke bilateral, but unilaterally opposite, effects in the nigro-striatal system (Nieoullon et al., 1978). There may, for example, be evoked an increased dopamine release on the side contralateral to the stimuli and an accompanying decreased dopamine release on the ipsilateral side (Nieoullon et al., 1977a, 1977b). The increased dopamine release in the side receiving the visual stimulus may facilitate arousal or attention to the stimulus while at the same time the decreased release on the other side may reduce the potential for arousal or attention so that the overall effect may be that of lateralized focussing. A similar relationship has been observed within the nigro-striatal system for ascending cerebellar output: Unilateral stimulation of the cerebellar dentate nuclei may evoke bilateral, but unilaterally opposite, effects in the nigro-striatal system (Nieoullon et al., 1978); for example, stimulation of the right dentate nuclei will cause a decreased dopamine release in the contralateral substantia nigra and an accompanying increased dopamine release in the ipsilateral substantia nigra (Nieoullon et al., 1978).

Lateralized Information Transmission through the Brain Stem in Relation to Lateralized Function of the Cerebral Hemispheres

The basic lateralized pathways for the transmission of information from the environment to the cerebrum, and between the cerebellum and cerebrum are shown in Figure 10. For simplicity, in Figure 10, representation of reticular transmission to the cerebellum and cerebrum has been omitted and only one pathway from the environment to the thalamencephalon and one from the cerebellum to the thalamencephalon are shown.

The unilateral focussing effect will allow cerebrally mediated attention to be directed predominantly to information travelling to one of the two cerebral hemispheres. A number of pathways including the reticular formation and related monoamine systems may be involved in this lateralized control process. The lateralized focussing may be on information from one half of the environment (focus on pathway 1 or 2) or it may be on information from one of the two cerebellar hemispheres (focus on pathway 3 or 4). In theory it would also be possible for one cerebral hemisphere to focus on information transmitted from the environment while the other cerebral hemisphere focussed on information transmitted from the cerebellum—the cerebral hemisphere receiving information predominantly from the environment would simultaneously inhibit its cerebellar input, whereas the cerebral hemisphere receiving information predominantly from the cerebellum would simultaneously inhibit its environmental input as shown in Figure 11.

Such an arrangement as that shown in Figure 11 would allow the cerebral cortex to receive a certain amount of cerebellar input during the awake state without totally interfering with the cerebral interaction with the environment. It is proposed that the minor cerebral hemisphere—the one with the lower level of abstract representation most suited to receive and process input from the cerebellum—would be the one most often in receipt of cerebellar input during the awake state. As the minor cerebral hemisphere is below the dominant hemisphere's level of consciousness, the cerebellar input to the cerebrum would not necessarily interfere with the activity of the dominant and conscious sub-system. The results of the minor cerebral hemisphere low-level abstract processing of cerebellar information could be transmitted to the dominant cerebral hemisphere for its attention as necessary.

Seen from this perspective, the minor cerebral hemisphere may be considered to fulfil a translatory role in handling low-level abstract data received from the association cortex, which in turn receives information from the cerebellum, before transmitting it to the highest-level abstract sub-system within the dominant cerebral

Figure 10
Basic Lateralized Pathways from Environment to Cerebellum and Cerebrum, and between Cerebellum and Cerebrum

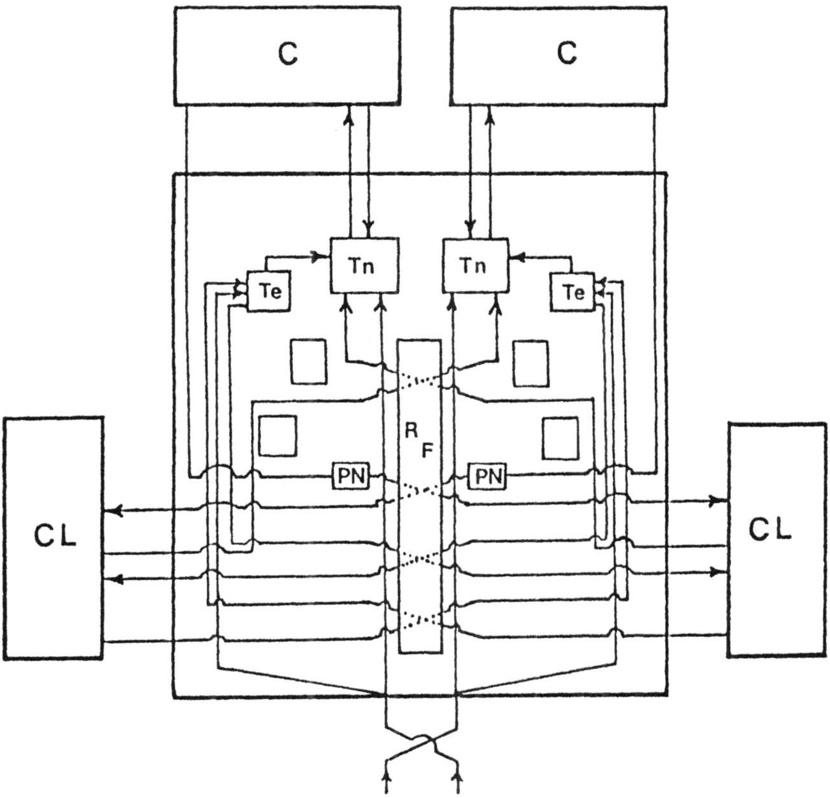

hemisphere. The minor cerebral hemisphere would therefore be more strongly involved with the processing of naturomorphic information than would the dominant cerebral hemisphere, and its removal or malfunction would be accompanied by a deterioration of the *cerebral* capacity to handle naturomorphically processed information.

The above described predominantly lateralized cerebral receipt of information from the cerebellum during the awake state could, in part, be related to the process of normal imagination. It is suggested that there may normally be automatic recall of images within the minor cerebral hemisphere prior to their utilization by the dominant cerebral hemisphere. Once the information has been transferred to the dominant cerebral hemisphere, it may then be most abstractly and consciously processed.

Figure 11
Cerebrally Lateralized Attention for Input from the Environment and Cerebellum

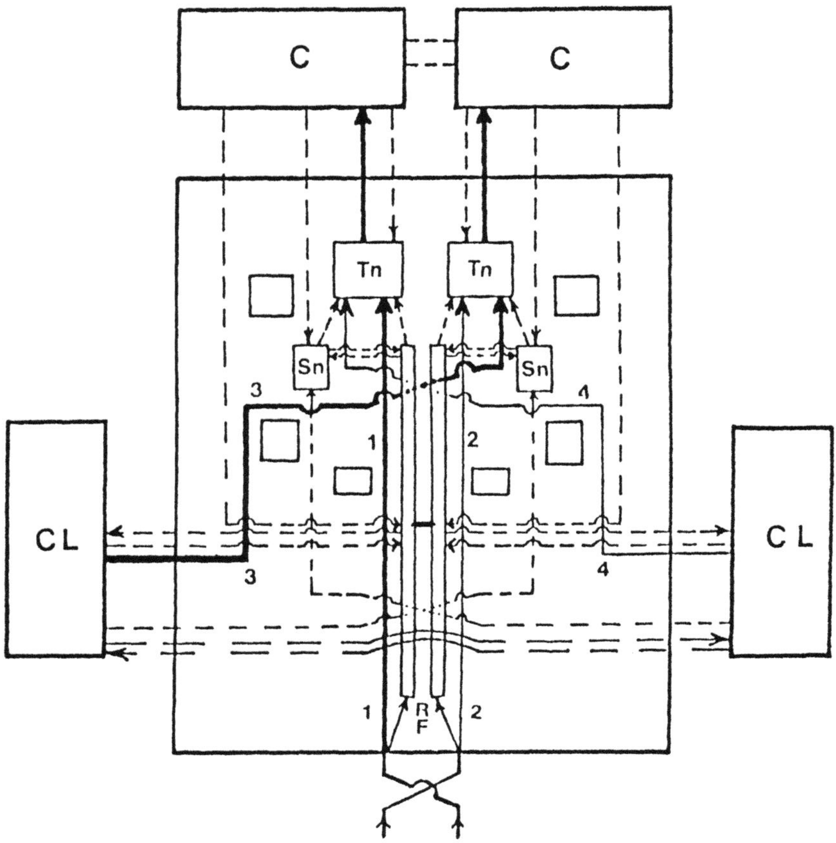

SUMMARY OF MAIN POINTS FROM THE NEUROLOGICAL DESCRIPTION

Basically, the brain is composed of the brain stem, the cerebellum, and the cerebrum. The brain stem, together with the spinal cord, facilitates homeostatic control at an innate level. Additionally, the brain stem provides a transmission system between the cerebellum and the environment, between the cerebrum and the environment, and between the cerebrum and the cerebellum.

The cerebellum and the cerebrum serve as learning-based controllers. Of these, the cerebrum appears to operate at a conscious level, whereas, relative to this, the cerebellum appears to operate at an unconscious level. On the basis of their neurostructural and processing characteristics and their developmental relationship to one another, the cerebellum would appear to correspond to a naturomorphic sub-system whereas the cerebrum would appear to correspond to an abstract sub-system.

6

The Brain, Sleep, and Dreaming

It is thought that for cerebral representations to be modified or updated, the cells over the whole cerebral cortex should become modifiable, and that at such times ordinary information (from the external environment) should be rigorously excluded (Marr, 1970). The time when such a condition normally exists is during sleep (Evans & Newman, 1964; Marr, 1970; Young, 1964).

THE BASIC NEUROPHYSIOLOGY OF SLEEP AND DREAMING

During sleep, the cerebral EEG periodically alternates between desynchronization (D sleep) and synchronization (S sleep). Correspondent with these EEG changes is a periodic alternation between sleep with rapid eye movements (REM sleep) and sleep without rapid eye movements (NREM sleep, Aserinsky & Kleitman, 1953, 1955). It is thought that mental activity takes place during D/REM and S/NREM sleep (Berger, 1969; Foulkes, 1967; Snyder, 1969), but that the mental activity during D/REM sleep is the most dream-like (Dement & Kleitman, 1957; Shapiro, 1967; Snyder, 1969), while that occurring during S/NREM sleep is much more awake-like (Berger, 1969; Shapiro, 1967). Consequently, it is the D/REM sleep phase that is thought to be correspondent with the actual experience of dreaming, while the subsequent S/NREM phase is correspondent with mental activity related to the experience of the preceding dream phase (Berger, 1969).

Normally, dream sleep appears at 70-90 minute intervals throughout the sleep period in adults (Berger, 1969; Oswald, 1974). There is, however, evidence that the physiological and neurophysiological activity normally correspondent with dream sleep also occurs with the same periodicity, but less intensely or evidently, throughout the awake state (Giora, 1972; Jouvet, 1962; Snyder, 1963).

Underlying the two psychological systems considered to interact during the process of dreaming may be two physiological or neuroanatomical systems (French, 1954; Pavlov, 1958). Dream sleep may involve the preponderant or emergent activity of a neuroanatomical region different from the region that normally is preponderantly active in the awake state (Pavlov, 1958).

One factor thought to contribute to the onset of sleep, particularly dream sleep, is a reduction of externally generated stimuli that reach the higher and conscious level of the brain (Pavlov, 1958). As a result of this reduction there may be facilitated a release of internally generated past impressions or memories from within the lower neuroanatomical and unconscious levels (Freud, 1900; Kubie, 1954). Within the higher, or cerebral, level of the brain, the emergence of information released from the lower level may also involve a decreased activity of processes, or switching off of the system that would normally in the awake state inhibit such preponderant emergence (Pavlov, 1958; Torda 1968).

PHYSIOLOGICAL AND NEUROPHYSIOLOGICAL CHANGES IN THE D/REM-S/NREM CYCLE

Relative to the S/NREM sleep phase, the D/REM sleep phase is accompanied by increased cerebral blood flow (Risberg & Ingvar, 1973); increased activity of the autonomic nervous system (Hartmann, 1967); increased "spontaneous" activity of the reticular formation (Hodes & Suzuki, 1965); a higher response threshold in the midbrain reticular formation to auditory as well as direct stimulation (Bizzi & Brooks, 1963; Hodes & Suzuki, 1965; Huttenlocher, 1961); and a higher threshold for behavioral awakening (Thompson, 1967).

Among the phenomena evident during D/REM sleep are cerebral desynchronization (Pompeiano, 1973); hippocampal theta waves of 5-6 Hertz (Grosser & Siegal, 1971; Smythies, 1970), a depression of spontaneous and reflex activity in the muscles (Pompeiano, 1967a) and a general atonia, especially of the antigravity muscles (Grosser & Siegal, 1971; Hartmann, 1967). The preceding phenomena constitute a tonic background on which are superimposed the following phasic phenomena: large amplitude waves occurring in the pontine reticular formation, lateral geniculate nuclei and occipital cortex, which are referred to as PGO activity and which normally occur coincidentally with REM bursts (Grosser & Siegal, 1971; Hartmann, 1967; Molinari & Foulkes, 1969; Morrison & Bowker); short-term increases in the frequency of the hippocampal theta rhythm (Harper, 1973); increased muscle activity and myoclonic twitches (Grosser & Siegal, 1971; Hartmann, 1967); and short fluctuations within the autonomic nervous system (Grosser & Siegal, 1971; Hartmann, 1967). Also involved in D/REM sleep are the parietal lobe (Humphrey & Zangwill, 1951), the temporal lobe (Penfield & Perot, 1963; Yamaguchi et al., 1967), the cerebral limbic regions (Broughton, 1973; Morgane, 1972), and the pulvinar of the thalamus (Alihanka et al., 1975; Psatta & Constantinescu, 1980).

Both the tonic and phasic phenomena of dream sleep may be regarded basically as an ascending excitatory component involving activity of the cerebral cortex and ascending sensory systems (reticular and PGO activity), and a desynchronizing component that is largely inhibitory.

Ascending Component

The most frequently described route for REM-related ascending impulses travelling to the cerebral cortex is from the pontine brain stem to the lateral geniculate nucleus and thence to the occipital cortex (Brooks & Bizzi, 1963; Jouvet et al., 1965). Input to the lateral geniculate, as evidenced in part by the PGO activity, is not from the eye muscle afferents or retina (Brooks, 1976; Cespuglio & Valtax, 1976; Munson, 1974); that is, it does not first descend to the pontine region and then ascend from there: It travels only in an ascending direction from the pontine region (Brooks & Bizzi, 1963; Michel et al., 1964). It is thought that, of the phasic phenomena of D/REM sleep, the PGO spikes in particular reflect the neurological activity underlying the experience of dreaming (Dement et al., 1970; Hartmann, 1967).

Descending Component

There are thought to be two inhibitory processes acting on motor output during sleep. There is atonic depression which lasts throughout the sleep episode, and there is a phasic depression, or enhancement of depression, which occurs synchronously with the bursts of REM or PGO activity during dream sleep (Morrison & Bowker, 1973; Pompeiano, 1970). Despite the phasic depression, there are muscular twitches during the REM bursts. These twitches are thought to occur whenever the excitatory volley that accompanies the REM burst is strong enough to overwhelm the inhibitory impulses (Pompeiano, 1967b). Phasic increases of excitatory output synchronous with REM bursts are evident in the pyramidal system (Marchiafava & Pompeiano, 1964), the mesencephalic reticular formation (Huttenlocher, 1961), and the red nucleus (Gassel et al., 1965), and may contribute to the muscular twitches (Pompeiano, 1967b). The phasic inhibitory output appears to particularly involve the vestibular nuclei (Moruzzi, 1963; Pompeiano, 1967b). It is thought that the predominance of inhibition upon the motor system during dream sleep prevents the motor execution of a behavioral response to (or within) the internally generated stimuli of the dream (Morrison & Bowker, 1975).

THE PHYLOGENY AND ONTOGENY OF DREAMING

Phylogeny of Dreaming

Behavioral and physiological sleep, including the dream-sleep phase, have been observed in higher reptiles, birds, and mammals, but not in lower reptiles, amphibians, or fish (Jouvet, 1974; Valtax, 1973). It is in some reptiles that the cerebral neocortex makes its first appearance during phylogeny (Barr, 1979; Yeo, 1979). Thus, the dream-sleep phase seems to make its first appearance along with the cerebral neocortex.

It is speculated that for some reason evolution beyond the reptilian (or lower reptilian) stage brings about the need to dream, but that dreaming may represent the functioning of the reptilian (or pre-reptilian) brain (Sagan, 1978). Alternatively expressed: dreaming may represent a necessary sleep time interaction between the pre-cerebroneocortical and cerebroneocortical systems within the brain, but predominantly involving activity of the pre-cerebroneocortical system.

Ontogeny of Dreaming

Upon the basis of sleep terror awakenings in infants it has been argued that dreams must be occurring by about 8-12 months of age (Erickson, 1941; Metcalf, 1974). Self-reported dreams by infants are evident at 1-1/2–2-1/2 years of age (Garcia-Uria et al., 1980; Metcalf, 1974). The neurophysiological characteristics of dream sleep are evident in humans at birth (Petre-Quadens, 1974; Valtax, 1973), and, according to some reports, even as early as the 7-8th month of gestation (Petre-Quadens, 1980; Parmelee et al., 1967). This indicates that at such an age the generator of these characteristics must already be functional.

Excepting the prenatal period, the percentage of REM time during total sleep time is greatest at birth (Roffwarg et al., 1966). Some reports indicate that there is a rapid decrease in this percentage during the period from birth to 2-3 years of age, followed by a slower decrease during the period from 3 to 6 years of age (Roffwarg et al., 1966), while elsewhere it is reported that there is a fairly steady high percentage of dream time over the period birth to 2 years of age, followed by great variability between 3 and 5 years of age (Catani & Findji, 1980). However, reports concertedly indicate some kind of significant change in the direction of reduced REM time at around 2-3 years of age (Catani & Findji, 1980; Roffwarg et al., 1966; Waldhorn, 1967). A number of reports also indicate that from 5 or 6 years of age onwards, the dream time remains approximately the same as it is in the adult (Catani & Findji, 1980; Hartmann, 1967; Roffwarg et al., 1966).

As the cerebral cortex is largely undeveloped at birth and over the first 2 years (see Chapter 5), when dream sleep time is most prominent, it would seem that the cerebral cortex is not necessary for the production of dream sleep characteristics. Taken together, the phylogenetic and ontogenetic data indicate that the neurological system responsible for the production of dream sleep characteristics is sub-cerebrocortical, but that dreaming involves the interaction of these sub-cerebrocortical regions with the cerebral cortex. The cerebral cortex seems to be particularly involved in the S/NREM sleep phase.

THE BRAIN STEM, CEREBELLUM, AND CEREBRUM IN RELATION TO DREAMING

The Brain Stem in Relation to Sleep and Dreaming

The region most often implicated as being critically involved with the production of sleep and dream sleep is the brain stem reticular formation (Oswald, 1974). All levels of the brain stem at midbrain level and below have been implicated: the midbrain level (Cadilhac et al., 1961; Rossi et al., 1961); the pontine level (Jouvet, 1962; Laurent et al., 1973; Markand & Dyken, 1976); and the medullary level (Pompeiano 1967b; Pompeiano & Morrison, 1966). The critical brain stem region, as indicated by EEG activity, has been determined by two levels of brain stem transection: (1) a pre-collicular transection that disconnects the whole cerebrum from the lower brain stem and totally prevents desynchronization of the EEG during sleep (Moruzzi, 1964); and (2) a mid-pontine pretrigeminal transection that results in a normal sleep EEG—one with D and S phases (Batini et al., 1959a, 1959b). Within this critical brain-stem region, more detailed studies, using various evaluative criteria, have implicated the raphe system (Jouvet, 1969), the nucleus sub-coeruleus (Laurent et al., 1973), the locus coeruleus (Jouvet, 1962), the nucleus reticularis pontis caudalis (nrpc) (Jouvet, 1962; Jouvet & Mounier, 1962), and the nucleus reticularis pontis oralis (nrpo; Batini et al., 1959b; Jouvet, 1962; Rossi et al., 1963). Other brain stem nuclei that have also been implicated but are below this critical region include various vestibular nuclei (Pompeiano, 1967b; Pompeiano & Morrison, 1966).

The brain stem monoamine systems are also significantly involved with various aspects of sleep. Norepinephrine (NE) neurons of the reticular formation, including those of the locus coeruleus, seem to be involved in the production of the D/REM sleep phase (Chu & Bloom, 1973; Jouvet, 1974) while the 5-Hydroxytryptamine (5HT) neurons of the raphe system seem to be involved with the production of the S/NREM sleep phase (Dement, 1969; Jouvet, 1974).

The NE and 5HT systems may play antagonistic or complementary roles in the D/REM—S/NREM sleep cycle (Adrien, 1976; Fuxe, 1971; Jouvet, 1974). Prior to the PGO activity the 5HT neurons cease firing and remain inactive throughout the D/REM sleep episode (McGinty et al., 1973; Yang et al., 1976). Moreover, impairment of the 5HT system may result in permanent PGO discharge (Brooks & Gershon, 1972; Delorme et al., 1966). The 5HT system therefore seems to inhibit PGO spikes (Adrien, 1976; Morrison & Bowker, 1975). Conversely, cells in the pontine reticular formation, including the regions of the nrpc and nrpo, selectively increase their firing just before the onset of the D/REM sleep phase and maintain this activity throughout it (Hobson et al., 1974a, 1974b). Interaction of the NE and 5HT systems may, in part, be facilitated by diffuse projections from the locus coeruleus to the raphe system (Morgane, 1972; Olson & Fuxe, 1971).

It is thought that the NE and 5HT systems may act in combination to produce dream sleep (Hartmann, 1967; Torda, 1968). The 5HT neurons may ordinarily first facilitate the production of S/NREM sleep, which then allows for the subsequent production of D/REM sleep (Bogdanski et al., 1958; Costa et al., 1960). During the S/NREM sleep phase the 5HT system may, in part, inhibit the production of PGO and dream activity; then, immediately preceding the onset of D/REM sleep and continuing throughout it, cells in the pontine reticular formation, for example the nrpc, nrpo, or locus coeruleus, may in part inhibit the influence of the 5HT neurons and thereby facilitate the release of PGO activity (Yang et al., 1976).

The above described monoamine systems are thought to have only a regulatory role in sleep (Adrien, 1978; Corner, 1978); that is, as facilitators or inhibitors that permit the real generating systems of D/REM and S/NREM activity to express themselves (Corner, 1978). This conforms to the earlier description of the brain-stem monoamine systems as regulators of information transmission (see Chapter 5).

As noted, the characteristics of the D/REM—S/NREM phases of the sleep cycle appear at regular periods throughout each 24-hour day, but only emerge predominantly during sleep. It has been observed that 5HT activity follows a 24-hour rhythm (Cramer, 1980); consequently, the 24 hour D/REM—S/NREM cycle may be related most directly to this. However, the formation of melatonin in the pineal exhibits a circadian rhythm (Cramer, 1980), and melatonin influences the activity of 5HT neurons (Cramer, 1980). It is thought that the pineal may play a fundamental role in the circadian distribution of D/REM sleep (Cramer, 1980). In turn, the activity of the pineal is regulated by light-darkness cycles (Barr, 1979; Cramer, 1980). It may therefore be that the pineal control of D/REM sleep distribution is light-sensitive and exists to ensure that the D/REM sleep normally only predominates during hours of darkness when sleep would most often naturally occur.

The Cerebellum in Relation to Sleep and Dreaming

The area that is thought to be most involved in the D/REM sleep phase is the brain stem. The particular regions implicated in the dream-sleep process, the raphe system, the nucleus subcoeruleus, the locus coeruleus, the nrpc and nrpo, and the vestibular nuclei all receive projections from the cerebellum. The most crucial region of the brain stem reticular formation involved in dream sleep is the region bounded by pre-collicular and mid-pontine pretrigeminal transections. Throughout the brain stem, including the reticular formation, information may be transmitted from the cerebellum to the cerebrum. Simple anatomical observation shows that the brain stem region enclosed by the two above-mentioned transections is that to which the cerebellar peduncles are attached and through which ascending cerebellar output must travel. Detailed physiological studies indicate that a precollicular transection prevents ascending cerebellar impulses from reaching the cerebrum and desynchronizing the EEG (Sawyer et al., 1961), while a mid-pontine pretrigeminal transection does not (Arduini & Hirao, 1959). On the basis of these points alone, it would seem that the cerebellum could quite easily be involved in the D/REM—S/NREM sleep cycle.

There are a number of direct physiological indications that the cerebellum is involved in sleep and dreaming: (1) Stimulation of the cerebellum may induce drowsiness (Manzoni et al., 1968), sleep (Sawyer et al., 1971; Zimkina, 1946), or a cerebral EEG pattern that resembles sleep (Manzoni et al., 1968; Sawyer et al., 1971); (2) REM sleep deprivation strongly affects the nitrogen level of particular areas of the brain, which has been taken to indicate that such areas are involved in the genesis of dream sleep—the two most affected areas are the brain stem and cerebellum (Leventhal et al., 1973); (3) during REM sleep the blood flow through the cerebellum is greater than during ordinary sleep (Reivich et al., 1969), thus indicating greater cerebellar activity during the REM phase; (4) the activity of Purkinje cells is as a whole greater during desynchronized sleep than during synchronized sleep (Pellet, 1967), and even greater during the REM bursts within the D/REM phase (Berlucchi et al., 1967; Hobson & McCarley, 1970, 1972); and (5) responses within the cerebellar cortex, evoked by peripheral stimuli (including auditory) are tonically reduced during sleep and even more reduced phasically during REM bursts (Hobson & McCarley, 1972; Marchesi et al., 1970; Pellet, 1973).

In particular, Purkinje cell activity changes along with the transition from S/NREM to D/REM sleep (Hobson & McCarley, 1970, 1972; Mano, 1970; Marchesi & Strata, 1970). It is thought that this change may be brought about by catecholaminergic projections to the cerebellum (Hoffer et al., 1971), from, for example, the locus coeruleus. Changes of Purkinje cell activity occur during, and in relation to, the phasic phenomena (REMs, PGO spikes, and myoclonic twitches) of D/REM sleep (Harlay et al., 1974; Hobson & McCarley, 1970; Mano, 1970; Marchesi & Strata, 1970; Pellet, 1976). Overall, the Purkinje cell activity during the phasic phenomena of D sleep is greater than during D sleep without the phasic phenomena (Berlucchi et al., 1967; Hobson & McCarley, 1972). Often the Purkinje cell bursts of activity, or spikes, precede the phasic phenomena (Hobson & McCarley, 1972). It is thought that this phasic cerebellar activity may be a cerebellar equivalent of PGO activity (Pellet & Harley, 1977). Concerning the latter physiological correlation, it has been noted that, anatomically, the PGO pathways appear to be connected to the brachium conjunctivum (Laurent et al., 1973)—which is the major output pathway from the cerebellum to the cerebrum.

The Descending Component of Cerebellar Influence upon the Characteristics of Dream Sleep. On the basis of anatomical and physiological data, it has been suggested that the cerebellum may be involved with the somatic changes that take place during sleep; for example, the collapse of antigravity muscle tonus (Gugliemino & Strata, 1971; Moruzzi, 1963). Although the basic somatic changes may occur in the absence of the cerebellum (Jouvet, 1961, 1962), detailed studies indicate that under normal circumstances the cerebellum is involved with a modulatory inhibition of muscle tone during D/REM sleep (Gadea-Cirea, 1976; Marchesi & Strata, 1971; Pellet & Harlay, 1977), in particular during the phasic activity (myoclonic twitches) of D/REM sleep (Pellet, 1976; Pellet & Harlay, 1977). This modulatory influence may be in the form of phasic cerebellar inhibition superimposed on a tonic reticular inhibition of muscle tone (Marchesi & Strata, 1971).

The Ascending Component of Cerebellar Influence on the Characteristics of Dream Sleep. Although large-magnitude, long-lasting effects have not been observed following removal of the cerebellar anterior lobe (Hobson, 1965) or complete cerebellum (Gadea-Cirea, 1976; Giannazzo et al., 1969; Jouvet, 1961, 1962) a number of studies have shown that lesions of the cerebellar cortex, nuclei, or peduncles do produce a long term effect on the sleep-dream cycle, including effects upon D/REM sleep (De Andres & Reinoso-Suarez, 1979; Fernandez-Guardiola et al., 1974; Garcia-Uria et al., 1980; Giannazzo et al., 1969; Manzoni et al., 1968; Morrison & Bowker, 1973; Raffaele et al., 1971). Generally, lesions of the cerebellar nuclei or peduncles (including the superior peduncle of which the brachium cunjunctivum is part) cause a decreased D/REM sleep time (De Andres & Reinoso-Suarez, 1979; Giannazzo et al., 1969; Raffaele et al., 1971), whereas lesions of the cerebellar cortex cause an increase of the D/REM sleep time (De Andres & Reinoso-Suarez, 1979; Garcia-Uria et al., 1980). The opposite effects of cerebellocortical lesions compared with nuclear or peduncular lesions (De Andres & Reinoso-Suarez, 1979) is consistent with the inhibitory nature of cerebellocortical output (Bantli et al., 1976; Eccles, 1967; Ito, 1967); and the excitatory nature of cerebellar nuclei output (Eccles, 1967; Ito, 1967; Munson & Hurd, 1973; Riklan et al., 1974) suggests that the overall ascending contribution of the cerebellum during D/REM sleep is excitatory.

A detailed analysis of the data obtained by observation of cerebellectomized cats reveals that although the basis characteristics of D/REM sleep were normal, the more detailed form of those characteristics was not the same (Gadea-Cirea, 1976; Gadea-Cirea & Fuentes, 1976; Munson & Hurd, 1973). The form of the phasic component of the basic characteristics, as exemplified by the amplitude of the monitored eye movements (which are directly related to REMs and PGO spikes) was significantly different (Gadea-Cirea, 1976; Gadea-Cirea & Fuentes, 1976). This small magnitude difference could normally be indicative of a *modulation* of the ascending phasic component of D/REM sleep (Gadea-Cirea, 1976; Gadea-Cirea & Fuentes, 1976).

The above-described direct neurophysiological evidence of cerebellar involvement with the ascending component of D/REM sleep is consistent with the ontogenetic data: Dream sleep is evident at birth; at birth the archi-cerebellum is well developed, as are ascending projections from the cerebellum to the highest level of the brain stem (see Chapter 5).

The Cerebrum in Relation to Sleep and Dreaming

Periodic emergence of the characteristics of dream sleep are still evident after total cerebral neodecortication (Jouvet, 1962, 1965), and in anencephalic children

(Pierce et al., 1965). These observations, together with ontogenetic data, indicate that the cerebral neocortex is not necessary for the production of many of the characteristics of dream sleep. The cerebral cortex does, however, appear to be essential for the normal production of the S/NREM sleep phase (Jouvet, 1962). Moreover, it appears to be able to exert an inhibitory influence on the brain stem structures that are involved with the facilitation of D/REM sleep (Koella & Ferry, 1963). Although the cerebral neocortex may not be responsible for the production of the sensory information that provides the dream content, it may well be responsible for the experiencing of that sensory information, that is, for experiencing the dream.

A SYSTEMATIC DESCRIPTION OF THE NEUROPHYSIOLOGY OF DREAMING

A Proposed Neurological System Responsible for the Generation of the Ascending Information that Constitutes Dreams

The cerebral cortex is not responsible for the production of the sensory information that provides the dream content. This information appears to come from or through the pontine brain stem. The cerebellum projects to the cerebrum through the pontine brain stem, and could therefore be the source of the dream content. The cerebellum is evidently involved with the modulation of the muscular, REM, PGO spike, and cerebral EEG desynchronization components of the phasic activity during D/REM sleep, that is, with virtually every component of phasic activity both ascending and descending. Evidence indicates that the cerebellum may contribute to the descending and ascending components in different ways—exerting an inhibitory influence in a descending direction while exerting an excitatory influence on the ascending direction. In relation to this there is evidence that the archi-cerebellum has an excitatory output via the fastigial nuclei, part of which travels in an ascending direction to the cerebral cortex; from the archi-cerebellum there are also direct inhibitory projections from the Purkinje cells in a descending direction to the vestibular nuclei (including Deiter's) (Palay & Chan-Palay, 1973); and physiological data indicates that from the fastigial nuclei the ascending influences are quite independent of the descending influence on muscle tone (Manzoni et al., 1968).

Although the cerebellum does not appear to be necessary for the basic D/REM sleep characteristics as monitored in terms of physiology, it does appear to be involved in some sort of secondary regulation (Pellet, 1973), which must be important for the manifestation of certain aspects of D/REM sleep (Pellet & Dermonville, 1971). Given the above points, together with the information presented in Chapter 5 which indicated the cognitive facility of the cerebellum, it is suggested that the cerebellum not only exerts a secondary modulatory influence on the physiological phenomena such as muscle tone, but that it is the source of the sensory information that provides the psychological content of dreams.

A Neurological Mechanism for Dreaming and the Updating of the Cerebrum/Abstract Sub-System

The most basic rhythm of the sleep-dream cycle may be governed by the pineal gland. This would ensure that the dream process would normally occur during times of darkness, when sleep would most likely take place and when the cerebral cortex would be least likely to attend to the external environment. It would also ensure that the dream process would normally occur regularly, that is, nightly. Control exerted by the pineal could be in the form of a general modification of the brain stem monoamine levels, which would allow the dream-producing system to become relatively predominant during times of darkness. Of the monoamine systems the 5HT system could prepare the brain for the dream sleep process by bringing about a general state of atonia and a synchronization of the cerebral cortex. During this preparatory phase, output from the cerebellum to the cerebrum would be inhibited by the projections from the raphe system to the cerebellum. The D/REM sleep phase would then be facilitated by the NE system, which would inhibit the 5HT system and thereby facilitate cerebellar ascending excitatory output to the cerebrum. Anatomical location of the pineal and the 5HT and NE systems within the brain stem would be consistent with such a basic role in the sleep-dream process.

The basic D/REM sleep characteristics may be considered as those that correspond to the preparation for and facilitation of dream sleep. In a descending direction the basic characteristics would include a tonic inhibition of the motor system. This would prevent the sensorimotor data of the dream from being accompanied by an overt expression of the motor component; in the absence of atonia, the phasic bursts of activity during dream sleep are capable of eliciting (or are accompanied by) behavioral responses (Morrison & Bowker, 1975). Another "descending" component would be the inhibition of the transmission pathways for externally generated stimuli (diminished evoked responses within the brain stem and an accompanying higher response threshold for behavioral awakening). This latter component would serve as an additional measure to prevent environmental interference with the transmission of dream information. In an ascending direction the basic characteristics correspondent to the facilitation of dream sleep—cerebral EEG desynchronization, PGO spikes, REMs—could be a manifestation of the transmission system's state of operational readiness but without meaningful information transmission taking place. The subsequent transmission of dream information, possibly during the PGO spikes, may manifest merely as a modulation of these basic characteristics.

Although the dream sleep process would seem to be controlled primarily at brain-stem level, both the cerebellum and cerebrum may be involved in some kind of secondary control: The cerebellum is reciprocally connected to both the locus coeruleus and the raphe system; it may exert an inhibitory influence on the raphe system, and it may be involved with the secondary facilitation of D/REM sleep; the cerebrum may be involved with the secondary facilitation of S/NREM sleep and the secondary inhibition of D/REM sleep.

It is suggested that the information constituting the dream is transmitted from the cerebellum, through the brain stem, to the cerebrum. To fulfil the requirements of the updating process, the dream material should include information from the part of the cerebellum that is not directly influenced or sub-programmed by the cerebrum. The part of the cerebellum not directly influenced by the cerebrum is the archi-cerebellum (Karamjan et al., 1969; Palay & Chan-Palay, 1974). It is this part of the cerebellum which is most strongly implicated in the sleep process through its projections to the raphe system (Morrison & Bowker, 1975), and which can exert an excitatory influence on the cerebral cortex while at the same time directly inhibiting motor activity. It is also the part of the cerebellum most highly developed at birth, when D/REM sleep is evident.

As the cerebellar output would be polymodal, it would normally automatically excite the sensory and motor systems. To prevent excitation of the motor effectors by the release of polymodal information from the cerebellum during dreaming, the motor system would have to be simultaneously depressed. While overall motor inhibition may be facilitated directly by the brain stem, it may also be synchronously depressed during phasic D/REM sleep by a direct inhibitory output from the archi-cerebellar Purkinje cell to the vestibular nuclei. The evidence suggests that the projections from the locus coeruleus to the cerebellar cortex may be involved in the activation of this descending archi-cerebellar inhibitory output.

It has been suggested that PGO spikes in particular may correspond to dream activity. In relation to this, a naturomorphic sub-system could release the entire content of a dream sequence as a whole in a very short time. This suggestion conforms to subjective reports that dreams take place almost instantaneously. The overall duration of the D/REM sleep phase may be equivalent to a cerebral "after-discharge" following the PGO spikes: following brief stimulation of the cerebellum there is often a prolonged desynchronized after-discharge within the cerebral cortex, lasting up to 15 minutes (Fanardjian, 1965; R. Snider, 1970; Ward, 1970).

Although the first S/NREM sleep period may be a preparatory phase for the D/REM sleep activity, the subsequent S/NREM sleep periods would appear to be related to non–dream-like processing in relation to the preceding dream period. It may therefore be the case that the precise timing of the D/REM–S/NREM cycles (within the sleep-dream cycle controlled by the brain stem) is secondarily controlled by the cerebellum and cerebrum together on the basis of the processing time that they require for each individual dream sequence.

This description is consistent with the neurophysiological data presented in this section on dreaming, the correspondence of the cerebellum and cerebrum with naturomorphic and abstract sub-systems, the psychological description of the process of dreaming, and the theoretical requirements for the updating process.

LATERALIZATION OF FUNCTION IN RELATION TO DREAMING

Both cerebral hemispheres may normally be involved with the experience of dreaming (Hoppe, 1977). There is, however, evidence of lateralized differences in the functional characteristics of the two cerebral hemispheres during dreaming (Foisoreanu et al., 1980; Goldstein et al., 1972; Webster, 1977). The minor hemisphere seems to be more involved than the dominant hemisphere (Dimond, 1979; Galin, 1974; Myslobodsky et al., 1976), especially in D/REM sleep (Goldstein et al.; 1972, Webster, 1977), whereas the dominant hemisphere seems to be more involved with S/NREM sleep (Goldstein et al., 1972; Myslobodsky et al., 1976; Webster, 1977). In relation to this it is the minor rather than the dominant hemisphere that is considered to represent and process information in a manner compatible with dreams (Galin, 1977). Thus, whereas both hemispheres may be involved with the experience of dreams or with the reception of dream information, it seems to be the minor hemisphere that is mainly involved with the processing of the dream information in its initial form. The minor hemisphere may be involved with the initial, relatively holistic, cerebral processing of dreams (Geschwind & Levitsky, 1968) while the dominant hemisphere may be involved in subsequently processing the information in a relatively more abstract manner. In theory, the minor hemisphere would be necessary for the intermediate translation of the dream information into a form that could be more readily handled or understood by the dominant hemisphere.

THREE

PSYCHOLOGICAL PROCESSES AND DEVELOPMENT

7

Psychological Processes: An Integrated Description

CURRENT ISSUES IN COGNITIVE PSYCHOLOGY

In an article entitled "Twelve issues in cognitive science," Norman (1981) selected 12 major issues that in his opinion needed to be addressed in order for cognitive science to make substantive advances. The 12 issues were belief systems (knowledge); emotion, learning, performance, consciousness, interaction (social), memory, skill, development, language, perception and thought. Motivation he considered as a derived issue. Norman also emphasized the need to consider the cognitive system in relation to regulation.

Sternberg, a leading theorist in cognitive psychology, has developed a triarchic theory (1984) which presents intelligence in terms of (1) adaptation, selection or choice, and shaping; (2) novelty or problem solving, and automatization; and (3) learning how to do things, planning, and actually doing things. His triarchic theory is presented in a componential manner. There are metacomponents that enable us to monitor and later evaluate actions, and that involve directing attention and the process of selection in planning. There are also performance components to execute plans, and knowledge acquisition components. Sternberg proposes that controlled information processing is under the conscious direction of the individual and is hierarchical in nature, with the executive processes (which are used to plan, monitor, and revise strategies of information processing) directing nonexecutive processes (which are used actually to carry out the strategies that the executive processes select, monitor, and revise). Automatic information processing is preconscious, not under the conscious direction of the individual, and nonhierarchical in nature. The range of processes and components considered in this triarchic theory is quite extensive.

Both Norman and Sternberg assert it is necessary to consider cognitive functioning in relation to biological adaptation or regulation. In combination, the processes or components to which they give particular attention are perception, knowledge (including the social aspect), learning (including the social aspect), memory, development, language, consciousness, motivation and emotion, attention, thought, novelty or problem solving, planning and choice, and automatization and skill.

The description of the representation and processing of information and the process of control presented in Chapters 3 and 4 of this work have already dealt with perception, knowledge (including the social aspect), learning (including the social aspect), memory, development, and, to some extent, language. The remaining issues of consciousness—motivation and emotion, attention, thought, novelty or problem solving; planning and choice, and automatization and skill will be dealt with in this chapter. In addition, a number of other important processes or features will be considered. Furthermore, these issues will be considered in relation to the description presented in Chapters 3 and 4, and will therefore be related to one another in an integrated system for equilibration or biological adaptation/regulation.

CONSCIOUSNESS AND CONSCIOUS CONTROL

Consciousness

One important characteristic of consciousness is thought to be that of serial processing of information (Mandler, 1975; Posner et al., 1973). Another is that conscious awareness restricts information processing in certain ways, in particular by selective attention (Williams et al., 1988). Conscious processes may occur at a relatively late stage in information processing (Shevrin & Dickman, 1980). These characteristics clearly link consciousness with abstract sub-system processing.

Conscious perception is thought to involve *introspection* or *awareness* of perception (Gibson, 1979; Natsoulas, 1982; Rock, 1975). Thus, consciousness involves two components in that to be conscious of sensations, experiences, perceptions, or responses there must be one system that senses, experiences, perceives, or responds, and another system that senses or perceives these sensations, experiences, perceptions, or responses from the first system (Arbib, 1972; Dixon, 1972; Powers, 1974). Consciousness must involve an interaction between two systems (Grey-Walter, 1954; Shallice, 1972).

It has been suggested that consciousness could not take place in one person's brain as it apparently involves the interaction of two or more brains (Rioch, 1954). However, an alternative could be that there is interaction between two different levels of a system (Shallice, 1972), or between two discrete but functionally interacting sub-systems within the whole brain.

The two component sub-systems could be arranged as shown for the naturomorphic sub-systems in Figure 4. The lower naturomorphic sub-system could receive sensory information from the external world directly through the sensors and thereby form an internal representation during perception. The higher abstract sub-system also could receive sensory information from the external world directly through the sensors, but in addition it might, via the naturomorphic response feedback connection, receive sensory information in the form of a naturomorphic re-presentation of the sensations. So arranged, the higher sub-system would be in receipt not only of the sensory information going to the lower sub-system but also of the perception of representation formed from the sensory information of the lower sub-system (McKellar, 1979). Thus, with this arrangement the perceptions of, or the re-presentations of perception within, the lower sub-system might serve as the objects of consciousness of the higher sub-system (Arbib, 1972; Grey-Walter, 1954; Powers, 1974).

As both the naturomorphic and abstract sub-systems are capable of perceiving the existence and actions of an organism's own body, there is the facility for consciousness of both body and actions, and therefore consciousness of these aspects of the organism itself; that is, aspects of self-consciousness.

Conscious Control

Consciousness is considered to be involved in controlling action (Kremyanskiy, 1960; Razran, 1965). As a result of consciousness there is thought to be the potential for volitional or conscious control (Powers, 1974). Furthermore, as a result of self-consciousness there is the possibility of self-referent thought and thus of self-control (Bandura, 1978a).

With the arrangement shown in Figure 4, the *action* output of the naturomorphic sub-system could be perceived by the abstract sub-system as sensory information from the external world directly through the sensors, and via the naturomorphic response feedback connection as sensory information in the form of a naturomorphic re-presentation. Thus, the *action* output of the naturomorphic sub-system would be the object of consciousness for the abstract sub-system, and would be subject to conscious control. The otherwise automatic response of the naturomorphic sub-system could therefore be monitored and controlled by the abstract sub-system in a conscious manner. This aspect of abstract sub-system functioning can be considered metacognitive.

UNCONSCIOUSNESS AND UNCONSCIOUS CONTROL

Unconscious Processes

Elsewhere it has been suggested that unconscious processes may operate with rules that are different from those of conscious processes (Shevrin & Dickman, 1980), and it is considered that the balance of evidence supports this suggestion (Marcel, 1980; Williams et al., 1988). According to Marcel (1983), one characteristic of nonconscious processing is that representations are not segmented in any way (for example, in terms of objects, events, or episodes). Another characteristic is that perceptual hypotheses are activated automatically if any of their criterial features can be detected among the records within the nonconscious system. Marcel suggests that within the nonconscious sub-system, many hypotheses will be simultaneously activated and processed in-parallel in terms of such factors as frequency and expectancy. These characteristics of nonconscious processing as described by Marcel are essentially the same as those of the naturomorphic sub-system described in Chapter 3. While it is recognized that nonconscious processes can affect conscious processes (Shevrin & Dickman, 1980; Williams et al., 1988), they may also serve a control function independent of the conscious sub-system.

Independent Operation of the Naturomorphic Sub-System and Unconscious Control

As noted in Chapter 4, while the higher sub-system may control the motor output directly or bias the low level sub-system, it is possible that the low-level sub-system may be allowed to operate on its own without interference from above. This may occur because the higher-level sub-system is busy "attending to other things" and so "not attending to" what the lower level sub-system is doing. Also, if an immediate response is required, there may not be time to use the planning facility of the abstract sub-system, and so the naturomorphic sub-system will act on behalf of the system as a whole.

MOTIVATION AND EMOTION

Motivation

Most theories of motivation present descriptions of the driving force for behavior in terms of one or more of the following three concepts: instinct, need-drive, or cognition. These three concepts facilitate a description of motivation at difference "levels." At the most basic biological or innate level, motivation may be described in terms of an *environmental sign stimulus* or an *innate releasing mechanism* such that certain stimuli automatically release a particular pattern of behavior that is of direct value in terms of survival at the most basic level (Lorenz, 1966; Tinbergen, 1951).

The need-drive theories are also described in terms of the most basic biological requirements. According to Blundell (1975), the need-drive description of motivation incorporates the following elements: (1) a need that arises when the conditions necessary for the optimal chances of survival depart from their respective optima; (2) a drive that is the purposeful activity initiated by the existence of a need state within the organism, and that is necessary to maintain homeostasis; (3) a goal that refers to conditions toward which the motivated behavior is directed; and finally, (4) satiation or the cessation of drive.

Although the need-drive theories are descriptions in terms of the most basic biological requirements, they also extend the descriptions to take learning into account. For example, according to Hull (1943), behavior is reinforced when it succeeds in reducing the drive or the need. The drive may be to directly reduce a basic biological need, and as such would be referred to as a primary drive. However, if a primary-driven behavior that results in a reduction of basic needs also frequently brings about another nondetrimentally-stimulating result, then there will develop a secondary drive to behave in a manner that will bring about this associated result. These secondary learned drives may in some instances be related to social needs (Murray, 1938).

Cognitive theories of motivation may be considered as even further extensions that incorporate more sophisticated aspects of learned behavior and involve more complex processes. Maslow's theory of motivation (1970) proposes that human desires or motives are arranged in an ascending hierarchy: basic physiological needs, safety needs, belongingness and loving needs, self-esteem needs, and self-actualization needs. Rotter (1966) describes motivation in terms of behavior potential, expectancy, reinforcement value, and the "locus of control." Bandura (1978a, 1978b) considers both vicarious and self-monitoring aspects of motivation in learning. One particularly important and subtle aspect of motivation common to these three cognitive theories is the notion of *self*.

The control model presented in Chapter 4 was developed from consideration of the basic features of homeostatic control. At the simplest level, the response of the system would be "motivated" by an error signal determined in relation to innate homeostatic requirements. This clearly corresponds to the description of motivation in terms of the concept of instinct.

The model in Chapter 4 was them systematically elaborated to incorporate learning-based control. Within the first learning-based level, the naturomorphic sub-system would be "motivated" by an error signal that contains information about the appropriate corrective action and gives an indication of how things should be—an "image of achievement." The removal of error in the naturomorphic sub-system would then "probably" result in removal of error from the innate sub-system. This level of the model corresponds to the description of motivation in terms of concept of need-drive, and in a manner that is systematically related to the innate level.

With the addition of the abstract sub-system and its referential representations, there will arise the possibility of "motivation" by an error signal that contains abstract referential information. This referential information may concern laws, rules, or social conventions. Furthermore, with the addition of the abstract sub-system, there arises for each individual the facility for consciousness of his or her own actions and body, and therefore his or her "self." This level clearly relates to the description of motivation in terms of the concept of cognition, and, once again, it does so in a manner that is systematically related to the two preceding levels.

Emotion

Emotion is a multifaceted phenomenon; it has been widely accepted that comprehensive theories of emotion must include different facets (Williams et al., 1988), for example, by taking into account physiological, behavioral, and cognitive components (Lang, 1985; Scherer, 1984). It has been suggested that an information-processing approach to emotion may provide a framework for integrating these various components (Williams et al., 1988).

Emotional responses are generally considered to be evoked by stimuli that are pleasant/beneficial or unpleasant/detrimental (Brady, 1975; A. Kagan, 1975; MacLean, 1975). However, such responses are not only dependent on the "actual" (direct) beneficial or detrimental nature of the stimulus, but also on a process of interpretation whereby objects, events, or ideas are seen as having indirect value or "meaning" (Lazarus et al., 1980; Scherer, 1984). Emotion is therefore inextricably linked with the cognitive processes (Kagan, 1975; Leventhal, 1982).

The stimulus interpretation and response that together make up the emotional process are considered to be a whole within which the physiological, behavioral, and cognitive components are integrated (Leventhal, 1982). Once the emotional response has been elicited by a given stimulus, its release at an autonomic and motor level is considered to be "automatic" (Leventhal, 1982; Zajonc, 1980). This process would be facilitated by a memory that stores a perceptual representation or analog of the features of the stimulus situation, a record of autonomic and motor responses, and an "implicit meaning" (Leventhal, 1982). New similar-stimulus situations subsequently reactivate these schematic structures and the resultant emotional response without necessarily involving any conscious cognitive processes (Mandler, 1982; Zajonc, 1980); that is, the evaluation of the emotional quality of a stimulus and the production of the response constitute an automatic process that can proceed in the complete absence of awareness (Zajonc, 1980).

Although the emotional responses can be evoked without conscious involvement, it does not follow that they are and that consciousness is completely uninvolved. On the contrary, consciousness may indeed be involved, and would necessarily be if there were an awareness of emotion (Scheier & Carver, 1977; Tomkins, 1962).

Leventhal and Scherer (1987) have presented a hierarchical model of emotion. In their model there is a sensorimotor level that operates in terms of innate-level preferences and without volitional effort, then a schematic level that contains concrete representations of specific emotional experiences (these schemata are activated atically), and the highest level, which is conceptual, is based on the capacity to draw propositional conclusions about two or more emotional episodes, and operates by conscious volition. Checks for "pleasantness" are based on innate preferences at the sensorimotor level, on learned preferences at the schematic level, and on recalled, anticipated, or derived evaluations at the conceptual level. At the conceptual level, emotions may involve a propositional evaluation that is social and includes reference to the self (Oatley & Johnson-Laird, 1987). Ideas that are similar to many of the concepts of Leventhal have been presented by Zajonc (1980, 1984), but with the additional suggestion that events can be appraised by the different levels relatively independently.

Therefore, the cognitive processes encompassed by all aspects of emotion evidently include both sensory and abstract forms. The sensory/imagistic, more holistic form of cognition is clearly the most involved at the primary-learning-based "evaluation and response" level (Aylwin, 1985; Horowitz, 1983; Leventhal, 1982), whereas the abstract form is involved at the secondary-learning-based "evaluation and response" level, and involves consciousness of emotion.

It is clear that emotion and motivation are related (Scherer, 1984), and that the various levels of motivation may be systematically related to the various levels of emotion. By relating the cognitive aspect of emotion to the cognitive level of motivation described in the preceding section, and by appreciating the systematic relationship between the cognitive level of motivation and the lower levels of motivation, it is possible to see how the more subtle cognitive motivations described by Maslow (1970) can be (although may not necessarily be) accompanied by quite definite emotional responses.

Considering the above information in relation to Chapters 3 and 4, the naturomorphic sub-system can provide a polymodal re-presentation of the changes in the external environment, the corresponding changes in the internal environment, and the relationship between them. It can evaluate a present stimulus on the basis of past experience and facilitate an anticipatory response that is released automatically. The naturomorphic sub-system therefore has the wherewithal to facilitate the interpretive and responsive aspects of emotion at a primary-learning-based level. It is the abstract sub-system, however, that has the capability to be conscious of the emotional interpretation and response, and therefore to "experience" emotion—provided it receives response information from the naturomorphic sub-system.

IMAGINATION AND THOUGHT

A given stimulus input to the organism from the environment would evoke from the naturomorphic sub-system a response in the form of a polymodal or sensorimotor sequence containing a motor component, which would normally constitute the overt response along with a sensory component, which would contain information concerning the expected consequences. The abstract system may receive information concerning this sequence in the feedback sample of naturomorphic response information. However, the re-presentation from the naturomorphic sub-system of the polymodal sequence, containing autonomic and motor components, would normally result in an autonomic and motor response. Somehow, the sensory component in the "imagination" process must become free of any overt manifestation of the motor component (Bruner et al., 1966; Dunlap, 1927). This requires that the motor component be inhibited, in terms of its expression through the effectors, by the abstract sub-system. This inhibition could occur through direct abstract sub-system control to the effectors. The overall result would be that the abstract sub-system could perceive the imagistic sequence, including the probable consequences, without actually having to execute the sequence. This may be considered as the process of imaginative thought—the substitution of virtual sensory images or actions for real images or actions (Aylwin, 1985). Imagination may also apply to the action of speaking, where the imagination of speech may otherwise be described as "internal speech" and be considered a particular aspect of thought (Watson, 1925).

Autonomous and Controlled Imagery

The representation of recorded information in image form may be autonomous or controlled (McKellar, 1979; Richardson, 1972). Similarly, it may either be conscious or unconscious (Bugelski, 1970). In the former instance some input to the naturomorphic sub-system, either from the innate sub-system or directly from the sensors, may evoke the imagery, which may then be forwarded to the abstract sub-system. In the latter instance the abstract sub-system may call up from the naturomorphic sub-system the imagery that it requires. For the abstract sub-system to be able to do this it will need to possess a cue referring to the "to-be-recalled" item within the naturomorphic sub-system (D. Thompson & Tulving, 1970). The registering of the cue, and the linking of it to the "to-be-recalled" item would normally be made at the time they were both stored.

Autonomous/Passive Creative Imagery

As a result of some initiating stimulus from the abstract sub-system, the innate sub-system, or the external environment, a novel sequence of images naturomorphically derived from a number of significantly associated images may be released from the naturomorphic sub-system. When the formation of this sequence is not controlled by the abstract sub-system, it may be considered to be autonomous and not under conscious control, and its combination by statistically significant association will in effect be passive.

Information in image form may be as the sensory component of an evoked polymodal response sequence which is in an "unmodified" form and so is reproductive imagery. Alternatively, the evoked sequence may be made up of a novel combination of component parts from a number of sequences and so may be regarded as passive, creative imagination.

PROBLEM SOLVING, INDUCTION, AND INTUITION

A Brief Outline of Some of the Basic Component Processes in Problem Solving

In order to solve a given problem it is first necessary to have a clear internal representation of it (Newell & Simon, 1972). In particular, it is necessary to represent the principal feature, pattern, or structure of the problem (Greeno, 1980; Newell & Simon, 1972). Having obtained a structural representation of the problem, it is then necessary to recognize a possible solution. This second stage of the process is thought to depend on past experience of solving similar or resemblant problems; that is, on internally represented knowledge of solutions to problems that are structurally similar to the given one (Greeno, 1980; Raaheim, 1965).

The Process of Induction

Induction is considered to be an important aspect of information processing which is evident in animal behavior and in human thought (Popper, 1963; Uttley, 1956c). Temporal induction may be considered to embody a primitive mechanism and to facilitate and anticipatory type of response (Reichenbach, 1956; Uttley, 1956b, 1956c).

Induction is sometimes referred to as synthetic thought in contrast to deductive or analytic thought, and it is considered to constitute the essence of originality or creativity (Payne, 1958). As a process it is considered a form of extrapolation by resemblance (Quine, 1972). For example, it may be induced that an event *A* is governed by the same law, or has the same properties, as another event, or class of events *B* because it sufficiently resembles that other event or class of events even though it may not be identical (Uttley, 1956c; J. Van Heerden, 1968). As a procedure, induction is considered to be of a probabilistic (Uttley, 1956c; J. Van Heerden, 1968) or an analogical form (Holland et al., 1986; Sloman, 1971). Induction is not considered to be a logically describable procedure (Ayer, 1946; B. Russell, 1950). Unlike deductive (logical) procedures, induction may be concerned directly with empirical data (Minsky, 1958).

Naturomorphic Representation and Processing Characteristics in Relation to the Basic Component Processes in Problem Solving

Information concerning structure or pattern can readily be represented in analogical form. Furthermore, analogical reasoning involves the application of past experience to new but similar experience (Holyoak, 1984; Winston, 1978). Analogical reasoning could therefore be involved at both stages of the problem-solving process previously described. In fact, there is substantial evidence that analogical reasoning plays a prominent role in problem solving (Beveridge & Parkins, 1987; Crisafi & Brown, 1986; Gick & Holyoak, 1983). It has even been suggested that possibly all problem solving is fundamentally analogical (Newell & Simon, 1972). Similarly, images are thought to facilitate discovery and problem solving (Beveridge & Parkins, 1987; Kaufman, 1984; Paivio, 1971). Naturomorphic representation and processing would therefore appear to be well suited to carrying out these two particular aspects of the problem-solving process.

Naturomorphic and Abstract Sub-System Interaction in Relation to the Process of Induction and Creative Problem Solving

Earlier, in Chapter 3, the point was made that the word *resemblance* could logically be replaced by the phrase "roughly the same." It may be that both the naturomorphic and the abstract sub-systems are capable only of recognizing things as "the same" or "not the same," and that neither is capable of recognizing things as similar or resemblant; consequently, neither of them would therefore be capable of the process of induction. Because of the difference in resolving power of the two sub-systems, it may be that two items A.1 and A.2 might at the high resolution of the abstract sub-system be viewed as "not the same" but at the low resolution of the naturomorphic sub-system might instead be viewed as "the same." The evaluation by the naturomorphic sub-system of the two items A.1 and A.2 as "the same" will, from the perspective of the abstract sub-system, appear to have involved treating two "not-the-same" items as though they were "the same." Thus, from the perspective of the abstract sub-system, the naturomorphic sub-system will appear to have detected a resemblance and to have processed information inductively when in fact it has done no such thing. It may therefore be the case that the detection of similarity or resemblance, and the process of induction, are phenomena that exist in the naturomorphic sub-system only from the point of view of the abstract sub-system; that is, they are phenomena that depend on the interaction of the two sub-systems and not on either one alone.

As noted earlier, problem solving is supposed to depend on the recognition of similarities or the detection of resemblances. Insofar as this is so, in the light of the preceding suggestion, it must depend on the interaction of the naturomorphic and abstract systems. Moreover, insofar as the discovery of novel solutions is thought to entail the crossing of a logical gap (Mackay, 1958; Polanyi, 1957)—the inability to perceive logical separation—it must also depend on the interaction of the two systems.

Naturomorphic and Abstract Sub-System Interaction in Relation to Intuition

Images are thought to be particularly involved in "intuitive" thought (Rugg, 1963; Yukawa, 1973). Insofar as the response information fed forward to the abstract sub-system from the naturomorphic sub-system is the result or "conclusion" of naturomorphic processing, it may be considered to be a naturomorphically derived solution to a problem. Thus, the abstract sub-system will be in receipt of a solution to a problem without necessarily having any information as to how the solution was arrived at and without necessarily having had anything to do with the naturomorphic production of the solution. This "receipt" of a solution in image or analogical form may be what is normally referred to as "intuition."

DREAMING

Dreaming: An Overview of the Conventional Psychological Description of Its Information Representation and Processing Characteristics and Function

Dreams are considered to be the expression of a particular kind of thinking or information processing, the activation of which is made possible by the conditions of sleep (Freud, 1900; Torre et al., 1980). Representation and processing of information within dreams is considered to have spatially atemporal, synaesthetic (polymodal), and associative characteristics (Jacobi, 1974; D. Schneider, 1948). Its form is considered to be analogical and exemplified by images (Dimond, 1979; Jones, 1970; Ullman & Krippner, 1970). Dream thought may be experienced during the dream as action, and the emotional content of the dream may be experienced as if real or as if in response to real events (Hartmann, 1967; Jones, 1970; Pugh, 1978). The characteristics of information representation and processing within dreams are different from abstract or logical mental processes (Freud, 1915; Jacobi, 1974; McDougall, 1926). The kind of thinking expressed in dreams is generally regarded to be phylogenetically and ontogenetically primitive (Berger, 1967; Freud, 1900; Jones, 1970; Pavlov, 1958).

Dreams are considered to be products of the unconscious (Freud, 1900; Jacobi, 1974) and, with regard to their content and unfoldment, to be spontaneous, autonomous, or outside the control of consciousness (Hilgard, 1977; Jacobi 1974). Although dreams may be produced by the psychological system referred to as the unconscious, the dream process may also involve interaction of two psychological systems—the unconscious and the conscious (Freud, 1910; Jacobi 1974; M. Ullman, 1958). Dream-like processing and the periodic preponderant activity of the dream-producing system may also be present throughout the awake state (Giora, 1972; Jacobi, 1974; Oswald, 1974) but be unnoticed because it is at a level below that of the conscious system (Jacobi, 1974; Kubie, 1966), or because its emergence is obscured or inhibited by attention to the outer world (Giora, 1972), that is, by attention to externally generated input to the conscious system.

It is considered that dreams are a means of self-regulation and are necessary for mental health (Hartmann, 1973; Jung, 1933; Lowy, 1942; Oswald, 1974). Dreams may provide information that serves to evaluate the concepts of the conscious (abstract) system to compensate for "errors" in conscious processing and thereby to correct an imbalance resulting from the conscious system's errors (Jung, 1933; Ullman & Krippner, 1970). Daydreams, to some extent, may fulfil a similar function (Klinger, 1971). The compensatory function of dreams may result from the fact that in some respects the prelogical form of information representation and processing in dreams is superior to that of awake/conscious information representation and processing (Jacobi, 1974; Ullman & Krippner, 1970). In particular, it is considered that the dream process may be more comprehensive than the conscious process, partly because it may reveal information that has been ignored, insufficiently appreciated, or discarded by the conscious system (Faraday, 1975; Hadfield, 1954; Jacobi, 1974).

Dreaming is therefore considered to be a form of information processing that facilitates control (Jung, 1933), and that has a re-programming function (Dewan, 1970; Greenberg & Pearlman, 1972). The particular re-programming functions attributed to dreaming include reviewing past experience of current relevance and restructuring perceptual models or concepts in terms of that review (Gaarder, 1965; Hennevin & Leconte, 1971; Ullman & Krippner, 1970). Dreaming is also considered to be a form of information processing that facilitates problem solving (French & Fromm, 1964; Garma, 1966; Jones, 1962).

In support of these suggestions concerning the function of dreams there is evidence that shows that the amount of dream sleep is in some way related to the process of learning (Giora, 1972; Greenberg & Dewan, 1969; Oswald, 1974). There is also evidence that, following lost dream time, there is compensatory recovery of it (Dement & Fisher, 1963; Sampson, 1965; Snyder, 1963), and that dream sleep deprivation may result in psychological changes that, in extreme instances, are comparable with those of schizophrenia (Bliss et al., 1959; Cartwright & Ratzel, 1972; Puca et al., 1976; West et al., 1962).

Dreaming Considered in Relation to the Cognitive Requirements for Equilibration

Representation and processing of information within dreams is considered to have spatially atemporal, polymodal and associative characteristics, to be analogical, to be exemplified by images, and to have emotional content. These are all characteristics of the naturomorphic sub-system.

The dream process involves interaction of two psychological systems: the prelogical unconscious and the logical conscious. During this interaction, the prelogical system provides information that has been ignored, insufficiently appreciated, or discarded by the conscious system. This information is provided in order to compensate for "errors" that have arisen in the conscious system. The dream process is thus considered to be a means of self-regulation and to be necessary for mental health (psychological equilibration).

In Chapter 4 it was indicated that the abstract representation and processing sub-system, as the uppermost controller in the homeostatic circuit, would have a number of disadvantages in relation to ensuring equilibration mainly because of the problem of information loss during selective attention and then during representation formation. It was pointed out that these sources of error would be detrimental to the homeostatic process and would have to be compensated for. The erroneous information or schemata would need to be corrected, and outdated schemata updated in terms of new experience, and past data relevant to new experience, to maintain correspondence with the environment. The efficiency of the whole homeostatic process would depend on this updating and the frequency with which it occurred. Naturomorphic information concerning relevant past events could be fed to the abstract sub-system, which could then treat that information as though it had been directly perceived and process the information according to its current needs. The abstract sub-system could in this way obtain the relevant data that it might not have selected or attended to itself when the (now relevant) past events took place. In providing the abstract sub-system with this information, the naturomorphic sub-system would facilitate the updating of the abstract sub-system.

Dreams are considered to be the expression of a particular kind of information processing, the activation of which is made possible by the conditions of sleep. Normally, the naturomorphic sub-system would be involved in responding to the environment and, while doing so, would be unable to specifically output any updating information to the abstract sub-system. Furthermore, during normal interaction with the environment, the hierarchically dominant abstract sub-system may have to, or may choose to, focus its attention on information input from the environment and therefore may only allow minimal input from the naturomorphic sub-system. Under these circumstances, uninhibited transmission of information from the naturomorphic sub-system to the abstract sub-system could not be guaranteed. It was therefore proposed that there must exist the facility for periodic naturomorphic sub-system dominance over the abstract sub-system, during which time the abstract sub-system could not inhibit input from the naturomorphic sub-system. It was proposed that this periodic dominance should occur selectively during times when neither the naturomorphic sub-system nor the abstract sub-system were interacting with the environment, and that it should occur often enough for the updating process to be efficient. These requirements could be fulfilled by the conditions of sleep.

PLANNING

Planning: Imagination and the Choice of Response Sequence

A given stimulus input to the organism from the environment would evoke from the naturomorphic sub-system a response in the form of a polymodal sequence that would contain information concerning the expected consequences. The abstract system could receive this information in the sample of naturomorphic response information. Provided that the stimulus did not demand an immediate response but rather allowed enough time for planning, the abstract sub-system could inhibit the motor output component of this naturomorphic sub-system response. As a result of this process of imagination, the organism would be able to view and therefore evaluate a number of response sequences, including their probable consequences, without the responses actually having to be executed. As such, the process of imagination would contribute to the process of planning (Berlyne, 1965; Horowitz, 1972a; Powers, 1974).

This process may also apply to the action of speaking, where the imagination of speech may otherwise be described as "internal speech" and be considered a particular aspect of thought (Watson, 1925).

Planning: The Ordering and Reordering of Fragments within a Response Sequence

The ordering of a number of elements within a response sequence such as a skilled action, or speech, is considered to take place at a level of processing that is below consciousness (Lashley, 1951, 1954). It is thought that the facility for a variable ordering of elements within a sequence requires that the neural representations of past experience must be stored in such a manner that all the temporal elements are represented in an atemporal or simultaneous manner (Lashley, 1951). Within such a sub-system, the individual parts of sequences would be completely interchangeable and could be expressed in a variety of orders (Lashley, 1951). This would be facilitated by the naturomorphic sub-system.

The temporal order in which the elements so stored are recalled in response to external conditions may be determined in two ways:

1. Considering the naturomorphic sub-system only, the fragments may be evoked passively as a routine sequence or as a novel sequence (see Chapter 4).
2. Considering the naturomorphic sub-system in combination with the abstract sub-system, if the stimulus does not demand an immediate response but allows enough time for planning, the probable naturomorphic sub-system response may be viewed by the abstract sub-system. The parts of the sequence could then be rearranged in their order of release by inhibition from the abstract sub-system. However, the general order of the fragments within the action sequence would to some extent be predetermined by the final condition that was envisaged (Piaget, 1927).

SUB-PROGRAMMING, SKILL ACQUISITION, AND AUTOMATIC PROCESSES

The abstract sub-system may, via its bias control connection, modulate the output of the naturomorphic sub-system. If an output sequence is used often as a result of conscious repetition or practice to develop a skill, it may "in effect" become "transferred" to lower-level automatic or sub-conscious control (Legge & Barber, 1976; Pugh, 1978; Williams et al., 1988). Thus, the naturomorphic sub-system may in effect be programmed with the sequence and thereafter respond to a cue from the abstract sub-system via the bias connection, or to the appropriate environmental stimulus, by releasing the entire programmed sequence without further involvement of the abstract sub-system. This process may be regarded as skill development through sub-programming (Mackay, 1980; Miller et al., 1960).

These automatic processes, once established through practice, are executed without awareness. They are rapid, unconstrained by capacity, and occur in-parallel (Hasher & Zacks, 1979; W. Schneider & Shiffrin, 1977). As such, they contrast with consciously controlled processes, which are capacity-limited, relatively slow, and usually serial in nature. Not only are they executed without conscious involvement, they can also be activated by a particular internal or external input configuration without the need for attention or conscious effort (Williams et al., 1988)

It is possible for the conscious repetition of a sequence to take place covertly by use of the imagination, a fact that is demonstrated in sports psychology (Suinn, 1983). Furthermore, the practiced sequence may be concerned with any "level" of activity; that is, it may be concerned with a lecture presentation, a series of chess moves, or a mathematical proof. The particular advantage of this rehearsal process is that the naturomorphic sub-system may learn a response sequence more quickly than during normal naturomorphic interaction with the environment. However, there is an attendant disadvantage: The response learned by repetitive evocation would acquire connective statistical significance values that were disproportionately high in comparison to what they would normally be if evoked only by the environment directly. Consequently, the sub-programming of the naturomorphic sub-system could disturb the naturomorphic sub-system's "correspondence" with the external environment. The sub-programming process would also decrease the probability of nonhabitual responses; that is, of low-probability, unusual, or novel responses.

SELECTIVE ATTENTION

When considering the process of abstraction in Chapter 4 it was noted that by selectively attending only to the significant information within the whole of what was possibly available, the load on the perceptual system in receipt of the selected information would be reduced. For selective attention to operate, it must be possible to shift attention selectively from one source of input to another within the whole of the available input from the environment (D. Allport et al., 1972; Treisman, 1964). This requires the simultaneous monitoring of the selected input and the remaining unselected inputs (Treisman, 1964). It is thought that this process of selective attention cannot be explained in terms of one processing system alone (D. Allport et al., 1972): More than one system must operate.

One system may determine the perceptual *set*, contextual perspective, or significant data for attention at a preattentive stage, while a second system attends to the selected information (Dixon, 1971; Douglas, 1967). In the preattentive stage, information may be evaluated at a very general contextual level (Barber & Legge, 1976; Neisser, 1976) by an analogical or Gestalt type of process (Mackay, 1949; Newell & Simon, 1959). Evidence suggests that the preattentive stage operates automatically and at a level below consciousness relative to the attentive stage (Dixon, 1971; Hilgard, 1973). This automatic processing system may interrupt the ongoing controlled and attentional processing at the conscious level in order to facilitate the reallocation of attention (W. Schneider et al., 1984).

In relation to this, the naturomorphic sub-system can receive the whole of the information available and process this so that the most significant pattern emerges. It can then forward this information to the abstract sub-system within the sample of the naturomorphic response information. Insofar as the significant information for attention is selected by the naturomorphic sub-system prior to its acceptance by the abstract sub-system, the phenomenon may be considered to exemplify a feedforward process in which the naturomorphic sub-system first rapidly processes all the available information and then forwards the result to the abstract sub-system, thereby potentially biasing the latter's area of activity (Mackay, 1966; Mittelstaedt, 1968). This forwarded information will indicate the naturomorphically determined "information for attention."

The significant information for attention may then be processed in a more detailed and analytical manner because of the higher resolution of the abstract sub-system (Neisser, 1976). Furthermore, the information may be evaluated to determine whether it is important in terms of the abstract sub-system's reference standards. If the information is important, the abstract sub-system, via control over the filtering process, may attend selectively to part or all of this significant pattern of information from the external environment. If the information is considered unimportant, the abstract sub-system may disregard it. Thus, the abstract sub-system would be involved only with deeper, detailed analysis, and would therefore expend time only on the most important fraction of the available information.

It is important to remember that the abstract sub-system is hierarchically above the naturomorphic sub-system in the control sense (at least during normal operation). Thus, although the naturomorphic sub-system determines what is selected for attention on the basis of processing all the available information, the abstract sub-system determines whether the naturomorphically selected information will be attended to in further detail on the basis of its previously abstracted information and controls the filtering process accordingly: It may choose to attend to, or to disregard, the naturomorphically selected information.

In a sense, the attention responses can become "automatized" (Shiffrin & Schneider, 1977). Initially, the naturomorphic sub-system will forward information regarding nonattended information to the abstract sub-system on the basis of naturomorphically determined significance. However, if the abstract sub-system repeatedly chooses to attend to certain of those naturomorphically selected features, the biased or sub-programmed naturomorphic sub-system will in this respect automatically increase the statistical significance values of those features and so they will become even more likely to be brought to the attention of the abstract sub-system. Conversely, if the abstract sub-system repeatedly chooses to disregard (consciously avoid) certain of the naturomorphically selected features, the biased or sub-programmed naturomorphic sub-system will in this respect automatically decrease the statistical significance values of those features and so they will become even less likely to be brought to the attention of the abstract sub-system. This latter instance may perhaps be described as "automatized" disregarding.

8

Psychological Development: An Integrated Description

A BRIEF REVIEW OF INFORMATION REPRESENTATION AND PROCESSING DEVELOPMENT IN PSYCHOLOGICAL ONTOGENY

Psychological Development from Birth to 2 Years of Age

Classical (Pavlovian) conditioning has been reported to be possible in the fetal state (Lipsitt & Kaye, 1964) and at birth (Papousek, 1965). At birth there is a demonstrable learned association between cutaneous and auditory stimuli, and by 4 weeks there is evidence of visuo-motor coordination (Bruner, 1973)—both of which require multimodal interaction. There is considerable evidence that by 2-3 months the child can make learned discriminative responses involving multimodal interaction (Macfarlane, 1975; Piaget, 1936; M. Russell, 1976). Between 3-6 months there is clear evidence of the regulation of innate responses on the basis of learning (past experience; J. Kagan, 1967; Papousek, 1965). By 9 months there is evidence of discriminative responses to different patterns of expression in intonation and of application of learned behavior patterns to new situations (Piaget, 1953; Smith & Miller, 1966). At 1 year, words may be used in a most generalized way, and it is considered that the child may represent the environment to him- or herself by an image or spatial schemata (Bruner et al., 1966; Oldfield & Marshall, 1968; Rayner, 1971). Up to 2 years—that is, up to the end of the sensorimotor period—perceptions appear to be holistic, the language used is imitative (echolalic) and holistic (holophrases), and information or events are linked or associated by similarity (Bruner et al., 1966; Brierly, 1976; Piaget, 1947). In terms of primary and secondary thought, it would appear that primary thought is manifest between birth and 2 years.

Psychological Development from 2-4 Years of Age

From 2-4 years there is a gradual emergence of the more specific meaning of concrete words (Vernon, 1962) together with the emergence of the significant features within holistic perceptions. Children as young as 2-3 years can analogically apply learned solutions to problems (Crisafi & Brown, 1986). At about 4 years there is evident recognition of symmetry, ability to match patterns, and use of analogical processes in thought and linguistic expression (Piaget, 1977b; Pickard, 1970).

Despite a basic development of perception as evidenced by more precise use of words and by pattern recognition, perception at 4 years is still basically holistic (Piaget, 1959), and there is difficulty in isolating complex figures from their backgrounds (Bruner et al., 1966; Witkin, 1959). Nevertheless, by 4 years it is thought that the normal child has a complete basic knowledge of his or her native language (Lennenberg, 1967; Oldfield & Marshall, 1968).

Psychological Development from 4-7 Years of Age

Between 4 and 7 years of age, the child's mode of thought has been described as largely intuitive (Piaget, 1947). This is considered to be an extension of sensorimotor thought (Piaget, 1947). The representation of information before 6-7 years is considered to be iconic or imagistic, still largely holistic, and limited in discrimination (Bruner, 1964; Bruner et al., 1966; Piaget, 1977b). However, as the child approaches the age of 7 years, a number of phenomena begin to make their appearance: the development of much greater self-control in action involving a certain degree of selectivity (Vernon, 1962), and more discriminate perception (Vernon 1962). It is thought that the characteristics of information representation and processing within dreams are basically the same as those of mental processes before about 7 years of age (Jones, 1970).

Psychological Development from 7 to 11-14 Years of Age

At around 7 years there is evidence of detailed perception, abstract thought, analysis, and logical or "reasoned" thought (Bruner et al., 1966; Piaget, 1927). Also around 7 years, external speech during thought has largely stopped (Vygotsky, 1962), and there is a development of a sense of left and right (Kagan, 1967). A variety of other psychological data further indicate that around 7 years there is an important transition phase for the mental processes (Paivio, 1971; Pellegrino, 1987; Piaget & Inhelder, 1971; Witkin, 1975).

From 7 years onward there is a continued development of the abstract-logical characteristics until the child roughly reaches full development at around 11-14 years (Inhelder & Piaget, 1958; Pellegrino, 1987). Coincidentally, the imagistic mode of representation, as exemplified in extreme form by eidetic imagery, declines sharply after about 11 years (Hunter, 1964; Schatzman, 1980). In terms of primary and secondary thought, it would therefore seem that the secondary level of thought begins to appear at around 7 years and is fully developed by around 11-14 years.

DEVELOPMENT OF MIND/BRAIN: A CORRESPONDENCE OF DEVELOPMENT IN NEUROLOGY AND PSYCHOLOGY

Studies in developmental psychology and in neuroanatomy and neurophysiology (see Chapter 4) concertedly indicate that there are significant transitions or completions that generally take place at around 2, 4, 7, and 10-12 years of age. It must be stressed, however, that these "ages" are essentially statistical means and therefore allow for variation in maturational rate from individual to individual. With this caution for interpretation, the main points can be summarized.

Birth to 2 Years of Age

At birth the archi-cerebellum is well developed and there are both descending and ascending cerebellar projections. The cerebral neocortex is immature. There is physiological evidence of a high percentage of D/REM sleep. Psychological development at birth includes classical conditioning to auditory and visual stimuli.

From birth to 2 years of age is the period of most rapid cerebellar growth. The inferior and superior cerebellar peduncles become fully myelinated. Over this period the cerebrum is still largely immature relative to the cerebellum. The percentage of D/REM sleep is still high. Speech is bilaterally represented. Psychological development includes sensorimotor or enactive representation and processing, and is characteristically holistic. Behavior and spoken language are largely imitative.

From 2-4 Years of Age

Over this period the cerebrum grows most rapidly, with the frontal and parietal lobes being well developed by 4 years of age, and there is a marked reduction in the percentage of D/REM sleep. Also by 4 years of age the middle cerebellar peduncle, with its descending cerebro-cerebellar tracts, is fully myelinated. Psychological features over this period include analogical or holistic thought with the recognition of significant features. It is considered that a basic knowledge of the native language will have been acquired, and that approximately half the intellectual growth will have occurred.

From 4-7 Years of Age

From 4-7 years of age the frontal and prefrontal lobes fully develop and the corpus callosum becomes largely developed. The percentage of D/REM sleep declines to its adult level. This is a critical period for lateralization. Psychological features over this period still include analogical or holistic thought but with the sensory image increasingly dissociated from the motor component with the transition from enactive to iconic thought—thought is therefore more purely imaginative.

From 7-12 Years of Age

There is continually increasing hemispheric specialization over this period. By around 12 years of age the corpus callosum is virtually fully developed and the complete adult EEG is evident. Psychological features over this period include the appearance and development of abstract thought with its greater power of discrimination. The sense of left and right develops. By the end of this period there appears to be decline in the use of imagistic thought.

AN INTEGRATED DESCRIPTION OF THE DEVELOPMENT OF MIND/BRAIN

Development Up to 2 Years of Age

Innate responses of the fetus and neonate are mediated at brain-stem level. As the child develops, these responses will be controlled, elaborated, and applied more discriminatively as a result of learning. The developmentally earliest learning based form of representation and processing is naturomorphic. This form of representation and processing has characteristics that may be described as polymodal, sensorimotor, holistic, imitative, and associative. It is ideally suited to represent information concerning the organism in terms of its interaction with the environment, and it facilitates emotional representation and processing. Its characteristics are most clearly evident in human development roughly between birth and 2 years of age, and are manifest in perception, behavior, and linguistic expression. Over this period it is the cerebellum, especially the archi-cerebellum, that is most well developed and the predominant learning-based neural sub-system.

Progressing from birth to 2 years of age there is increasing control, elaboration and discrimination, but within the limits of the cerebellum/naturomorphic sub-system. Significant perceptual and motor patterns (including linguistic patterns) emerge first as the largest significant features and then as increasingly smaller features. Learning occurs largely be repetition and, as the naturomorphic sub-system is essentially passive, is largely dependent on stimulation from the environment (including the internal environment).

Memories formed during this period are stored in the archi-cerebellum, are permanent, and form the lowest substratum of experience on which will be based, or to which will be referred, all subsequent learning and learning-based behavior. Frequently used behavioral patterns, frequently observed behavioral patterns, traumatic experiences, and very strongly beneficial experiences will be recorded with relatively high significance values and will most strongly influence subsequent behavior.

The cerebral cortex does not appear to have direct access to the archi-cerebellum, and so memories formed over the period of birth to 2 years of age will, in later years, be unconscious (relative to the cerebrum) and not volitionally accessible by the abstract sub-system. However, it has been suggested that such early memories from the preverbal stage of childhood may be evoked by using appropriate imagery as a stimulus (Kepecs, 1954).

Memories from these early years that are permanently stored in the archi-cerebellum may continue to contribute to behavior in later years, but the influence will be at an unconscious level. It may be that in later years the behavior based on these archi-cerebellar memories will be no longer appropriate or relevant. Because the cerebellar memory is permanent, these habitual responses or traumatic associations cannot simply be forgotten. Either they must be replaced "in effect" by more presently appropriate behavior, or, on being evoked, their expression must be inhibited by the cerebrum. To do this, however, the cerebral sub-system would first have to be aware that the inappropriate behavior was occurring: There would have to be a constant conscious effort to inhibit the inappropriate behavior. In order for the inappropriate behavior to be replaced "in effect," it would be necessary to repeat the preferred behavior to such a degree that the probability of eliciting the new behavior became greater than the probability of eliciting the inappropriate behavior: The old habit would have to be replaced by a "stronger" new habit.

Over the first year or so, sleep time is almost entirely D/REM sleep with very little or no S/NREM sleep. The absence of S/NREM sleep may be taken to indicate that there is little or no cerebral processing of the dream material, that is, no updating of cerebral reference standards or representations on the basis of dream information from the cerebellum. This may be explained by the fact that the cerebrum is largely undeveloped and contains few if any abstract representations—updating would therefore be unnecessary. It has been suggested that, over the first year or so, the high percentage of D/REM time during sleep serves merely to assist the maturation of the cerebrum by providing it with sensory stimuli (Roffwarg et al., 1966).

Development from 2-7 Years of Age

The period between 2 and 7 years of age may be considered an intermediate phase that is sub-divided into one period from 2-4 years of age and another from 4-7 years of age.

From 2-4 years of age the cerebellum/naturomorphic sub-system is still predominant and is not fully influenced by the cerebrum/abstract sub-system. During this period, the representation and processing of information is still largely naturomorphic, although there is the emergence of smaller and smaller significant features within the holistic perceptions up to the limit of the sub-system. However, the cerebrum/abstract sub-system develops markedly and receives information from the environment and from the cerebellum/naturomorphic sub-system. The increasing influence of the cerebrum/abstract sub-system may be evidenced by more "active" behavior over this period. The earliest cerebrally accessible memories would, in theory, be of experiences from this period.

Processing by the cerebrum of the information received from the cerebellum during D/REM sleep is evidenced by a marked increase in the percentage of S/NREM sleep time from 2-4 years of age. By 4 years of age, the cerebro-corticopontine tract of the middle cerebellar peduncle is fully myelinated and the cerebral frontal lobe is well developed. From this age onward, the cerebrum/abstract sub-system is able to fully influence the neocerebellar/naturomorphic (biased) sub-system either by selectively inhibiting cerebellar responses during their release or by sub-programming the cerebellum. This cerebral/abstract sub-system influence may be partly responsible for the increasing dissociation of the sensory image from the manifest motor component within the whole sensorimotor output of the cerebellar/naturomorphic sub-system beyond 4 years of age.

From 4 years of age onward, learning may most simply be regarded as (1) relatively unconscious learning at the cerebellar level without cerebral involvement (as for birth to 2 years of age); (2) conscious sub-programming of the cerebellum from the cerebrum; and (3) conscious learning at a cerebral level. Similarly, responses may most simply be regarded as (1) relatively unconscious responses from cerebellar level without cerebral involvement (as for birth to 2 years of age); (2) conscious control or bias of cerebellar responses by the cerebrum; and (3) conscious responses from the abstract/cerebral level.

Between 4 and 7 years of age, the activity of the cerebrum/abstract sub-system continues to increase relative to the cerebellum/naturomorphic sub-system but does not yet predominate. As the cerebrum/abstract sub-system is essentially "active," the child may now initiate learning, and, by selectively manipulating environmental variables, he or she may learn more quickly than with the "passive" naturomorphic sub-system. The cerebrum/abstract sub-system may sub-program or "teach" the cerebellum/naturomorphic sub-system by repetitively initiating sequences, for example by rote learning of *wholes* such as the alphabet string, the multiplication tables, songs, or poems. These sub-programmed sequences will be stored at the cerebellar level and will therefore be permanently recorded and will normally be released as *wholes* or *whole parts*.

Information recorded within the neo-cerebellum from 4 years of age onward may, in theory, be accessed by the cerebrum/abstract sub-system provided that it has also recorded a part of the same information which could subsequently serve as a cue (or cerebrally generated stimulus) to evoke the full information from the cerebellum. The information recorded within the cerebellum may, of course, also be evoked directly by a stimulus from the environment. Whatever the source of the stimuli, the information evoked from the cerebellum may emerge through the autonomic and motor systems as an emotional and action response or it may emerge within the cerebrum as a "would be" or "imagined" response.

Over the whole period from 2-7 years of age, as the cerebrum/abstract sub-system becomes increasingly involved in learning-based control, there is increased abstraction of detail, increased discrimination, increased cerebral/abstract sub-system inhibition of the cerebellar/naturomorphic sub-system, and increased dissociation of the naturomorphic sensory images from their naturomorphic motor component. Behavior responses become further refined, more discriminate, and less habitually applied. There is an increasing development of the ability to inhibit the expression of cerebellar sub-system responses and to plan. The sensorimotor image sequences evoked from the cerebellum/naturomorphic sub-system in response to an environmental stimulus, or cerebral cue, may, in the process of imagination, be received by the cerebral/abstract sub-system, where they will be abstractly evaluated, and, if necessary, modified in detail, perhaps by active reordering of the sequence. Thought, therefore, becomes less enactive, and less frequently accompanied by its motor component. This development would include the transition from overt speech towards "silent" speech and "silent" reading.

Development from 7 to 10-12 Years of Age

By 7 years of age, the sensory image is virtually totally dissociated from overt motor action, which indicates that the cerebrum/abstract sub-system can fully bias or inhibit the information transmitted to it from the neocerebellum naturomorphic (biased) sub-system during the awake state. By this age the percentage of S/NREM sleep time has reached it adult level, and this indicates that the interaction between the cerebellum and cerebrum during sleep has matured; that is, the process of updating the abstract representations must have matured.

Also by 7 years of age, the corpus callosum and a (conscious) sense of left and right has developed, and abstract thought has become predominant. These simultaneous developments indicate that from 7 years of age on the predominant learning-based sub-system is the cerebrum/abstract sub-system, in particular the dominant cerebral hemisphere.

Altogether the data indicates that full development of the basic interaction between the cerebellum/naturomorphic sub-system and the cerebrum/abstract sub-system coincides with the full development of the basic intermediate representational form within the cerebrum/abstract sub-system. It also coincides with the beginning of the predominance of the development of the high-level abstract sub-system within the dominant cerebral hemisphere. The intermediate representational form is retained by the minor cerebral hemisphere, but may also further develop in its own form with further experience. The role of the intermediate representational form (unimodal images/iconic) may be partly as a translatory language that enables the high-level abstract sub-system of the dominant cerebral hemisphere to more readily process (understand) the information transmitted to the cerebrum from the cerebellum/naturomorphic sub-system.

From this age onward the dominant cerebral hemisphere may inhibit the input it receives from the cerebellum but allow input to the minor cerebral hemisphere from the cerebellum. This allows for further abstract development of the dominant cerebral hemisphere. It also allows for the full operation of cerebral or conscious attention: The dominant cerebral hemisphere may fully attend to and process input from the external environment while the minor hemisphere attends to input from the cerebellum—only information determined to be relevant by both the cerebellum/naturomorphic sub-system and by the minor cerebral hemisphere/low-level abstract sub-system need then be attended to by the dominant cerebral hemisphere/high-level abstract sub-system. Over this period, the ability to focus attention or to concentrate will be able to develop. Lateralization of cerebral processing may then lead to sub-programming of the neo-cerebellum, especially in terms of left-hand side and right-hand side motor specialization.

From 7 years of age the cerebral/abstract sub-system, especially the dominant cerebral hemisphere/high-level sub-system, is predominant and may be regarded as the normal level of consciousness. The cerebellum/naturomorphic sub-system may now be regarded as unconscious relative to the cerebrum/abstract sub-system. In terms of the transmission of information from the cerebellum/naturomorphic sub-system to the dominant cerebral hemisphere/high-level abstract sub-system, the minor cerebral hemisphere/low-level abstract sub-system may be regarded as preconscious and as performing a largely translatory function. From this age on: learned responses may most simply be considered as originating from the cerebellum/naturomorphic sub-system or from the cerebrum/abstract sub-system.

Responses may be evoked: (1) directly and automatically from the cerebellum at an unconscious level either as a result of an environmentally generated stimulus or as a result of a cerebral cue; (2) directly from the cerebrum at a conscious level as a result of a directly perceived environmental stimulus or as a result of a cerebellar-generated cue. The two learning-based sub-systems may operate consecutively or simultaneously, and they may operate independently or in relation to one another. For instance the cerebral sub-system may deal with a behavior that requires attention, or with nonroutine processing, while the cerebellar sub-system may carry out a routine operation. However, the two sub-systems may both deal with nonroutine information, either each dealing with different problems or each dealing with the same problem in their respectively different ways. It is possible that in dealing with the same problem that the two sub-systems may arrive at essentially the same result. However, it is not impossible that the two sub-systems may arrive at conflicting "conclusions" with regard to some problem with which they are simultaneously dealing. Ideally, in the event of such a conflict the abstract sub-system would consider both possibilities before the whole system responded. However, time may not permit the delay entailed in such further consideration. Also, it may be that the motivational component of the naturomorphic sub-system is so strong that the response cannot be fully inhibited by the abstract sub-system, and so the naturomorphic sub-system response is executed even though the abstract sub-system "disagrees" with it in terms of logic. The processing by the two sub-systems may be consecutive or simultaneous.

In a similar, but more complex, manner, lateralized learned responses may be considered as originating from the dominant cerebral hemisphere/high-level abstract sub-system, the minor cerebral hemisphere/low-level abstract sub-system, the "minor" cerebellar hemisphere/biased naturomorphic sub-system, the "dominant" cerebellar hemisphere/biased naturomorphic sub-system, or the archicerebellum/unbiased naturomorphic sub-system.

Between 7 and approximately 12 years of age, the dominant cerebral hemisphere/high-level abstract sub-system develops fully. This is accompanied by an inhibition, or a decreased expression, of the forms or representation and processing utilized by the cerebellum/naturomorphic sub-system and the minor cerebral hemisphere/low-level abstract sub-system.

Although the sensorimotor and imagistic forms of representation and processing of information seem to disappear, their neurological substrates still exist, as does the facility (and need) for their expression. The dominant cerebral hemisphere/high-level abstract sub-system may normally largely inhibit or refine the motor expression of these lower sub-systems, or inhibit the transmission of information from these sub-systems to the dominant cerebral hemisphere/high-level abstract sub-system, in order to attend to the external environment. However, the lower sub-systems may normally be deliberately allowed expression in automatic/habitual actions (motor or mental) or in the recall of information from the experiential memory during imagination. The transmission of information from the cerebellum/naturomorphic sub-system to the cerebrum/abstract sub-system would be especially involved in the process of attention shifts and in problem solving. The lower sub-systems may also inadvertently be allowed expression when the conscious attention of the dominant cerebral hemisphere/high-level abstract sub-system is taken up in processing information other than that presented by the environment. An automatic cerebellar sub-system response is likely to occur when an immediate response is required or when the activity of the cerebral sub-system has been adversely affected, for example by fatigue or certain drugs.

Summary

Most simply, the developmental changes may be summarized as: from birth to 2 years of age, a predominance of the cerebellum/naturomorphic sub-system representation and processing; from 2-7 years of age an intermediate translatory/transition phase with some characteristics of both cerebellum/naturomorphic and cerebrum/abstract representation and processing; from 7 years of age onward a predominance of cerebrum/abstract sub-system representation and processing.

THE DREAM PROCESS IN RELATION TO DEVELOPMENT

The dream process enables the abstract representations to be updated or to continually develop on the basis of further experience, and is necessary for the overall efficiency of the learning-based homeostatic process. Dreams are formed of sequences from within the cerebellum/naturomorphic sub-system memory, and so provide the cerebrum/abstract sub-system with information that the latter does not possess. In addition to providing information for the updating of the cerebrum/abstract sub-system representations, the dreams also uniquely provide information from the period of birth to 2 years of age, and therefore serve to indicate the possible origins and nature of relevant inappropriate habits patterns, phobias, or attractions. Dreams may also provide a cerebellum/naturomorphic sub-system response sequence that could be most significant in relation to some problem; whether of current life or "intellect."

During sleep the minor cerebral hemisphere/low-level abstract sub-system and its intermediate representational form may play an important role in translating the dream information prior to its more abstract processing during S/NREM sleep by the dominant cerebral hemisphere/high-level abstract sub-system. Alternatively, upon awakening, the dreams that are remembered by the conscious dominant cerebral hemisphere/high-level abstract sub-system may be translated by the use of the intermediate representational form (characterized by images, analogies, associative linkage, similies, metaphors, concrete words, etc.), and then analyzed. While some images may have "universal" meanings, most may be uniquely determined by the individual's personal experience. It is possible that particularly important dreams have a motivational component strong enough to provoke awakening at the end of the dream in order to facilitate conscious "recall" and subsequent processing.

Those dreams that are not remembered on awakening may, in some instances, be subsequently cued by stimuli from the environment because dreams will most probably be concerned with current problems and will probably be made up partly of imagery from current environmental events. Those dreams that expressed the cerebellum/naturomorphic sub-system's solution or "would-be" response to pressing behavior problems, if not remembered and consciously dealt with, may eventually emerge as intrusive images or thoughts, or recurrent daydreams. In certain instances they may even emerge as "automatic responses." Familiarity with this intermediate representational form will be important for the understanding of dreams. It will also be of use for translating intuitions into a logical form so that they may be more easily communicated and tested.

THE IMPORTANCE OF THE BRAIN STEM TRANSMISSION SYSTEM IN RELATION TO DEVELOPMENT

Although the development of the brain/mind may be described largely in terms of the cerebellum/naturomorphic sub-system and the cerebrum/abstract sub-system, it is also dependent on the transmission of information between the environment and each of the two sub-systems, and between the two sub-systems themselves. Development of the cerebrum/abstract sub-system depends in part on the information that it receives from the cerebellum/naturomorphic sub-system: Information concerning what is naturomorphically significant and worthy of attention, information that provides a context or a meaning for "referential" abstract representations, information in the form of response sequences utilized in the process of imagination, and experiential memory information from the naturomorphic and information of use in the updating process. Successful interaction of the cerebellum/naturomorphic sub-system and the cerebrum/abstract sub-system in the process of attention, experiential memory recall, imagination, intuition, problem solving, and dreaming, all depend on the transmission of information through the brain stem. Development of the neo-cerebellum/naturomorphic (biased) sub-system in sub-programming also depends, in part, on the transmission of information through the brain stem from the cerebrum/abstract sub-system to the cerebellum/naturomorphic sub-system. Accordingly, the development and functioning of the brain stem, especially the reticular formation and the monoamine systems, will be of crucial importance for the overall development of the brain/mind.

MENTAL HEALTH IN RELATION TO DEVELOPMENT

One of the major problems in mental health promotion has been the difficulty in developing an adequate definition or model of mental health (Freudenberg, 1979; Sauber, 1973). It has been suggested that such a model should be developed from the knowledge of the behavioral sciences (Jahoda, 1958) and should be based on the concept of normal mental development and functioning (Allinsmith & Goethals, 1962). Consideration should not, however, be limited to information about the normal or healthy mind, for psychological health and disease may be regarded as parts of a continuum (Leighton et al., 1957; Wishner, 1955). Any model of mental health that is to be taken seriously should also provide some explanation of the causes and symptoms of mental illness. Similarly, consideration should also include information concerning the development and normal and abnormal functioning of the brain (Dalzell-Ward, 1967). The resultant model, if valid, should be consistent with material from all these areas, and it should have explanatory power within them. It should also relate information from the various fields of knowledge in an integrative manner.

One of the most frequently selected criterion for mental health is that of the individual's ability to successfully interact with the environment. Within this general ability may be others that are thought to be prerequisite to mental health, for example problem solving and adjustment or adaptation (Allinsmith & Goethals, 1962; Jahoda, 1958). In relation to these criteria, it has been suggested by a number of psychiatrists and psychologists that mental health may be viewed in terms of the principle of homeostasis (Dalzell-Ward, 1967; Menninger, 1963).

It is proposed that the description of the development of the mind and brain in terms of the principle of equilibration presented in Chapters 2–6 fulfil these requirements. On the basis of the description presented, it is possible to suggest a number of conditions that, in theory, would facilitate mental health. It should also be possible to consider a number of major disorders in terms of the description and the suggested conditions.

FACTORS AFFECTING PSYCHOLOGICAL DEVELOPMENT AND MENTAL HEALTH

Normal development and functioning of the brain/mind will depend on the anatomical development of the brain stem, cerebellum, and cerebrum, and on the normal functioning of each of these sub-systems both within themselves and in interaction with one another. It will also depend on the development of the naturomorphic, intermediate, and abstract forms of representation and processing, and on the utilization of these forms in themselves and in relation to one another.

Conditions that interfere with the anatomical development of, or cause damage in maturity to, the brain stem, cerebellum, and cerebrum, or that interfere with the normal functioning of these sub-systems in themselves or in interaction with one another, will be detrimental to the development or efficient utilization of the brain/mind. Similarly, conditions that interfere with the development of the naturomorphic, intermediate, and abstract forms of representation and processing, or that interfere with their utilization in maturity, will also be detrimental to the development and efficient utilization of the brain/mind.

Detrimental physiological conditions would be exemplified by neurological lesions as a result of "biological" disease or damage, or by neurotransmitter imbalance, possibly as a result of drug consumption (prescribed or otherwise) and possibly as a result of incorrect diet. Detrimental psychological conditions would be exemplified by inadequate interaction with the environment (inadequate stimulation) during the early years when the passive cerebellum/naturomorphic sub-system is predominant, by inadequate sleep/dream time, and by imbalanced or inadequate utilization of the different forms of representation and processing. Inadequate utilization could be caused by repeated failure of the conscious cerebrum/abstract sub-system to respond to the information it receives from the cerebellum/naturomorphic sub-system during sleep. Imbalanced utilization of the different forms of representation and processing could also result from too much or too little of any of the following: attention to input from the external environment, attention to input from the cerebellum/naturomorphic sub-system as in imagination or "day dreaming," use of the cerebellum/naturomorphic sub-system, and use of the cerebrum/abstract sub-system. Many of the aforementioned psychological conditions could, in part, be influenced by the education process, which may nurture either a balance or an imbalance.

It is argued that dream sleep is one of the natural mechanisms that facilitates updating. If the updating process is prevented from occuring naturally, for example by the absence of adequate dream sleep, then the updating transmission of information may take place during nonsleep times. This would result in the abstract sub-system receiving memory images at the same time as, or in place of, information input from the external environment, possibly resulting in disrupted train of thought, difficulty with attention/concentration, and confusion over what is real and what is imaginary.

Detrimental psychological conditions could also be exemplified by an unrepresentative or distorted learning environment. An unrepresentative or unnatural environment may lead to schemata that are maladaptive in the representative or natural environment. The learning environment obviously includes other people from whom a child can learn directly or vicariously. A child's early social learning may unfortunately involve parents or other "teachers" who serve as maladaptive models. Irrational beliefs, emotional sensitivity and expressiveness, and faulty reasoning processes are modelled in parent-child communication, and children internalize them into their cognitive schemata through social modelling and language imitation (Bernard & Joyce, 1984). This could be a particular problem in the extreme instances where the role models were severely neurotic or psychotic parents or other care-givers.

FOUR

DISORDERS OF THE MIND/BRAIN

9

Schizophrenia

SOME CHARACTERISTICS OF SCHIZOPHRENIA

Schizophrenia is considered to be a disorder of formal thought and to be the expression of a more primitive form of thought as exemplified by autochthonous images (Arieti, 1974; Birchwood et al., 1988; Matte-Blanco, 1975). In general, schizophrenics have a significantly poorer verbal IQ relative to performance IQ (Birchwood et al., 1988). Particular impairments associated with schizophrenia include persisting "positive" symptoms such as hallucinations, delusions, and thought disorder (Birchwood et al., 1988). The thought disorder includes phenomena such as thought insertion, where the subject experiences thoughts which are "not his own" but intruded into consciousness, and audible thoughts where the individual experiences his thoughts spoken out loud in his mind (Birchwood et al., 1988).

The above-described features of schizophrenia are considered to be "positive" symptoms. It has been suggested that the positive symptoms of schizophrenia involve a disorder of the filtering process (Weckowicz & Blewett, 1959), and may also involve a disorder of attention (Birchwood et al., 1988; McGhie & Chapman, 1961; S. Schneider, 1976). In addition to the aforementioned positive symptoms, there may also be "negative" symptoms such as apathy, emotional blunting, and a tendency to withdraw (Birchwood et al., 1988). Symptomatically, schizophrenia may therefore be considered to be composed of at least two identifiable pathological syndromes: type I, which is characterized by the presence of positive symptoms and is most typically seen in acute psychosis; and, type II, which is associated with negative symptoms, such as affective flattening and poverty of speech (Crow, 1980; Crow et al., 1982).

Schizophrenic Hallucinations

Schizophrenic hallucinations are perceptions that are often in the visual or auditory modality and occur in the absence of identifiable external stimulation. Often the hallucinations include memories which seem to be released in an uninhibited manner (Hernandez-Peon, 1965; Horowitz, 1975; West, 1962). Auditory hallucinations are frequently experienced as "voices" that "speak" in the third person and may offer comments on the person's action or thoughts. In most instances the individual will believe that the "voices" are alien but real; that they must be taken seriously and sometimes that they must be obeyed (Birchwood et al., 1988).

There is evidence that when schizophrenic subjects recall "images" from memory, they may experience the recollection as though it is a present reality. For example, Mintz and Alpert (1972) asked subjects to imagine (recall the memory of hearing) the words and music of the song "White Christmas." They found that 85 percent of hallucinated schizophrenic subjects reported either "hearing" the record and believing it was playing, or at least imagining its sound very clearly, while only 5 percent of nonhallucinated subjects reported hearing it with any vividness. Repeated failure to distinguish between imagination and reality at the time of occurrence would represent a psychotic state (Williams et al., 1988).

Ullman and Krasner (1975) suggest that "voices" may be viewed as "responses," citing McGuigan's (1966) reports of increased chin muscle amplitude, respiration, and faint whisperings immediately prior to a patient's reports of hallucinatory experiences. McGuigan had speculated that hallucinatory voices might therefore be initiated when a person "talks to himself." This suggestion is supported by P. Green and Preston (1981), who report a case study in which sensitive microphones were used to record a schizophrenic's faint whispering, previously observed at times when his self-reports and nonverbal behavior suggested him to be hallucinating. The schizophrenic's reports of hearing a hallucinatory female voice were reliably preceded by detectable episodes of whispering. When amplified, the whispers could be reliably detected as words, phrases, and sentences whose content corresponded closely to the patient's reports of what the voice had said.

It has been reported that hallucinatory voices are reduced if the subject has to attend to external task information and to make an overt verbal response (Margo et al., 1981; Slade, 1974). "Voices" were most markedly reduced when subjects were required to actively monitor external material by reading simple prose passages aloud and then describing their content (Margo et al., 1981).

Stress and resulting anxiety can precipitate hallucinatory experiences (Horowitz, 1975; Slade, 1976). For example, stressful films were followed by more intrusive thoughts and more intrusive imagery, which surfaced repeatedly in conscious representations. Such repeated surfacing is considered to be necessary to bring about a "completion" of information processing (Horowitz, 1975).

THE BRAIN STEM, CEREBELLUM, AND CEREBRUM IN RELATION TO SCHIZOPHRENIA

The Brain Stem in Relation to Schizophrenia

It has been suggested that schizophrenia involves a malfunction or over-activity of the reticular formation (Fish, 1961; Kornetsky & Mirsky, 1966; Mayer-Gross et al., 1969; McGhie & Chapman, 1961). Neurochemical data indicates that schizophrenia is likely to be associated with a malfunction of the DA/NE and 5HT systems (Birchwood et al., 1988; Crow, 1980; Crow et al., 1982; Richter, 1976). In particular, it is thought that there may be increased DA transmission (Crow, 1980; Richter, 1976). Drugs that release DA may induce schizophrenic symptoms whereas drugs that ameliorate schizophrenic symptoms are DA antagonists (Owen et al., 1978).

The Cerebellum in Relation to Schizophrenia

A number of years ago it was speculatively suggested that the psychotic symptoms of schizophrenia may involve the cerebellum (Schilder, 1951). More recently, this suggestion has been reiterated on the basis of contemporary research: "Based on anatomical, electrophysiological, biochemical, and pharmaco-logical evidence, there appears to be a capability of the cerebellum to influence behavior and thereby for cerebellar dysfunction to contribute to the symptomatology of schizophrenia" (S. Snider, 1982, 50). In fact, there have been numerous articles, including several on the basis of CAT scans and postmortem confirmation studies, that have indicated that cerebellar dysfunction is correlated with psychotic aspects of schizophrenia (Dewan et al., 1983; Diaz-Infante et al., 1982; Freedman, 1977; Hamilton et al., 1983; Heath et al., 1979; Kutty & Prendes, 1981; Lippman et al., 1982; Luchins et al., 1981; Reider et al., 1983; Weinberger et al., 1980; Yadalam, et al., 1985).

In relation to this it was noted earlier that stimulation of the cerebellum is involved in the production of hallucinatory-like behavior (McDonald, 1953; Pagano, 1902, 1905); that is, on stimulation of the cerebellum without spread of the stimulating current to extra-cerebellar regions (McDonald, 1953), there have been observed responses as if to external visual or auditory stimuli when in fact no such external stimuli existed. Furthermore, some data indicates that cerebellar stimulation may cause a subsequent reduction of hallucinatory-activity in humans (Heath, 1977). These opposite results of cerebellar stimulation may be related to different conditions of stimulation or to the rebound phenomenon—while cerebellar stimulation may cause hallucinatory activity at the time of stimulation, it may also result in a later reduction of the activity (possibly because the "need" for cerebellar output has thereby been temporarily reduced).

The Cerebrum in Relation to Schizophrenia

Evidence indicates that within the cerebrum, the hippocampus and the temporal lobe may be particularly involved in schizophrenic symptoms (Mayer-Gross et al., 1969). Cerebral malfunction in schizophrenia may partly be related to malfunction of cerebral control or filtering of ascending input to the cerebral cortex (Stevens, 1973; Weckowitz & Blewett, 1959).

Hemispheric Processes in Schizophrenia

On the basis of their detailed review of EEG and evoked potential studies, Birchwood et al. (1988) suggest that schizophrenia may entail both a dysfunctional dominant (left) hemisphere and a disturbance of interhemispheric integration. In turn, disturbed interhemispheric integration in schizophrenics might arise as a consequence of left hemisphere over-activation (Flor-Henry, 1983) or as a consequence of a disordered right hemisphere "driving" the left (Weller & Montagu, 1979). In effect, therefore, the various suggested defects include left hemisphere malfunction, right hemisphere malfunction, and disturbed interhemispheric integration. Most interpretations of schizophrenia suggest that the primary defect is in the dominant hemisphere. For example, it has been suggested that "voices" reflect right-hemisphere processing that is normally unavailable to consciousness but becomes manifest because of a failure in the dominance of the left hemisphere (Budzinski, 1977). However, contrary to most interpretations, several authors have raised the possibility that the primary defect state in schizophrenia is one of right-hemisphere dysfunction (Venables, 1982). For example, it has been argued that left-hemisphere over-activation observed in schizophrenics may represent a compensatory reaction to a fundamental right-hemisphere defect (Schweitzer, 1982; Weller & Montagu, 1979). The proponents of a primary right-hemisphere defect have tended to suggest that this occurs prior to the onset of schizophrenia, and that the symptoms only become apparent when the left hemisphere processes become involved (Birchwood et al., 1988).

In the presence of faulty interhemispheric communication, whatever the cause, the right hemisphere's activity may interfere with and intrude into the left hemisphere's awareness, leading to a subjective interpretation of the intrusions as hallucinations, feelings of control, thought insertion, and so forth arising from an independent source (P. Green et al., 1983; Nasrallah, 1982, 1985; Randall, 1983). This may lead to delusional constructs in order to rationalize these perceived external and independent influences. Other symptoms might also reflect a disorder in interhemispheric communication. Thus thought blocking might arise if the left hemisphere's ongoing train of thought were interrupted by disparate intrusions from the right hemisphere. If frequent, these might give rise to a fragmentation of thought and disordered verbalizations (Birchwood et al., 1988).

Although much of the psychological theorizing about schizophrenia has been in terms of the cerebral hemispheres, it has been stressed that sub-cortical systems, such as the limbic system and the brain stem, might also contribute to the problems evident in schizophrenia, and that future research needs to increasingly adopt a three-dimensional approach to CNS function rather than an "up-down" or "left-right" perspective (Birchwood et al., 1988).

SLEEP AND DREAMING IN RELATION TO SCHIZOPHRENIA

There have been numerous comparisons between the form of thought in schizophrenia, hallucinogenic thought, and the form of dream thought (Bridger, 1960; Freud, 1900; Jacobi, 1974; Katan, 1960; Schneider, 1948). Over 60 years ago it was suggested that schizophrenia was an emergence of dreams or dream-like thought during the awake state (Freud, 1900; McDougall, 1926). In relation to this, relatively recent evidence indicates that:

1. In animals, hallucinatory-like behavior is accompanied by PGO spikes similar to those in the dream state, and, conversely, in the awake state, PGO spikes may be accompanied by hallucinatory-like behavior (Bowker & Morrison, 1976; Dement, 1969, 1971). This hallucinatory-like behavior in animals has been described as dream sleep without atonia (Carli & Zanchetti, 1965; Dement, 1969; Morrison & Bowker, 1975); that is, as the sensory activity of dream sleep with the motor facility of the awake state.
2. Biochemically induced psychotic hallucinations are experienced in much the same way as dreams and are accompanied by EEG activity correspondent with that of dream sleep (Asgian et al., 1973; Itil, 1969). Moreover, the biochemicals that induce psychotic hallucinations may induce, or increase the quantity of, D/REM sleep (Dement, 1965; Green, 1969; Torda, 1968).
3. D/REM sleep activity is reduced in schizophrenics (Ornitz, 1970)—an experimental physiological observation supported by subjective experiential reports of no sleep-time dreaming (Janov, 1978). Moreover, the typical schizophrenic does not seem to exhibit the normal "rebound" increase of D/REM sleep time following a period of sleep deprivation (Gillin et al., 1974; Zarcone & Dement, 1969). In relation to the latter point it has been observed that prolonged periods of sleep deprivation in normal subjects may result in hallucinations (Bliss et al., 1959; E. Murray, 1959; West et al., 1962). It is therefore possible that the "rebound" of the schizophrenic manifests not as increased dream time but as increased hallucination time. In fact, hallucinosis in the schizophrenic is accompanied by EEG activity correspondent with that of dream sleep (Stevens, 1973), and such activity may manifest in 90–120 minute cycles correspondent with that of the D/REM-S/NREM sleep cycle (West et al., 1962).

On the basis of this more objective, scientifically obtained information, it has once more been suggested that schizophrenia may be a breakthrough of dreams during the awake state (Fisher, 1970; Ornitz, 1970; Snyder, 1963). Neurophysiological data indicates that normally there is a periodic preponderant activity of the dream-producing system during the awake state. The activity of this system may be unnoticed because it is at a level below that of the conscious system; for example, by emerging only within the preconscious minor cerebral hemisphere, and because it is "obscured" as a result of conscious attention to the external environment. The breakthrough in schizophrenia is thought to be the result of increased dream "pressure" and reduced inhibition of D/REM emergence (Fisher, 1970).

SUMMARY OF CHARACTERISTICS OF SCHIZOPHRENIA

Schizophrenia is considered to be a disorder of formal thought and to be the expression of a more primitive and imagistic form of thought. Positive symptoms include hallucinations, delusions, and thought insertion. Often the hallucinations include memories that seem to be released in an uninhibited manner and are experienced as reality. Auditory hallucinations and thought insertion are frequently experienced as "voices." These "voices" may be viewed as responses in the form of the person talking to him or herself but are experienced as reality. Intrusive thoughts and intrusive imagery that surface repeatedly in conscious representations may be precipitated by stress and resulting anxiety. Such repeated surfacing is considered to be necessary to bring about a "completion" of information processing.

Studies suggest that schizophrenia may entail both a dysfunctional dominant (left) hemisphere and a disturbance of interhemispheric integration. It has been suggested that the "voices" reflect right-hemisphere processing normally unavailable to consciousness but manifest because of a failure in the dominance of the left hemisphere. However, it is thought possible that the primary defect state in schizophrenia is one of right-hemisphere dysfunction. The primary right-hemisphere defect may, however, occur prior to the onset of schizophrenia, with the symptoms only becoming apparent when the left-hemisphere processes become involved.

Although much of the psychological theorizing about schizophrenia has been in terms of the cerebral hemispheres, it has been stressed that sub-cortical systems, such as the limbic system and the brain stem, might also contribute to the problems evident in schizophrenia. Evidence indicates that within the cerebrum, the hippocampus and the temporal lobe may be particularly involved in schizophrenic symptoms. Cerebral malfunction in schizophrenia may partly be related to malfunction of the cerebral control or filtering of ascending input to the cerebral cortex. In relation to this it has been suggested that schizophrenia involves a malfunction or over-activity of the reticular formation. Neurochemical data indicates that schizophrenia is likely to be associated with a malfunction of the DA/NE and 5HT systems. In particular, drugs that release DA may induce schizophrenic symptoms. Last, it has been suggested that the psychotic symptoms of schizophrenia may involve the cerebellum, and there is some evidence that stimulation of the cerebellum may result in hallucinatory behavior.

There have been numerous comparisons between the form of thought in schizophrenia, hallucinogenic thought, and the form of dream thought. A variety of scientifically obtained information supports the notion that schizophrenia may be a breakthrough of dreams during the awake state. The periodic activity of the dream-producing system may normally be unnoticed during the awake state because it is at a level below that of the conscious system, for example, by emerging only within the preconscious minor cerebral hemisphere, and because it is "obscured" as a result of conscious attention to the external environment. The breakthrough in schizophrenia in some instances is thought to be the result of increased dream "pressure" and reduced inhibition of D/REM emergence.

AN INTERPRETATION OF SCHIZOPHRENIA

As described earlier, in the process of imagination, the cerebrum/abstract sub-system may receive naturomorphic response information from the cerebellum/naturomorphic sub-system. The response information may be largely a visual image sequence, or it may be mainly the action of speaking, where the imagination of speech would be experienced as "internal speech." A similar process takes place during dream sleep but without the facility for cerebral inhibition or control of input from the cerebellum.

Dream-like processing and the periodic preponderant activity of the dream-producing cerebellum/naturomorphic sub-system may be present throughout the awake state but be unnoticed because it is at a level below that of the conscious system or because its emergence is obscured or inhibited by attention to the outer world, that is, by attention to environmental input.

Under normal circumstances, the unilateral focussing effect would allow the dominant cerebral hemisphere to focus on information transmitted from the environment while the minor cerebral hemisphere focused upon information transmitted from the cerebellum. The cerebral cortex could therefore receive a certain amount of cerebellar input during the awake state without totally interfering with the cerebral interaction with the environment. As the minor cerebral hemisphere is below the dominant hemisphere's level of consciousness, the cerebellar input to the cerebrum would not necessarily interfere with the activity of the dominant and conscious sub-system. The results of the minor cerebral hemisphere low-level abstract processing of cerebellar information could be transmitted to the dominant cerebral hemisphere for its attention as necessary.

A disruption of the normal interaction of the cerebrum/abstract sub-system and the cerebellum/naturomorphic sub-system that facilitates the bilateral cerebral emergence of cerebellar output, either trans-callosally or directly, would clearly result in a number of phenomena including disrupted attention, disrupted cerebrum/abstract sub-system processing, and increased experience of autonomous imagery, which, in certain instances, may virtually be dreams (with intact inhibition of the motor component). These characteristics of schizophrenia may therefore be seen as the result of excessive cerebellar excitatory input to the cerebrum.

The normal operation of this system may be disrupted by a number of conditions. For example, conditions that interfere with the anatomical development of, or cause damage in maturity to, the brain stem, cerebellum, and cerebrum, or that interfere with the normal functioning of these sub-systems in themselves or in interaction with one another, could disrupt the normal functioning of the above-described process. Such conditions could, for example, be neurological lesions resulting from "biological" disease or damage, or neurotransmitter imbalance possibly resulting from drug consumption (prescribed or otherwise) or incorrect diet.

The normal interaction of the cerebellar and cerebral sub-systems could also be disrupted as a result of repeated failure by the cerebrum/abstract sub-system to respond to the information it receives from the cerebellum/naturomorphic sub-system during sleep. During periods of stressful experience, such repeated failure could result in an increased dream sleep "pressure" and a cerebrally bilateral breakthrough during the awake state.

The conditions described in the preceding two paragraphs may largely be considered to be conditions not deliberately created, and also to be conditions that would result in symptoms that could not, in theory, be volitionally inhibited. In theory, symptoms of schizophrenia could also result from imbalanced utilization of the different forms of representation and processing. This could develop directly as a result of too much deliberate attention to input from the cerebellum/naturomorphic sub-system as in imagination or "day dreaming"—where such inward attention is for some reason preferable to attention to the "real world." In this particular instance, in theory, the experience/symptoms should be open to volitional inhibition. Alternatively, the symptoms of schizophrenia could develop indirectly as a "rebound" or compensatory reaction to too much deliberate inattention to input from the cerebellum/naturomorphic sub-system—where such outward attention is for some reason preferable to attention to the "inner world."

As indicated, the aforementioned characteristics of schizophrenia may be seen as the result of excessive cerebellar excitatory input to the cerebrum. Certain other general characteristics might be expected in the event of relatively excessive naturomorphic sub-system processing or a deficiency of abstract sub-system processing. Most generally, there would be a predominance of low-discrimination, holistic, analogical, associative, polymodal (synaesthetic), imaginative, and affective cognition.

Within the naturomorphic sub-system, information is represented and processed in a "continuous" form and as a whole within which the separate dimensions of space-time are merely implicit. A consequence of representing temporal relationships in this manner is that the parts of a sequence are not themselves bound totally by the temporal order in which they occurred in any one actually experienced sequence. A particular recorded sequence or event will, once recorded, cease to have its individual identity in space-time; it will coexist with all the other recorded information. Its individual identity may be retained by the relationship within its particular set of significance values, but only implicitly. If it has anything in common, in this respect, with the data already recorded, or with data subsequently recorded, its particular set of significance values will be altered (because of the cumulative nature of the memory) and it will no longer even implicitly have its original identity. Consequently, the individual parts of different but associated sequences would be interchangeable. This characteristic will inevitably make it difficult for the naturomorphic sub-system, in itself, to determine the temporal relationship between strongly associated items, and so there may be confusion in attempting to recall the order in which strongly associated events have taken place. Interaction with the abstract sub-system will be necessary to clarify such matters.

A stimulus from the environment would evoke from the naturomorphic sub-system a response in the form of a polymodal, or sensorimotor, sequence containing a motor component, which would normally constitute the overt response along with a sensory component containing information concerning the expected consequences. The integrated physiological, behavioral, and cognitive components constitute a response that is "characteristically" emotional. Once the emotional response has been elicited by a given stimulus, its release at an autonomic and motor level will be automatic.

Naturomorphic processing would have a limited and fairly low-power of resolution (relative to abstract representation and processing). There could be failure to distinguish between importantly different data at a detailed level, and under such circumstances inappropriate responses might occur. Furthermore a significantly large part of an often-experienced or otherwise important spatial or temporal pattern would be treated as if it were the whole pattern. In some circumstances this pattern completion can be inappropriate. For example, a largely familiar cue could evoke a habitual response (motor or mental) which, upon its completion, would be innappropriate because of the small but nonetheless important difference between the actual total stimulus and the inductively perceived total pattern. If behavior of this sort is repeated often enough, it can become habitual. The habitual response sequences would, in effect, be released as predetermined wholes, and could be regarded as ritualistic and, insofar as they are illogical, possibly as superstitious.

All these aforementioned naturomorphic processing characteristics are likely to be more evident when there is relatively excessive cerebellar activity, and thus are likely to be "characteristic" of schizophrenia.

10

Depression

SOME CHARACTERISTICS OF DEPRESSION

Clinical depression is considered to be a misery/malaise that occurs either spontaneously or, with respect to duration and intensity, is in excess of the normal reaction to the provocative circumstance. The depressive disorders may be categorized according to a variety of criteria, several of which are briefly reviewed by Gilbert (1984). Among those reviewed are:

1. The unipolar-bipolar distinction, between those individuals with depression who have no family history of depressive illness (unipolar) and those with depression who do (bipolar);
2. The primary-secondary distinction, between those with depression that is not preceded by any other psychiatric or physical disorder (primary) and those with depression that is preceded by, and may be accompanied by, psychiatric or physical disorder (secondary);
3. The hierarchical classification of (a) dysthymic states—anxiety, depression, and elation, (b) neurotic symptoms—dissociative, compulsive, and ruminative, (c) integrated delusions—delusions of contrition, grandeur, and/or persecution, and (d) delusions of disintegration—primarily of the schizophrenias.

Of these, the hierarchical classification arising from the work of Foulds (Foulds, 1973; Foulds & Bedford, 1975, 1976) is the most complex, and it clearly allows for the possibility of instability of diagnosis over time (Kendell, 1974), and the tendency of patients to shift between neurosis and psychosis (Akiskal et al., 1978). Two of these categorizations (1 and 2) clearly allow for the inclusion of psychotic characteristics.

Types of Cognitive Error in Depression

It has been suggested that depressed people tend to make at least six types of error that produce highly negative conclusions (A. Beck et al., 1979). These include:

1. *Arbitrary inference*—drawing a negative conclusion in the absence of supporting data.
2. *Selective abstraction*—focusing on a detail out of context, often at the expense of more salient information.
3. *Over-generalization*—drawing conclusions over a wide variety of things on the basis of single events.
4. *Magnification and minimization*—making errors in evaluating the importance and implication of events.
5. *Personalization*—relating external (often negative) events to the self where there is no connection for doing so.
6. *Absolutist, dichotomous thinking*—thinking in polar opposites (black and white). Something is all good, or totally bad and a disaster.

A substantial body of literature supports the view that depressives are prone to these cognitive errors (Coyne & Gotlib, 1983).

Some Particular Characteristics of Depression

Selective Attention to "Negative" Information. There is evidence that patients suffering from anxiety disorders appear to automatically attend to those aspects of the information input that are inherently threatening at the expense of more benign aspects (Landau & Godfried, 1981; Mathews & MacLeod, 1986). It has been suggested that, in a similar way, depressed patients might be particularly likely to notice "negative" things that are consistent with their depressed mood. Some depressed people may be particularly inclined to notice criticism of their competence; others may notice a lack of affection and intimacy (Williams et al., 1988). It is important to note that the attentive processes may be automated and nonconscious (Beck et al., 1986; Williams et al., 1988).

Interpretive Bias Toward Negative Thinking. A characteristic of depression is the predominance of negative aspects of the past (Williams et al., 1988). In part this may be because of a biased recall of information from memory, for it has been shown that in comparison with nondepressed controls, depressed subjects are more negative in their recall of performance feedback, evaluate themselves more negatively, and blame themselves more for failure (Blaney, 1986; Coyne & Gotlib, 1983).

Depression is said to be associated with schemata concerned with negative aspects of the self and the world (A. Beck et al., 1979, 1986). These schemata are activated when the patient is confronted with certain internal or external stimuli, and contribute to the characteristics of depression (Kovacs & Beck, 1978). For some reason the probability of these schemata being activated would appear to be particularly high in depressed persons. It may be that the depressive has negative schemata that have particularly high significance values as a result of either many negative experiences or a few very strongly negative experiences (direct or vicarious).

It may be that the activating stimuli in themselves actually are negative but are interpreted to be much more negative still. Alternatively, it may be that the activating stimuli are actually innocuous or ambiguous, such as pauses in conversation or half-smiles, but are misinterpreted due to the disproportionate influence of the schemata (Williams et al., 1988). In either instance, the schemata results in a biased interpretation.

More generally, the negative schemata may result in experiences being interpreted in a way that intensifies a negative mood state (Power & Champion, 1986). It would also appear to be a possibility that a negative mood state, in turn, could increase the accessibility of all emotionally congruent negative material in memory (Williams et al., 1988). This could then have an effect on both the preattentive and the interpretive phases. It is important to note that these interpretive processes may be automated and nonconscious (Beck et al., 1986; Williams et al., 1988). Clinical observations suggest that automatic thoughts are particularly important in maintaining a depressive mood state (Williams et al., 1988).

Ruminative Negative Thinking. Ruminative thinking (i.e., the tendency to dwell on the same thought or theme repetitively) is one of the characteristics of depression. It is more than four times as common in *melancholic* than in *nonmelancholic* depressives (Nelson & Mazure, 1985). Ruminative thinking may have a detrimental effect on subsequent cognitive processes. It has been shown that when subjects are asked to imagine themselves involved in a positive event or a negative event and then subsequently asked to make probability judgements about a similar class of events, there occur systematic shifts in their probability judgments toward increased likelihood of the event they had imagined (Carroll, 1978; Gregory et al., 1982). This effect can persist over at least a 3-day period (Anderson, 1983). Consequently, if depressed individuals allow themselves to simply dwell on memories of negative events, there may result an inflation of expected negative probabilities. This inflated expectation could be influential in terms of both the preattentive and interpretive phases.

Concentration. Concentration problems are pervasive in depression and cause considerable frustration (Watts & Sharrock, 1985). For example, the characteristic description that depressed patients give of their difficulties reading is that they cannot take in what they are reading, with the result that when they get to the bottom of the page they have no idea what they have just read (Williams et al., 1988). Current theories of the effects of depression on concentration or task performance assume that ruminations and worries occupy cognitive resources, leaving less for task performance (Williams et al., 1988). Studies show that the performance deficits found in depression are comparable to those produced in normal subjects by adding a secondary task (Krames & McDonald, 1985). It would appear that the disruptive effect of intrusive emotional thoughts on concentration or task performance results not so much from their frequency as from their meaning (Bruch et al., 1986).

Self-Esteem and Negative Self-Schemata. Self-esteem is seen as a central vulnerability factor in many theories of depression (P. Gilbert, 1984). In general terms, self-esteem develops according to an interaction between a person and significant others. Experiences that consistently lead the person to think badly of him- or herself or to be labelled by others as having bad attributes lay the foundations for the development of negative self-schemata. Thus, A. Beck (1967) believes that failure may be labelled as evidence of being inept or inadequate. For example, a child who gets the notion that he is inept, as a result of either a failure or being called inept by someone else, may interpret subsequent experiences according to this notion. Beck's model of depression suggests that the depression-prone individual, early on in life, develops particular negative schemata relating to the world, the self, and the future. Although these negative schemata may not be discernible at any given time, they are easily evoked by life events that are similar to those that were responsible for their formation. In relation to this it is of interest to note that parents of depressed children have been found to set higher standards for reinforcement and to reward their children less frequently than parents of nondepressed children (Cole & Rehm, 1986).

Physical Symptoms of Depression

In addition to the cognitive aspects of depression, there may also be certain physical symptoms. Typically, speech and bodily movements may be slowed down or restricted in scope (Leigh et al., 1977).

NEUROPHYSIOLOGICAL INFORMATION CONCERNING DEPRESSION

Neurochemical data indicates that depressive illnesses may involve a malfunction of the brain stem monoamine systems (Fillion & Fillion, 1981; P. Gilbert, 1984; Murphy et al., 1974; Wolfe et al., 1978). From a biological point of view it has been suggested that there are two types of depression: Type A depressions have a deficit in NE pathways, and type B depressions have a deficit in 5HT pathways (Akiskal, 1979; Maas, 1975; Schildkraut, 1976).

The evidence for either a "too little" or a "too much" neurotransmitter hypothesis of the affective disorders has been reviewed by Mass (1979). He makes it clear that there is evidence for both positions, and suggests that it is the stability and integrated functioning of neurotransmitter systems that might offer the best neurochemical clue to understanding depression. In relation to the treatment of depression, (1) most tricyclic antidepressants are thought to modulate NE transmission (Wolfe et al., 1978) and act upon the 5HT receptors (Fillion & Fillion, 1981);

(2) MAO inhibitors influence the monoamine systems (Oswald, 1974); and (3) electroconvulsive therapy (ECT) treatment is known to modify brain 5HT levels (Essman, 1978), and this modification is thought to be related to the effect of ECT on depression (Essman, 1978).

SLEEP AND DREAMING IN RELATION TO DEPRESSION

Depression is frequently accompanied by a disorder of sleep—notably a reduced sleep time (Leigh et al., 1977; Van Den Burg et al., 1980). In particular, McCarley (1982) has suggested that REM sleep and some depressive phenomena may in fact be mediated by the same neurobiological control mechanisms.

In addition to their effect upon the monoamine systems, ECT and most antidepressant drugs may reduce or abolish D/REM sleep (Depoortere & Santucci, 1980; Hartmann, 1969; Oswald, 1974; Polc et al., 1976; Pompeiano, 1969), but this may be followed by a rebound increase of D/REM sleep (Oswald, 1974). It has been suggested that the D/REM pressure resulting from the initial reduction of D/REM time, may be the mechanism underlying the success of antidepressant drugs (Vogel et al., 1973)—presumably this may also apply to ECT. This suggestion is supported by the observation that sleep deprivation has a therapeutic effect on depression—especially D/REM deprivation (Pompeiano, 1972; Vogel et al., 1973)—and that during improvement, depressed patients exhibit an increased D/REM time (Hawkins et al., 1967; Snyder, 1972).

It is difficult, from the above reports, to be sure exactly whether it is the reduction of D/REM sleep that directly contributes to a reduction of depression or the consequent rebound increase in D/REM sleep that reduces depression. Furthermore, it is not exactly clear whether it is the psychotic or the nonpsychotic symptoms that are reduced. However, one unequivocal conclusion is that D/REM sleep is in some way related to the depressive condition.

SUMMARY OF CHARACTERISTICS OF DEPRESSION

Two of the categorizations of depression referred to earlier (1 and 2) clearly allow for the inclusion of psychotic characteristics. Thus, depression may be considered to be made up of psychotic characteristics and nonpsychotic characteristics. Types of cognitive error common in depression include selective abstraction, absolutist/dichotomous thinking, arbitrary inference, over-generalization, and personalization. Concentration problems are also pervasive in depression.

Particularly characteristic of depression is the predominant awareness of "negative" aspects of experience and the "negative" interpretation of experience, where the experience may be either present or recalled. Awareness of both present and recalled experience is thought to involve selective attention to the negative aspects of the experience.

In depressed persons' schemata (memories) concerned with negative aspects of the self and the world appear to have a greater probability of being activated than in nondepressed persons. There is also a tendency to ruminate or dwell repetitively on the same thought (or memory). Schemata-recall probability, repetitive recall, interpretive processes, and direction of selective attention are thought to interact in a way that increases the "negative" influence. The interpretive and the selective attention processes and may be automated and nonconscious.

Neurochemical data indicates that depressive illnesss may involve a malfunction of the monoamine systems. From a biological point of view it has been suggested that there are two types of depression: Type A depressions have a deficit in NE pathways, and type B depressions have a deficit in 5HT pathways. Although inconclusive at a mechanistic level, it would appear that D/REM sleep is in some way related to the depressive condition.

AN INTERPRETATION OF DEPRESSION

Depression may be considered to be made up of psychotic characteristics and nonpsychotic characteristics. In relation to this it has been suggested that, from a biological point of view, there are two types of depression: Type A depressions have a deficit in NE pathways, and type B depressions have a deficit in 5HT pathways. According to the description of the brain-stem neurotransmitter system presented in Chapters 5 and 6, the NE deficit type would correspond to inhibition of cerebellum/naturomorphic sub-system input to the cerebrum/abstract sub-system, whereas the 5HT deficit type would correspond to enhancement of cerebellum/naturomorphic sub-system input to the cerebrum/abstract sub-system. Of these two, the 5HT deficit type would be associated with psychotic symptoms.

From a cognitive perspective, the six types of error described by A. Beck et al. (1979) may be considered in terms of the characteristics of abstract and naturomorphic representation and processing. Selective abstraction and absolutist/dichotomous thinking would appear to be characteristic of the abstract sub-system, whereas arbitrary inference, over-generalization, and personalization would appear to be characteristic of the naturomorphic sub-system. In cognitive terms, depression may therefore be considered to be made up of abstract sub-system and naturomorphic sub-system characteristics, analogous to its nonpsychotic NE deficit-type and psychotic 5HT deficit-type characteristics.

The psychotic characteristics may, for the sake of simplicity, be described and explained in essentially the same way as with their occurrence in schizophrenia. This simplification is not, however, meant to overlook the importance of an interplay of the psychotic characteristics with the nonpsychotic characteristics within the "whole" of the depressive illness.

The psychotic symptoms of depression, where they are secondary to the nonpsychotic symptoms, may develop as a "rebound" or compensatory reaction to too much deliberate inattention to input from the cerebellum/naturomorphic sub-system. Similarly, if, during periods of stressful experience, there was a repeated failure by the cerebrum/abstract sub-system to respond to the information it received from the cerebellum/naturomorphic sub-system during sleep, the normal interaction of the cerebellar and cerebral sub-systems could be disrupted by an increased dream sleep "pressure" and a cerebrally bilateral breakthrough during the awake state. This would result in the appearance of psychotic symptoms.

It would appear from the above information that the nonpsychotic characteristics of depression correspond to a prevalence of cerebrum/abstract sub-system characteristics and a deficit or inhibition of cerebellum/naturomorphic sub-system input to the cerebrum/abstract sub-system. This inference is augmented by the observation that the nonpsychotic aspects of depression frequently occur as a symptom of Parkinson's disease, where there is considerably more neurological evidence that the cause involves inhibition of cerebellar input to the cerebrum.

A disruption of the normal interaction of the cerebrum/abstract sub-system and the cerebellum/naturomorphic sub-system that produced a "general" inhibition of cerebellar output to the cerebrum would clearly result in a number of phenomena experienced at a "general" level, including difficulty in shifting attention, reduced ability to use the imagination in planning (alternative) responses, and reduced experience of cerebellar generated emotion.

As noted earlier the normal operation of this interaction may be disrupted by a number of conditions: damage to the brain stem, cerebellum, or cerebrum, or interference with the normal functioning of these sub-systems in themselves or in interaction with one another through lesion or neurotransmitter imbalance. A deficit of NE would in effect result in a general inhibition of cerebellum/naturomorphic sub-system input to the cerebrum/abstract sub-system. In theory, general nonpsychotic symptoms of depression could also result from imbalanced utilization of the different forms of representation and processing. This could develop directly as a result of too much deliberate inattention to input from the naturomorphic sub-system—where such outward attention is for some reason preferable to attention to the "inner world."

During normal operation, the cerebrum/abstract sub-system is hierarchically above the cerebellum/naturomorphic sub-system in the control sense, and so can determine whether the naturomorphically selected information will be attended to or disregarded. In particular, it would be possible for the abstract sub-system to attend only to those "negative" aspects of environmental input selected by the naturomorphic sub-system. The negative schemata of the abstract sub-system and their pervasive influence the depression could then be self-perpetuating if their influence on the selective attention process precludes further access to "positive" information (see section on the development of abstract reference standards in Chapter 4). Similarly, the abstract sub-system could selectively recall negative memories. Furthermore, if the abstract sub-system repeatedly chose to attend to (or disregard) certain of those naturomorphically selected features, within the biased naturomorphic sub-system the statistical significance values of those features would automatically change and they would become even more likely to be brought (or not to be brought) to the attention of the abstract sub-system. The same would apply to the process of abstract sub-system recall of information from the biased naturomorphic sub-system memory.

The repetitive selection of negative information could eventually result in what would effectively be an automatic selection of negative information by the cerebellum/naturomorphic sub-system for the attention of the cerebrum/abstract sub-system. The selective attention to negative information may therefore initially be directed by the abstract sub-system but eventually become habitual and be facilitated by the naturomorphic sub-system. Ultimately, however, the allocation of attention would be decided upon, or allowed, by the abstract sub-system.

As noted in Chapter 8, the homeostatic process could be adversely affected by the experience of an unrepresentative or a distorted learning environment, especially in the early years when the naturomorphic sub-system is the main learning-based sub-system in operation. An unrepresentative or unnatural environment may lead to schemata that are maladaptive in the representative or natural environment. The learning environment obviously includes other people from whom a child can learn directly or vicariously. For example, consider a child's early social learning which would involve parents or other teachers who could serve as maladaptive models. Negative experiences in the early years could result in the development of negative schemata relating to the world, the self, and the future, and in the development of poor self-esteem. The cumulative growth in memory in the cerebellum/naturomorphic sub-system would mean that a long established negative schemata could take a long time to change. That is, until the positive experiences accumulate a significance value equal to or greater than that of the old negative experiences. Old negative self-schemata would not, therefore, simply be eradicated from memory: they would have to be gradually replaced (on a probability of recall basis) by the newer, more positive memories.

11

Epilepsy

SOME CHARACTERISTICS OF EPILEPSY

Auras

At the onset of an epileptic seizure, there may be an *aura*, which often involves intense memory recall (Penfield, 1975a; Penfield & Jasper, 1954; Taylor, 1932). Frequently the memory that emerges during the aura is the same for the same patient in each new attack (Taylor, 1932); alternatively, the auras may contain different memories, but they will have some common feature or pattern (Penfield & Jasper, 1954). Often the aura contains the image, or some feature in common with the image, that accompanied or provoked the subject's very first seizure (Penfield & Jasper, 1954; Taylor, 1932). Auras may contain the contents of previous dreams (Taylor, 1932) or be experienced "as a dream" (Penfield & Jasper, 1954); they may also be experienced "as a hallucination" (Mayer-Gross et al., 1969). The aura is considered to be the initial feature of an epileptic attack, and not merely a warning of it (Penfield & Jasper, 1954).

It is thought that the memories contained within the auras originate in subcerebrocortical regions (Gastaut, 1954; Jasper, 1949; Taylor, 1932), and involve the hippocampus (Jasper, 1949; Penfield, 1975a), thalamencephelon (Penfield, 1975b), and brain stem (Penfield, 1954).

Automatisms

During epileptic automatism, the conscious system may lose both consciousness and control of the lower levels, but the lower levels may continue to execute stereotyped habitual responses which may be quite complex and involve sensorimotor processing in relation to a changing environment (Laidlaw & Richens,

1976; MacLean, 1958; Penfield, 1975b; Penfield & Jasper, 1954). The automatic sensorimotor system responsible for the execution of activity during the automatism is thought to be of sub-cerebrocortical origin and to involve the same neuroanatomical regions that are the source of the memories experienced during auras (Penfield, 1975b).

Grand Mal Seizures

Grand mal seizures or generalized convulsions are thought to be produced by an excessive discharge from the neuroanatomical region that is responsible for the ideas or type of thought that is necessarily bound up with movement, enactive thought, or from the region responsible for the automatic sensorimotor mechanism (Penfield, 1975b; Taylor, 1932).

Summary

Auras, automatisms, and generalized convulsions are evidently all thought to be the product of activity within the sub-cerebrocortical system, one that is capable of executing automatic sequences, involves enactive or sensorimotor thought, and contains a memory that is capable of recognizing patterns. The cerebrocortical experience of the information released from this system during auras has been compared with that of dreaming.

THE BRAIN STEM, CEREBELLUM, AND CEREBRUM IN RELATION TO EPILEPSY

The Brain Stem in Relation to Epilepsy

The origin of the neural impulses responsible for the epileptic phenomena is thought to be the brain stem (Penfield & Jasper, 1954), in particular the reticular formation (Gastaut et al., 1958; Kreindler, 1965; Smythies, 1970). Monoamine levels may influence seizure threshold (Laidlaw & Richens, 1976; Stevens, 1973). Some results indicate that catecholamines (DA and NE) may also be related to seizure threshold (Stevens, 1973). While the data indicates that the monoamine neurotransmitters are in some way involved in epileptic activity, they cannot be unequivocally interpreted. The apparently contradictory results may be related to dosage or rebound phenomena.

The Cerebellum in Relation to Epilepsy

It has been suggested that the cerebellum may be involved with seizural activity (Gastaut et al., 1958; Kreindler, 1965). Stimulation of the cerebellum during a cerebrally manifest seizure may alter the seizure pattern, inhibit it, or facilitate it, depending on the precise conditions of stimulation (Cooper et al., 1974; Dow,

1970; Dow et al., 1962; Fernandez-Guardiola et al., 1962). Periodic "chronic cerebellar stimulation" within epileptics may reduce or prevent seizures (Cooper et al., 1974; Dow, 1978). However, it is not known whether chronic cerebellar stimulation excites or inhibits the ultimate outflow of the cerebellum (Dow, 1978). Recent data indicates that cerebellar stimulation that reduces epileptic seizures may be a result of antidromic stimulation of the reticular formation rather than the result of Purkinje cell activity alone (Bantli et al., 1976; I. Cooper, personal communication, June 25, 1979). Taken in isolation, this data cannot be interpreted conclusively.

It is possible to biochemically induce an electrographic cerebellar seizure that is then followed by a cerebral electrographic seizure (Dow et al., 1962; Fernandez-Guardiola et al., 1962; Swank & Brendler, 1951). Seizural activity that progresses from the cerebellum to the cerebral cortex, in particular the temporal lobe, seems to do so via the hippocampus (Giannazzo et al., 1969; Heath, 1976). Cerebellar seizures may be accompanied by an activation pattern within the cerebral cortex (subsequent to the induction of cerebellar seizural activity; Clark & Ward, 1949), and by psychomotor symptoms (Gastaut et al., 1958).

It has been observed that during normal epileptic seizural activity, there is a discharge from the cerebellum (Heath, 1976) and a progressive reduction of Purkinje cell firing during the development of a major prolonged seizure (Cooper et al., 1974). This reduction of Purkinje cell discharge would be equivalent to a reduction of inhibition upon the overall cerebellar output; thus, there would be a progressive increase of excitatory output from the cerebellum as a whole during the development of a major seizure. In conformity with this is the observation that ablation of the cerebellar nuclei will inhibit epileptic seizures (Cooper et al., 1974).

The Cerebrum in Relation to Epilepsy

Epileptic convulsions may occur in the anatomical absence of the cerebrum (Taylor, 1932). Convulsions may occur in the newborn (Dreyfus-Brisac & Monod, 1964), where the cerebral cortex is thought to be essentially nonfunctional. Moreover, a number of studies have indicated that, beyond age 4 years, there is a fairly dramatic fall in the percentage of the population classified as epileptic (Robb, 1975)—this is the age beyond which the cerebrum may fully exert an inhibitory influence upon the neo-cerebellum via the cerebro-corticopontine tract. It has been suggested that epileptic activity is not necessarily, or normally, of cerebral origin (Dreyfus-Brisac & Monod, 1964; Kreindler, 1965; Penfield, 1975b). However, data indicates that the hippocampus may be critically involved with the emergence within the cerebrum of impulses from sub-cerebral regions (Laidlaw & Richens, 1976; Penfield, 1975a; Smythies, 1970).

SLEEP AND DREAMING IN RELATION TO EPILEPSY

Normal epileptic seizures may be enhanced during sleep, and some epileptic seizures may occur exclusively during sleep. Convulsive seizures such as grand mal are facilitated during S/NREM sleep (Angeleri, 1974; Passouant, 1976; Passouant et al., 1974; Vein et al., 1980; Wyler, 1974), but supressed during D/REM sleep (Angeleri, 1974; Passouant, 1976; Passouant et al., 1974)—especially during the REM bursts themselves (Pompeiano, 1969; Stevens et al., 1971). Conversely, local seizures (those manifest within the cerebral EEG), especially those of temporal lobe "origin," appear to be facilitated by D/REM sleep (Passouant, 1976; Passouant et al., 1974; Pompeiano, 1969).

There is evidence that during the daytime awake state, epileptic characteristics within the EEG, especially temporal lobe and typical petit mal absence discharges, increase cyclically approximately every 90 minutes; that is, with the same periodicity as the S/NREM-D/REM sleep cycle (Broughton, 1978; Stevens et al., 1971; Wyler, 1974).

Daytime epileptic activity disrupts the sleep cycle (Angeleri, 1974; Laidlaw & Richens, 1976; Vein et al., 1980), for example, generalized convulsive seizures result in subsequent reduction of REM sleep (Koridze, 1980; Passouant et al., 1976; Vein et al., 1980). Accordingly, it has been suggested that epileptic discharges may reduce or eliminate the need for REM sleep (Koridze, 1980)—from which it may be further suggested that the epileptic discharges are an alternative expression of dream sleep.

Disruption of the sleep cycle may influence epileptic activity: Sleep deprivation increases the appearance of epileptic characteristics within the EEG (Domzal et al., 1973), lowers the threshold to seizures (Passouant, 1976; Pompeiano, 1969; Wyler, 1974), and may even precipitate epilepsy in otherwise "normal" subjects (Broughton, 1978). In particular, REM sleep deprivation accentuates the manifestation of epileptic characteristics within the EEG and may precipitate clinical seizures (Bergonzi et al., 1973), whereas excess REM sleep maximizes the threshold for induced seizures (Wyler, 1974).

SUMMARY OF CHARACTERISTICS OF EPILEPSY

From the data it seems that the cerebral cortex is not the source of the impulses that result in an epileptic discharge, whether during petit mal, temporal lobe, or grand mal epilepsy. The impulses appear to be transmitted from, or through, the brain stem. As dream sleep is reduced following daytime epileptic seizures, it seems that, in part, epileptic seizures may be an alternative form of expression for the information normally released during dream sleep. There is evidence that the cerebellum may normally contribute to the onset of seizures.

AN INTERPRETATION OF EPILEPSY

A General Interpretation of Epilepsy

The characteristics of the sub-cerebral system responsible for the production of auras, automatisms, and generalized convulsions correspond to the characteristics of the cerebellum/naturomorphic sub-system. It is considered that the cerebellum is the source of the information transmitted to the cerebrum during dream sleep. It is therefore proposed that the cerebellum may normally be the source of the impulses that result in epileptic phenomena: The epileptic phenomena may be due to excessive cerebellar excitatory input to the cerebrum.

As noted in relation to schizophrenia, the normal interaction of the cerebellar and cerebral sub-systems could be disrupted by a number of conditions: damage to the brain stem, cerebellum, and cerebrum or interference with the normal functioning of these sub-systems in themselves, or in interaction with one another through lesion or neurotransmitter imbalance. It could also be disrupted as a result of repeated failure by the cerebrum/abstract sub-system to respond to the information it received from the cerebellum/naturomorphic sub-system during sleep. During periods of stressful experience, such repeated failure could result in an increased dream sleep "pressure" and a cerebrally bilateral breakthrough during the awake state. These conditions may largely be considered to be unintentionally created, and would result in symptoms that could not, in theory, be volitionally inhibited.

In theory, some of the symptoms of epilepsy could, as for schizophrenia, also result from imbalanced utilization of the different forms of representation and processing: directly, as a result of too much deliberate attention to input from the cerebellum/naturomorphic sub-system as in imagination or "day dreaming," in which instance the experience/symptoms should be open to volitional inhibition, or indirectly, as a "rebound" or compensatory reaction to too much deliberate inattention to input from the cerebellum/naturomorphic sub-system.

An Interpretation of Auras

It is suggested that auras are a vivid cerebral experience of image sequences transmitted from the cerebellum to the cerebrum. Auras may be explained in the same way as hallucinations (see the section on schizophrenia).

An Interpretation of Automatisms

It is suggested that, during automatisms, the cerebral cortex, for whatever reason, temporarily loses control of behavior, and so interaction with the environment is carried out by the cerebellum. As noted in Chapter 8, the cerebellar/naturomorphic sub-system may operate independently of the cerebral/abstract sub-system, and may normally be allowed to do so in the execution of habitual or well-programmed automatic activities.

It is possible that the automatic activity is facilitated by the cerebral/abstract sub-system "attending to other things" and so "not attending to" and "not being conscious of" what the lower-level sub-system is doing. It is also possible that if the subject experiences a particularly stressful situation, and "emotional" response will be released at an autonomic and motor level and proceed at an automatic level entirely in the absence of awareness.

An Interpretation of Grand Mal Seizures

When the excitatory output of the cerebellum become intense and exceeds a certain value, the descending motor component may not be inhibited strongly enough by the cerebrum, and the phasic descending inhibition from the cerebellum that is normally effective during dream sleep may not be activated; consequently, the descending motor component may be expressed as overt motor activity. The information released from the cerebellum may be released rapidly as during the dream process, so rapidly that it is manifest as a convulsion rather than as a purposeful sequence. Alternatively, the convulsion could be the uninhibited motor consequence of the cerebral after discharge following cerebellar input.

Intense cerebellar discharge that is transmitted bilaterally to the cerebrum would presumably result in a bilateral seizure or grand mal. It is possible that an intense neo-cerebellar discharge could be unilateral and so could manifest as a unilateral seizure. However, the unilateral neo-cerebellar discharge could also produce a bilateral seizure if the cerebral after-discharge involved trans-callosal transmission.

An Interpretation of Petit Mal Absences

It is considered that during petit mal absences there is a disorder of the attention with brief interruptions of consciousness during which time there is a dream-like state. These absences may occur with the same periodicity as the S/NREM-D/REM sleep cycle. In theory, the cerebellum would not normally transmit information to both cerebral hemispheres during the awake state. This would only occur in the event of a neurophysiological malfunction or in the event of significantly increased pressure for D/REM sleep. In the event of cerebellar input to both cerebral hemispheres, the cerebral cortex would not, at the same time, be able to attend to information from the environment. The result would be an "absence" of cerebral (conscious) interaction with the environment. At younger than 4 years of age, the facility for cerebral inhibitory control of input to it from the cerebellar would not be fully developed and so this would be a period when absences would most likely occur. Similarly, below 10–12 years, the lateralization of the cerebral hemispheres would not be fully developed, and so there would be the possibility of indirect cerebellar input to both cerebral hemispheres as a result of trans-callosal transmission. This too would result in an absence.

When cerebellar-cerebral interaction has become fully lateralized at around 10–12 years of age, the cerebellum should be able to transmit information to the minor cerebral hemisphere while the dominant cerebral hemisphere attends to the environment, and so absences should be less likely to occur. In theory, at all ages older than about 4 years of age, the periodic preponderant activity of the dream-producing system throughout the awake state should be unnoticed because its emergence is inhibited by attention to the outer world, that is, by attention to externally generated input to the conscious system. However, the subject may choose not to attend to the input from the external environment for some reason, for example when the environmental input is too uninteresting or "boring," or when it is too threatening. This inattention to the environmental input would facilitate the experience of cerebellar input and the accompanying absence.

An Interpretation of Nocturnal Epilepsy

During normal S/NREM sleep there is general atonia, whereas during normal D/REM sleep the motor system is additionally supressed by phasic inhibition. During very vivid dreams or intense and prolonged REM bursts, even the combined general atonia and phasic inhibition may be overcome by the excitatory output from the cerebellum, and muscular twitches may occur (Pompeiano, 1967b). These muscular twitches normally occur at the extremities (Pompeiano, 1969), that is, in the same place that the epileptic convulsions begin as twitches. During nocturnal epilepsy, however, the convulsive seizures appear to be facilitated by S/NREM sleep and inhibited by D/REM sleep—the opposite of what might be expected. It is proposed that during S/NREM sleep there is the general atonia but that there are also cerebellar discharges equivalent to dream bursts. As these "epileptic" cerebellar discharges occur during the S/NREM sleep, they will do so without the influence of the locus coeruleus projections to the cerebellar cortex that would normally inhibit the motor component of the cerebellar output; that is, the cerebellar output would not be accompanied by synchronous phasic depression of the motor system. The cerebellar output during D/REM sleep may result in twitches at the extremities even when there is general atonia and phasic atonia synchronous with cerebellar output. Thus, in the presence of general atonia alone the cerebellar discharge may be accompanied by grossly excessive twitches or convulsions. During D/REM sleep, however, the cerebellar output would be taking place under normal conditions and so the otherwise convulsive descending output would be reduced to normal dream twitches.

Seizures that manifest as discharges within the cerebral cortex are enhanced by D/REM sleep. This is consistent with the earlier suggestion that the cerebellum is the source of the information that is transmitted to the cerebral cortex, especially the temporal lobe, during D/REM sleep, and that constitutes dreams.

12

Parkinsonian Disorders

SOME CHARACTERISTICS OF PARKINSONIAN DISORDERS

The classical symptoms of Parkinson's disease, or analogous diseases, include tremor (postural and intention), postural rigidity, abnormal gait, disturbed phonation, and a fixed, mask-life facial expression (Barr, 1979; Cooper, 1961). These "physical" phenomena are often accompanied by psychological changes (Cooper, 1961) that include mental (perceptual, cognitive, and intellectual) impairment (Asso, 1969; Loranger et al., 1972; Murphy & Henry, 1972) and symptoms of depression (Cooper, 1961; Mayeux et al., 1984; Murphy & Henry, 1972)—the latter of which is so frequent as to be considered an endogenous feature of the disease. Not only do psychological changes accompany Parkinson's disease, they may be causally involved in the physiological manifestations (Buell & Biehl, 1949); for, regarding the tremor, it has been observed that emotional stress may greatly intensify the tremor (Cooper, 1961), and, under hypnosis, the tremor may be diminished or abolished (Buell & Biehl, 1949). Further concerning the psychological component, it has been suggested that the paralysis may be a pseudoparalysis that is a result of "motor disregard" (Mettler, 1967). Similarly it may be that the fixed facial expression is the result of "emotional disregard."

THE BRAIN STEM, CEREBELLUM, AND CEREBRUM IN RELATION TO PARKINSONIAN DISORDERS

The Brain Stem in Relation to Parkinsonian Disorders

Among the regions that appear to be particularly involved with Parkinson's disease are the ventrolateral thalamus (Cooper, 1961; Lin et al., 1961; Walsh, 1973); substantia nigra and the locus coeruleus (Ungerstedt et al., 1973). Lesions of the ventrolateral thalamus may abolish tremor (Cooper, 1961; Lin et al., 1961; Walsh, 1973) in relation to which it has been suggested that thalamo-cerebrocortical-thalamo interaction may be of importance in the genesis of Parkinsonian-like tremor (Jasper et al., 1972). Involvement of the substantia nigra may be related to motor disregard (or general disregard of ascending information), for it has been observed that nigrostriatal deficencies may result in sensory inattention or sensory disregard (Ungerstedt et al., 1973). Through its interaction with the ascending reticular formation, the locus coeruleus may also, in part, be involved with disregard phenomena.

The brain stem monoamine systems are strongly involved in Parkinson's disease. It is also thought that an abnormal concentration of 5HT and NE may be related to Parkinson's disease (Dinnerstein et al., 1962). Most data indicates that there is a deficiency in the DA (Hornykiewicz, 1975) content, in particular a nigro-striatal dopamine deficiency (Hornykiewicz, 1973, 1975). Often Parkinson's disease is treated by the administration of L-Dopa (Birkmayer et al., 1975; Hornykiewicz, 1975), the success of which may be thought to be related partly to its elevation of the NE level. However, drug treatment of the disease only provides transient relief (Cooper, 1961), and it does not ultimately slow the progressive worsening of the symptoms (Cooper, 1961).

The Cerebellum in Relation to Parkinsonian Disorders

Most often the cerebellum is regarded as an organ primarily concerned with motor function, and would, therefore, naturally be considered in relation to motor disorders. At the brain-stem level, the cerebellum may be involved in tremor through the rubro-cerebellar-rubro loop (Pecharde et al., 1976; Poirier, 1975; Poirier et al., 1974). Including the cerebral level, it seems that a cerebro-cerebellar-cerebral circuit is involved with the starting and stopping of movement without jerkiness (Ruch, 1951), and so malfunction of this circuit may be involved with intention tremor. Further concerning this circuit it has been suggested that cerebellar input to the cerebral cortex via the ventrolateral thalamus may in some way be involved in the production of tremor (Lin et al., 1961; Mettler, 1967).

Even in healthy animals a certain amount of tremor is usually present (Bell et al., 1968)—this tremor is greatly exaggerated in decerebellate animals (Bell et al., 1968). Several studies have indicated that removal of the cerebellum, or removal of cerebellar output, may enhance or induce tremor (Carrea, 1970; Goldberger & Growden, 1971; Narabayashi et al., 1974). The tremor resulting from cerebellar removal is normally associated with voluntary effort either in the maintenance of a posture or in the initiation of movement (Fulton, 1936; McIntyre, 1941; Thomas, 1912)—the latter of which has the same characteristics as intention tremor (Thomas, 1912). It has also been observed that cerebellar lesion or ablation may result in a poverty or loss of facial expression (Mills & Weisenberg, 1914; Sprague & Chambers, 1957). Lesions of the cerebellar nuclei may produce symptoms that have been explicitly referred to as "Parkinsonian-like" (Carpenter & Hanna, 1962).

In relation to the above data, it has been suggested that Parkinsonian-like symptoms may normally involve deprivation of cerebellar regulatory influence (Carpenter & Hanna, 1962).

The Cerebrum in Relation to Parkinsonian Disorders

It has been suggested that the cerebral hemispheres may be involved with the production of tremor and this is supported by the observation that cooling the cerebral motor cortex may reduce tremor (Jasper et al., 1972).

SLEEP AND DREAMING IN RELATION TO PARKINSONIAN DISORDERS

Concerning the relationship between Parkinson's disease and the S/NREM-D/REM cycle it has been observed that: (1) during sleep the tremor of Parkinson's disease patients is almost always lost (Buell & Biehl, 1949; Cooper, 1961); (2) untreated Parkinson's disease patients evidence a shortened D/REM time (relative to normal) (Murri et al., 1976; Schneider et al., 1980); (3) although L-Dopa may increase or decrease the D/REM period depending on the circumstances of administration (Fram et al., 1970; Gillin et al., 1973; Hartmann & Bridwell, 1970; Zarcone et al., 1970), in Parkinson's disease patients it appears to increase both S/NREM and D/REM periods (Kendel et al., 1972; Schneider et al., 1980)—this increase is thought to be related to the improvement of the Parkinson's disease symptoms during the awake state (Schneider et al., 1980).

AN INTERPRETATION OF PARKINSONIAN DISORDERS

Parkinsonian like symptoms of tremor and loss (rigidity) of facial expression (emotion) may be caused by removal of the cerebellar contribution to motor control. Normally, the cerebral cortex may also be involved with the production of these symptoms. It seems that the symptoms may be due to cerebral disregard of (or failure to receive) information transmitted through the brain stem, but that the removal of cerebral influence results in a decrease of these symptoms. All three brain stem regions involved with Parkinson's disease—the locus coeruleus, substantia nigra, and thalamus, are partly involved with interaction of the cerebellum and cerebrum. Data indicates that in the Parkinsonian condition there is a deficiency of DA or NE content and that the condition may be relieved by elevating the DA content. From the information presented in Chapters 5 and 6, it would appear that DA and NE potentiate input to the cerebrum from the cerebellum.

Taken together the information indicates that the Parkinsonian condition may be due to inadequate cerebellar input to the cerebrum, and that its alleviation may be the result of facilitating this input. It is proposed that the symptoms may be caused partly by cerebral disregard or cerebral inhibition of the cerebellar contribution to the control of the relevant motor functions. As the cerebellum is involved with the representation of autonomic, "emotional," and sensory information, and as the cerebellar information would be released as a polymodal whole, the cerebrum's lack of access to motor information would be accompanied by a lack of access to emotional and naturomorphically imagistic information. The accompanying characteristic of depression would be explained as in the previous section on depression.

Disruption of the normal interaction of the cerebrum/abstract sub-system and the cerebellum/naturomorphic sub-system which produces a "general" inhibition of cerebellar output to the cerebrum could be produced by the usual range of conditions: damage to the brain stem, cerebellum, and cerebrum, or interference with the normal functioning of these sub-systems in themselves, or in interaction with one another, through lesion or neurotransmitter imbalance. In theory, cognitive and affective symptoms of Parkinsonian disorders could also result from imbalanced utilization of the different forms of representation and processing. They could develop directly as a result of too much deliberate inattention to input from the cerebellum/naturomorphic sub-system.

As the abstract sub-system is hierarchically above the naturomorphic sub-system in the control sense (at least during normal operation), the abstract sub-system can determine whether the naturomorphically selected information will be attended or not: it may choose to disregard or "repress" the naturomorphically selected emotional or imagistic information, and it may do so repeatedly. In some instances it may be that long-term repetitive cerebral inhibition of the cerebellar/naturomorphic sub-system input to the cerebral/abstract sub-system eventually results in a neurotransmitter system equivalent of atrophy through lack of use (possibly evidenced as depleted NE/DA), and that it eventually causes the accompanying inhibition of the motor information. In some instances the motor symptoms may therefore be a consequence of the cognitive processes rather than the other way around.

13

Interrelationship between Schizophrenia, Depression, Epilepsy, and Parkinsonian Disorders

SCHIZOPHRENIA AND EPILEPSY

Epileptics may exhibit schizophrenic-like symptoms (Mayer-Gross et al., 1969). In particular, there seems to be an inverse relationship or periodic alternation between epilepsy (especially temporal-lobe type) and schizophrenia (Slater et al., 1963; Stevens, 1973): psychotic phases may be followed by reduced psychosis together with increased epilepsy whereas epileptic phases may be followed by reduced or "controlled" epilepsy together with increased psychosis (Fish, 1961; Slater et al., 1963); the epileptic threshold is high during severe psychotic phases, whereas it is low during mild or nonpsychotic phases (Asgian et al., 1973). It has been suggested that there may be a common background disorder underlying epilepsy and schizophrenia (Flohr-Henry, 1976), either neuroanatomically (e.g., reticular formation and hippocampus) (Heath, 1962; Stevens, 1973) or neurochemically (e.g., monoamines) (Stevens, 1973). It is proposed that most epileptic and schizophrenic phenomena may be explained fundamentally in terms of excessive cerebellar excitatory input to the cerebrum.

DEPRESSION AND PARKINSONIAN DISORDERS

Parkinsonian phenomena and the nonpsychotic aspects of clinical depression may both be explained fundamentally in terms of inadequate, or excessively inhibited, cerebellar excitatory output. Parkinsonian phenomena that involve malfunction of motor activity may result from inadequate, or excessively inhibited, cerebellar excitatory output ascending to the cerebrum and descending indirectly to the motor system. Clinical depression without motor symptoms may result from inadequate, or excessively inhibited, cerebellar excitatory output ascending to the cerebrum.

SCHIZOPHRENIA/EPILEPSY AND DEPRESSION/PARKINSONIAN DISORDERS

When the various disorders considered in the preceding sections are looked at in detail in terms of their sub-groups it becomes quite clear that, symptomatically at least, they "overlap": There are depressed schizophrenics (P. Gilbert, 1984), psychotic depressives (P. Gilbert, 1989; Williams et al., 1988), and psychotic epileptics. It has been questioned whether psychotic depressives are really depressed schizophrenics or whether they are shifting across disorders (Akiskal et al., 1978). The same might also be enquired in relation to psychotic epileptics.

The intimate relationship between these disorders is particularly evident when the effects of treatment are considered. Upon treatment by DA administration, there may be a decrease of Parkinsonian-like symptoms accompanied by an increase or emergence of schizophrenic-like symptoms (Barbeau, 1971; Birkmayer et al., 1975; Celesia & Barr, 1970; Godwin-Austen et al., 1969; Jenkins & Groh, 1970). Similarly, upon treatment by antidepressant drugs there may be a decrease in the symptoms of depression accompanied by an increase or the emergence of schizophrenic-like symptoms (R. Fisher, 1975). Conversely, drugs that reduce schizophrenic-like symptoms may cause the emergence of Parkinsonian-like symptoms (Birchwood et al., 1988; Hasse & Jansen, 1965). There is therefore direct biochemical evidence of an inverse relationship between schizophrenia and Parkinsonian disorders/depression. Dream-sleep deprivation may reduce the symptoms of depression but enhance the symptoms of epilepsy and schizophrenic. This indicates that there is a biochemical or psychological inverse relationship between epilepsy-schizophrenia and depression. Together, the biochemical and dream-sleep–deprivation data indicate that there is a biochemical and possibly a psychological inverse relationship between epilepsy/schizophrenia and Parkinsonian disorders-depression. The possibility of an inverse psychological relationship is further supported by evidence that increased emotional pressure may cause a change from Parkinsonian-like symptoms to schizophrenic-like symptoms (Cooper, 1961).

Epileptic and schizophrenic phenomena both seem to involve excessive cerebellar excitatory output whereas Parkinsonian disorders and nonpsychotic depressive phenomena seem to involve inadequate cerebellar excitatory output (which may result from excessive inhibition by the cerebrum). In terms of interaction between the cerebellum and the cerebrum, the fundamental characteristics of epilepsy/schizophrenia thus appear to be the inverse of the fundamental characteristics of Parkinsonian disorders/depression.

SOME POSSIBLE CAUSES OF SCHIZOPHRENIA, EPILEPSY, DEPRESSION, AND PARKINSONIAN DISORDERS

Flor-Henry's (1983,3) conceptual position is that there is a bilateral dysfunction in all psychoses and that "the severity of dysfunction is least in depression and maximal in schizophrenia with a right hemisphere emphasis in depression and a left hemisphere emphasis in schizophrenia.'' The limitations of a 'cerebral hemispheres' interpretation of psychological processing have already been outlined in Chapter 5. The same limitations, and the same elaborated explanation in terms of the cerebellum, also apply to psychiatric issues.

Most of the characteristics of epilepsy, schizophrenia, Parkinsonian disorders, and clinical depression may be explained fundamentally in terms of disordered interaction between the cerebellum/naturomorphic sub-system and the cerebrum/abstract sub-system. They may therefore be described as disorders within the learning based homeostatic process. Each of the four disorders, to different extents, also involves sleep and dream sleep either in their symptoms or their treatment. In particular, the four disorders may therefore be described, to different extents, partly as disorders of the ''updating'' process. Clearly, however, this suggestion does not imply that all or even many instances of these disorders are a result of disorders of the updating process, nor does it deny neurophysiological or biochemical causes; what it does do is indicate that it is possible that in some instances there may be 'psychological' causes.

Insofar as these four disorders may be described fundamentally in terms of interaction between the cerebellum/naturomorphic sub-system and the cerebrum/abstract sub-system, they may be the result of a disorder of one of the following: the anatomical development of the brain stem, cerebellum, or cerebrum; the normal functioning of the brain stem, cerebellum, or cerebrum either in themselves or in interaction with one another; the development of the naturomorphic, intermediate, and abstract forms of representation and processing of information; and the utilization of these forms of representation and processing of information in themselves and in relation to one another. These disorders may therefore be the result of inadequate neurological or psychological development, of neurological or psychological trauma; of imbalance of neurotransmitters or in the utilization of the different forms of representation and processing of information: in other words, they may be of physiological or psychological origin. Obviously, however, it may not be sensible to view the causes of these disorders as due only biological changes, or only to cognitive changes. Rather, these factors are locked together in complex relationships (P. Gilbert, 1984).

Parkinsonian disorders or depression could, for example, be the result of: (1) excessive cerebral inhibition of cerebellar input to the cerebrum (possibly involving hippocampal or temporal lobe malfunction); (2) inadequate DA/NE facilitation or excessive 5HT inhibition of cerebellar input to the cerebrum; (3) inadequate expression of the cerebellum/naturomorphic sub-system through dreaming because of insufficient sleep; (4) excessive conscious cerebrum/abstract sub-system inhibition of its input from the cerebellum/naturomorphic sub-system, for example, by excessively inhibiting the imagination or emotions; and (5) failure of the conscious cerebrum/abstract sub-system to utilize (take notice of) naturomorphic input.

Epileptic or schizophrenic phenomena could, for example, be the result of: (1) inadequate inhibition of cerebellar input to the cerebrum (possibly involving hippocampal or temporal lobe malfunction); (2) excessive DA/NE facilitation or inadequate 5HT inhibition of cerebellar input to the cerebrum; (3) inadequate expression of the cerebellum/naturomorphic sub-system through dreaming because of insufficient sleep (as a result of this there would eventually be increased "pressure" from the cerebellum/naturomorphic sub-system; see below; (4) failure of the conscious cerebrum/abstract sub-system to inhibit excessive input from the cerebellum/naturomorphic sub-system. The excessive input from the cerebellum/naturomorphic sub-system may be simply as excessive daydreaming or as the naturomorphic release of excessively emotionally charged image sequences. In the latter instance these highly emotionally charged sequences may be evoked by an environmental stimulus pattern similar to one strongly associated with an earlier traumatic experience. In relation to the inhibition of this input, there is evidence that abstract sub-system activities such as "concentration" or "attention" to a task may completely arrest an epileptic discharge at its onset (Laidlaw & Richens, 1976; Okuma & Akimoto, 1966; Penfield & Jasper, 1954) or at the aura phase, and as noted earlier, schizophrenic hallucinations may be similarly inhibited by such activities; (5) finally, there is failure of the conscious cerebrum/abstract sub-system to utilize (take notice of) naturomorphic input; as a result of this, there could eventually be increased pressure and a breakthrough of strong cerebellum/naturomorphic sub-system input to the cerebrum/abstract sub-system (in which event the content of the hallucination could be the "pressing" naturomorphic information).

A PERSPECTIVE ON THE TREATMENT OF SCHIZOPHRENIA, EPILEPSY, DEPRESSION, AND PARKINSONIAN DISORDERS

When the disorders are of a physiological origin such as a biochemical imbalance, they may logically be dealt with best by physiological means such as drug treatment or even diet control. Recent work has demonstrated the interactions between diet and neurochemical processes (Anderson, 1981; Growdon & Wurtman, 1979), and examined the effect of diet on mood, sleep, and neurotransmitter (5HT) activity (Crisp, 1980). Following this the suggestion was made that clinical ecology has a place in psychiatry (Rippere & Adams, 1982).

Concerning treatment of psychiatric disorders by means of medication, the following points need to be considered. Continued use of neuroleptic medication following discharge from hospital has been advocated because of high rate of relapse which in one study was reported to be as high as 80 percent within 2 years (Hogarty et al., 1974). Continued medication is of proven efficacy in the prevention of relapse particularly in those who manage to survive for 1 year (Hogarty, 1984). However, those who continue to take medication even though asymptomatic are at risk of relapse if medication is discontinued (Hogarty, 1984). Thus, although drugs may successfully control the symptoms of schizophrenia, they do not seem to resolve the underlying process (Birchwood et al., 1988). This would be particularly so in those instances where the psychiatric disorder was of psychological origin. Furthermore, because of the interrelationships between the four disorders previously described, those drugs which alleviate one disorder would inevitably be likely to induce the symptoms of the inversely related disorder during treatment. It must therefore be stressed that when a disorder is of psychological origin, physiological treatment such as drug administration could temporarily alleviate the symptoms, but would not directly, or permanently, remove the cause. When the disorders are of psychological origin they may logically be best dealt with, in the long term, by psychological means (although this approach may be logically best, it may appear to be economically not the best).

SUMMARY

The disorders of epilepsy, schizophrenia, Parkinsonian disorders, and clinical depression have been discussed in terms of their physiological and psychological characteristics and in relation to interaction between the cerebellum/naturomorphic sub-system and the cerebrum/abstract sub-system. It is proposed that the characteristics of each of these disorders in themselves, and in relation to one another, may be interpreted in terms of interaction between the cerebellum/naturomorphic sub-system and the cerebrum/abstract sub-system. That is, they may be interpreted in terms of the learning-based homeostatic process, and in particular, partly in terms of the updating process of dreaming.

Bibliography

Abbie, A. (1941). The anatomy of the cerebellum. *Medical Journal of Australia*, 28, 159–163.

Adams, D. (1969). The anatomy of memory mechanisms in the human brain. In G. Talland & N. Waugh (Eds.), *The pathology of memory.* New York: Academic.

Adey, W. (1965). Personal communication. Cited in S. Smythies (1970), *Brain mechanisms and behaviour.* Oxford: Blackwell Scientific.

Adey, W., & Tokizane, T. (Eds.) (1967). *Progress in brain research: Vol. 27. Structure and function of the limbic system.* Amsterdam: Elsevier.

Adrian, E. (1943). Afferent areas in the cerebellum connected with the limbs. *Brain, 66,* 289–315.

Adrien, J. (1976). Ontogenesis of PGO activity in the kitten. In W. Koella & P. Levin (Eds.), *Sleep. Proceedings of the third European Congress on sleep research.* Basel: Karger.

Adrien, J. (1978). Ontogenesis of some sleep mechanisms. In M. Corner et al. (Eds.), *Progress in brain research: Vol. 48. Maturation of the nervous system.* Amsterdam: Elsevier.

Akiskal, H. (1979). A bio-behavioural approach to depression. In R. Depue (Ed.), *The psychobiology of the depressive disorders.* New York: Academic.

Akiskal, H., et al. (1978). The nosological status of neurotic depression. *Archives of General Psychiatry, 35,* 756–766.

Albe-Fessard, D., & Fessard, A. (1961). Thalamic integrations and their consequences at the telencephalic level. In G. Moruzzi et al. (Eds.), *Progress in brain research: Vol. 1. Brain mechanisms.* Amsterdam: Elsevier.

Albe-Fessard, D., & Rougeul, A. (1955). Activities bilaterales tardives evoquees sur le cortex du chat sous choralose par stimulation d'une voie somesthesique. *Journal of Physiology* (Paris), *47,* 69–72.

Albe-Fessard, D., & Rougeul, A. (1958). Activities d'origine somesthesique evoquees sur les cortex non-specifique du chat anesthesie au chloralose. *EEG Clinical Neurophysiology, 10,* 131–152.

Albus, J. (1971). A theory of cerebellar function. *Mathematical Bioscience, 10,* 25–61.

Alihanka, J., et al. (1975). Oculomotor outflow and its relation to electrical activity of supra sylvian gyrus and pulvinar during paradoxical sleep in the cat. *EEG Clinical Neurophysiology, 39,* 9–19.

Allinsmith, W., & Goethals, G. (1962). *The role of schools in mental health.* New York: Basic.

Allport, D., et al. (1972). On the division of attention. *Quarterly Journal of Experimental Psychology, 24,* 225–235.

Allport, G. (1924). Eidetic imagery. *British Journal of Psychology, 15,* 99–120.

Anderson, C. (1983). Imagination and expectation. *Journal of Personality and Social Psychology, 45,* 293–305.

Anderson, G. (1981). Diet, neurotransmitters and brain function. *British Medical Bulletin, 37,* 95–100.

Angeleri, F. (1974). Partial epilepsies and nocturnal sleep. In P. Levin & W. Koella (Eds.), *Sleep. Proceedings of the second European Congress on sleep research.* Basel: Karger.

Appell, M., & Goldberg, L. (Eds.). (1977). *Topics in cognitive development* (Vol. 1). London: Plenum.

Arbib, M. (1972). *The metaphorical brain.* New York: Wiley.

Arduini, A., & Hirao, T. (1959). On the mechanism of the EEG sleep pattern elicited by acute visual deafferentation. *Archives of Italian Biology, 97,* 140–155.

Arieti, S. (1966). Creativity and its cultivation. In S. Arieti (Ed.), *American handbook of psychiatry* (Vol. 3). New York: Basic.

Arieti, S. (1970). Cognition and feeling. In M. Arnold (Ed.), *Feelings and emotions.* London: Academic.

Arieti, S. (1974). *Interpretation of schizophrenia.* London: Crosby.

Aserinsky, E., & Kleitman, N. (1953). Regularly occurring periods of eye motility and concomitant phenomena during sleep. *Science, 118,* 273–274.

Aserinsky, E., & Kleitman, N. (1955). Two types of ocular motility occurring in sleep. *Journal of Applied Physiology, 8,* 1–10.

Asgian, B., et al. (1973). Investigations on the effects of LSD-25 in schizoid syndromes with paroxysmal EEG manifestations of the temporal lobe. In W. Koella & P. Levin (Eds.), *Sleep. Proceedings of the first European Congress on sleep research.* Basel: Karger.

Ashby, W. (1956a). Design for an intelligence amplifier. In C. Shannon & J. McCarthy (Eds.), *Automata studies.* Princeton: Princeton University Press.

Ashby, W. (1956b). *An introduction to cybernetics.* London: Chapman & Hall.

Ashby, W. (1960). *Design for a brain.* New York: Wiley.

Asso, D. (1969). W.A.I.S. scores in a group of Parkinson patients. *British Journal of Psychiatry, 115,* 555–556.

Attneave, F. (1972). Representation of physical space. In A. Melton & E. Martin (Eds.), *Coding processes in human memory.* Washington, DC: Winston.

Ayer, A. (1946). *Language, truth and logic.* London: Victor Gollancz.

Aylwin, S. (1985). *Structure in thought and feeling.* London: Methuen.

Baldwin, M., & Bailey, P. (Eds.). (1958). *Temporal lobe epilepsy.* Springfield IL: C. C. Thomas.

Bandura, A. (1977). *Social learning theory.* Englewood Cliffs, NJ: Prentice-Hall.

Bandura, A. (1978a). Reflections on self-efficacy. *Advances in Behavior Research and Therapy, 1,* 237–269.

Bandura, A. (1978b). The self system in reciprocal determinism. *American Psychologist, 33,* 344–358.

Bantli, H., et al. (1976). Activation of neurons in the cerebellar nuclei and ascending reticular formation by stimulation of the cerebellar surface. *Journal of Neurosurgery, 45,* 539–554.

Barbeau, A. (1971). Long term side-effects of Levodopa. *Lancet, 1,* 395.

Barber, P., & Legge, D. (1976). *Perception and information.* London: Methuen.

Barr, M. (1979). *The human nervous system.* London: Harper & Row.

Basser, L. (1962). Hemiplegia of early onset and the faculty of speech with special reference to the effects of hemispherectomy. *Brain, 85,* 427–460.

Batini, C., et al. (1959a). Effects of complete pontine transections on the sleep-wakefulness rhythm. *Archives of Italian Biology, 97,* 1–12.

Batini, C., et al. (1959a). Neural mechanisms underlying the enduring EEG and behavioral activation in the midpontine pretrigeminal cat. *Archives of Italian Biology, 97,* 13–25.

Bechterew, W. (1905). *Principles of the theory of brain function* (4th ed.). Leningrad.

Beck, A. (1967). *Depression.* New York: Harper & Row.

Beck, A., et al. (1979). *Cognitive therapy of depression.* New York: Wiley.

Beck, A., et al. (1986). *Anxiety disorders and phobias.* New York: Basic.

Beck, D. (1978). Metaphor as a mediator between semantic and analogic modes of thought. *Current Anthropology, 19,* 83–97.

Bell, G., et al. (1968). *Textbook of physiology and biochemistry.* Edinburgh: Livingstone.

Berger, R. (1967). When is a dream is a dream is a dream? *Experimental Neurology Supplement, 4,* 15–18.

Berger, R. (1969). The sleep and dream cycle. In A. Kales (Ed.), *Sleep. A symposium.* Philadelphia: Lippincott.

Bergonzi, P., et al. (1973). Selective deprivation of sleep stages in epilepsies. In W. Koella & P. Levin (Eds.), *Sleep. Proceedings of the first European congress on sleep research.* Basel: Karger.

Berlucchi, G., et al. (1967). Changes in click evoked responses in the auditory system and cerebellum of free moving cats during sleep and waking. *Archives of Italian Biology, 105,* 118–135.

Berlyne, D. (1965). *Structure and direction in thinking.* New York: Wiley.

Bernard, M., & Joyce, M. (1984). *Rational-emotive therapy with children and adolescents.* New York: Wiley.

Bernston, G., et al. (1973). Evidence for higher functions of the cerebellum. *Proceedings of the National Academy of Sciences,* U.S.A., *70,* 2497–2499.

Bernston, G., & Torello, M. (1982). The paleocerebellum and the integration of behavioural function. *Physiological Psychology, 10,* 2–12.

Beurle, R. (1956). Properties of a mass of cells capable of regenerating impulses. *Philosophical Transactions of the Royal Society, 240,* 55–94.

Beurle, R. (1962). Storage and manipulation of information in random networks. In C. Muses (Ed.), *Aspects of the theory of artificial intelligence.* Proceedings of First international symposium on biosimulation. New York: Plenum.

Beveridge, M., & Parkins, E. (1987). Visual representation in analogical problem solving. *Memory and Cognition, 15,* 230–237.

Birchwood, M., et al. (1988). *Schizophrenia.* London: Longman.

Birkmayer, W., et al. (1975). Dopaminergic supersensitivity in Parkinsonism. In D. Calne et al. (Eds.), *Advances in neurology: Vol. 9. Dopaminergic mechanisms.* New York: Raven.

Bishop, G. (1959). The relation between nerve fibre size and sensory modality. *Journal of Nervous and Mental Disorders, 128,* 89–114

Bize, P. (1976). The comparator function in the regulation of mental life. *Kybernetes, 5,* 177–180.

Bizzi, E., & Brooks, D. (1963). Pontine reticular formation: relation to lateral geniculate nucleus during sleep. *Science, 141,* 270–272.

Blaney, P. (1986). Affect and memory. *Psychological Bulletin, 99,* 229–246.

Bliss, E., et al. (1959). Studies of sleep deprivation relationship to schizophrenia. *Archives of Neurological Psychiatry, 81,* 348–359.

Bloedel, J. (1973). Cerebellar afferent systems: A review. *Progress in Neurobiology, 2,* 1–68.

Blomfield, S., & Marr, D. (1970). How the cerebellum may be used. *Nature, 227,* 1224–1228.

Blundell, J. (1975). *Physiological psychology.* London: Methuen.

Bobrow, D. (1975). Dimensions of representation. In D. Bobrow & A. Collins (Eds.), *Representation and understanding.* New York: Academic.

Bobrow, D., & Collins, A. (Eds.). (1975). *Representation and understanding.* New York: Academic.

Bobrow, D., & Norman, D. (1975). Some principles of memory schemata. In D. Bobrow & A. Collins (Eds.), *Representation and understanding.* New York: Academic.

Boden, M. (1982). Is equilibration important?—A view from artificial intelligence. *British Journal of Psychology, 73,* 165–173.

Boden, M. (1983). Interdisciplinary epistemology. In S. Modgil, et al. (Eds.), *Jean Piaget.* London: Routledge & Kegan Paul.

Bogdanski, D., et al. (1958). Pharmacological studies with the serotonin precursor 5-hydroxytryptophane. *Journal of Pharmacology and Experimental Therapeutics, 122,* 182–194.

Bohm, K. (1980). *Wholeness and the implicate order.* London: Routledge & Kegan Paul.

Bower, G. (1972). Mental imagery and associative learning. In L. Gregg (Ed.), *Cognition in learning and memory.* New York: Wiley.

Bowker, R., & Morrison, A. (1976). The PGO spike. In W. Koella & P. Levin (Eds.), *Sleep. Proceedings of the third European congress on sleep research.* Basel: Karger.

Brady, J. (1975). Toward a behavioural biology of emotion. In L. Levi (Ed.), *Emotions: Their parameters and measurement.* New York: Raven.

Brain, W. (1958). The physiological basis of consciousness. *Brain, 81,* 426–455.

Brain, W. (1963). Some reflections on brain and mind. *Brain, 86,* 381–402.

Brand, M., & Harnish, R. (Eds.). (1986). *The representation of knowledge and belief.* Tuscon: University of Arizona Press.

Brazier, M. (1963). How can models of information theory be used in neurophysiology? In W. Fields & S. Abbot (Eds.), *Information storage and neural control.* Springfield, IL: C. C. Thomas.

Bridger, W. (1960). Signalling systems in the development of cognitive functioning. In M. Brazier (Ed.), *The central nervous system and behaviour.* New York: Josiah Macy Jr. Foundation.

Brierly, J. (1976). *The growing brain.* Slough, England: N.F.E.R. Publishing.

Broadbent, D. (1958). *Perception and communication.* London: Pergamon.

Brodal, A. (1957). *The reticular formation of the brain stem.* London: Oliver & Boyd.

Brogden, W., & Gantt, W. (1937). Cerebellar conditioned reflexes. *American Journal of Physiology, 119,* 277–278.

Brogden, W., & Gantt, W. (1942). Intraneural conditioning: Cerebellar conditioned reflexes. *Archives of Neurological Psychiatry, 48,* 437–455.

Bronson, G. (1965). The hierarchical organisation of the central nervous system. *Behavioral Science, 10,* 7–25.

Brooks, D. (1976). The PGO phenomena. In W. Koella & P. Levin (Eds.), *Sleep. Proceedings of the third European congress on sleep research.* Basel: Karger.

Brooks, D., & Bizzi, E. (1963). Brainstem electrical activity during sleep. *Archives of Italian Biology, 101,* 648–665.

Brooks, D., & Gershon, M. (1972). An analysis of the effect of reserpine upon ponto-geniculo-occipital activity in the cat. *Neuropharmacology, 11,* 499–510.

Broughton, R. (1973). Confusional sleep disorders. In P. MacLean *A triune concept of brain and behaviour.* Toronto: University of Toronto Press.

Broughton, R. (1978). Sleep and epilepsy. In British Epilepsy Association (Ed.), *Epilepsy 1978* (pp. 57–62). Leeds: British Epilepsy Association.

Brown, G., & Desforges, C. (1979). *Piaget's theory.* London: Routledge & Kegan Paul.

Bruch, M., et al. (1986). Beliefs and the subjective meaning of thoughts. *Cognitive Therapy and Research, 10,* 51–69.

Bruner, J. (1964). The course of cognitive growth. *American Psychologist, 19,* 1–15.

Bruner, J. (1973). *Beyond the information given.* London: Allen & Unwin.

Bruner, J. (1986). *The narrative mode of thought.* Paper presented at the Annual Conference of the British Psychological Society. Sheffield, April.

Bruner, J., et al. (1966). *Studies in cognitive growth.* New York: Wiley.

Buchtel, H. (1970). Visual learning deficits following cerebellar damage in rats. *Journal of Comparative Physiological Psychology, 72,* 296–305.

Budzinski, J. (1977). Turning on in the twilight zone. *Psychology Today, 11,* 38–44.

Buell, F., & Biehl, J. (1949). The influence of hypnosis on the tremor of Parkinson's disease. *Diseases of the Nervous System, 10,* 20–23

Bugelski, B. (1970). Words and things and images. *American Psychologist, 25,* 1002–1012

Bullock, T. (1969). Discussion. In R. Llinas (Ed.), *Neurobiology of cerebellar evolution and development* (p. 536). Chicago: American Medical Association.

Buser, P., & Borenstein, P. (1956). Observations sur les responses corticales visuelles recueillies dans le cortex associatif suprasylvien schez le chat sous chloralose. *Journal of Physiology* (Paris), *48,* 422–424.

Cadilhac, J., et al. (1961). Modifications de l'activite de l'hippocampus suivant les divers stades du sommeil spontanee chez le chat. *Revue Neurologique, 105,* 171–176.

Calne, D. (Ed.). (1973). *Advances in neurology: Vol. 3. Progress in the treatment of Parkinsonism.* New York: Raven.

Calne, D., et al. (Eds.). (1975). *Advances in neurology: Vol. 9.* New York: Raven.

Carli, G., & Zanchetti, A. (1965). A study of pontine lesions suppressing deep sleep in the cat. *Archives of Italian Biology, 103,* 752–788.

Carmon, A. (1971). Sequential motor performance in patients with unilateral cerebral lesions. *Neuropsychologia, 9,* 445–451.

Carnap, R. (1958). *Introduction to symbolic logic and its application.* New York: Dover.

Carpenter, M., & Hanna, G. (1962). Effects of thalamic lesions upon cerebellar dyskinesia in the Rhesus monkey. *Journal of Comparative Neurology, 119,* 127–147.

Carrea, R. (1970). In discussion. In W. Fields & W. Willis (Eds.), *The cerebellum in health and disease.* St. Louis: Green.

Carroll, J. (1978). The effect of imagining an event on expectations for the event. *Journal of Experimental Social Psychology, 14,* 88–96.

Cartwright, R., & Ratzel, R. (1972). Effects of dream loss on waking behaviours. *Archives of General Psychiatry, 27,* 277–280.

Catani, P., & Finji, F. (1980). Paradoxical sleep and rapid eye movements during normal child development. In L. Popoviciu et al. (Eds.), *Sleep. Proceedings of the fourth international congress on sleep research.* Basel: Karger.

Celesia, G., & Barr, A. (1970). Psychosis and other psychiatric manifestations of levodopa therapy. *Archives of Neurology, 23,* 193–200.

Cespuglio, R., & Valtax, J. (1976). Genetic factors of the phasic phenomenon of paradoxical sleep. In W. Koella & P. Levin (Eds.), *Sleep. Proceedings of the third European congress on sleep research.* Basel: Karger.

Chafe, W. (1975). Creativity in verbalisation as evidence for analogic knowledge. In R. Schank & B. Nash-Weber (Eds.), *Theoretical issues in natural language processing.* Cambridge, MA: Bolt Beranek and Newman Inc.

Chalupa, L., et al. (1976). Effect of pulvinar lesions on visual pattern discrimination in monkeys. *Journal of Neurophysiology, 39,* 354–369.

Chambers, W., & Sprague, J. (1955). Functional localisation in the cerebellum. *Archives of Neurological Psychiatry, 74,* 653–680.

Chase, M. (Ed.). (1972). *The sleeping brain.* Los Angeles: Brain Information Service.

Chomsky, N. (1966). *Cartesian linguistics.* New York: Harper & Row

Chu, N., & Bloom, F. (1973). Norepinephrine containing neurons. *Science, 179,* 908–910.

Clark, M., & Fiske, S. (Eds.). (1982). *Affect and cognition.* Hillsdale, NJ: Erlbaum.

Clark, S., & Ward, J. (1949). The electroencephalogram in cerebellar seizures. *Electroencephalography and Clinical Neurophysiology, 1,* 299–304.

Cole, D., & Rehm, L. (1986). Family interaction patterns and childhood depression. *Journal of Abnormal Child Psychology, 14,* 297–314.

Conel, J. (1963). Postnatal development of the human cerebral cortex. Cambridge MA: Harvard University Press.

Cooper, I. (1961). *Parkinsonism.* Springfield IL: C. C. Thomas.

Cooper, I. (Ed.). (1978). *Cerebellar stimulation in man.* New York: Raven.

Cooper, I., et al. (Eds.). (1974). *The cerebellum, epilepsy and behavior.* New York: Plenum.

Cooper, L., & Shepard, R. (1973). Chronometric studies of the rotation of mental images. In W. Chase (Ed.), *Visual information processing.* New York: Academic.

Corballis, M. (1983). *Human laterality.* New York: Academic.

Corner, M. (1978). During discussion. In M. Corner et al. (Eds.), *Progress in brain research: Vol. 48. Maturation of the nervous system.* Amsterdam: Elsevier.

Corner, M., et al. (Eds.). (1978). *Progress in brain research: Vol. 48. Maturation of the nervous system.* Amsterdam: Elsevier.

Costa, E., et al. (1960). Brain concentrations of biogenetic amines and EEG patterns of rabbits. *Journal of Pharmacology and Experimental Therapeutics, 130,* 81–88.

Courchesne, E., et al. (1987). Abnormal neuroanatomy in a non-retarded person with autism. *Archives of Neurology, 44,* 335–341.

Coyne, J., & Gotlib, I. (1983). The role of cognition in depression. *Psychological Bulletin, 94,* 472–505.

Cracco, R., & Cracco, J. (1976). Somatosensory evoked potentials in man. *EEG clin. Neurophysiology, 41,* 460–466.

Cramer, H. (1980). Melatonin and sleep. In L. Popoviciu et al. (Eds.), *Sleep. Proceedings of the fourth internal congress on sleep research.* Basel: Karger.

Crisafi, M., & Brown, A. (1986). Analogical transfer in very young children. *Child Devlop-ment, 57,* 953–968.

Crisp, A. (1980). Sleep activity, nutrition and mood. *British Journal of Psychiatry, 137,* 1–7.

Crow, T. (1980). Molecular pathology of schizophrenia. *British Medical Journal, 280,* 66–68.

Crow, T., et al. (1982). Two syndromes in schizophrenia and their pathogenesis. In F. Henn & H. Nasrallah (Eds.), *Schizophrenia as a brain disease.* Oxford: Oxford University Press.

Dalzell-Ward, A. (1967). Health education for mental health. *Health Education Journal, 26,* 192.

Dawis, R., & Siojo, L. (1972). *Analogical reasoning: A review of the literature.* (ERIC Document Service No. ED 077 947).

De Andres, I., & Reinoso-Suarez, F. (1979). Participation of the cerebellum in the regulation of the sleep-wakefulness cycle through the superior cerebellar peduncle. *Archives of Italian Biology, 117,* 140–163

De Bono, E. (1969). *The mechanism of mind.* London: Jonathan Cape.

De Crinis, M. (1934). *Aufbau und abbau der grosshirnleistungen und ihre anatomischen grunde.* Berlin: Karger.

Delafresnaye, J. (Ed.). (1954). *Brain mechanisms and consciousness.* Oxford: Blackwell Scientific.

Delorme, F., et al. (1966). Supression du sommeil par la chlorometamphetamine et par la chlorophenylalanine. *Comptes Rendus de Seances, Societe de Biologie et des Ses Filiales, 160,* 2347–2350.

Dement, W. (1965). Studies of the function of rapid eye movement (paradoxical) sleep in human subjects. In M. Jouvet (Ed.), *Aspect anatomo-fonctionells de la physiologie du sommeil.* Paris: CRS.

Dement, W. (1969). The biological role of REM sleep. In A. Kales (Ed.), *Sleep. A symposium.* Philadelphia: Lippincott.

Dement, W. (1971). The effects of the chronic administration of parachlorophenylanaline on sleep parameters. In M. Chase (Ed.), *The sleeping brain.* Los Angeles: Brain Information Service.

Dement, W., et al. (1970). A sleep researcher's odyssey. In L. Madow & L. Snow (Eds.), *The psychodynamic implications of the psychological study of dreams.* Springfield, IL: C. C. Thomas.

Dement, W., & Fisher, C. (1963). Experimental interference with the sleep cycle. *Canadian Psychiatric Association Journal, 8,* 400–405.

Dement, W., & Kleitman, N. (1957). The relation of eye movements during sleep to dream activity. *Journal of Experimental Psychology, 53,* 339–346.

Dennis, M., & Whitaker, H. (1976). Language acquisition following hemidecortication. *Brain and Language, 3,* 404–421.

Depoortere, H., & Santucci, V. (1980). The influence of antidepressant drugs on the rebound phenomena following paradoxical sleep deprivation and on the PGO activity induced by reserpine. In L. Popoviciu et al. (Eds.), *Sleep. Proceedings of the fourth international congress on sleep research.* Basel: Karger.

Dewan, E. (1970). The programming of "P" hypothesis for sleep. In E. Hartmann (Ed.), *Sleep and dreaming.* Boston: Little, Brown.

Dewan, M., et al. (1983). Cerebellar morphology in chronic schizophrenic patients. *Psychiatric Research, 10,* 97–103.

Diamond, I., & Hall, W. (1969). Evolution of neocortex. *Science, 164,* 251–262.

Diaz-Infante, L., et al. (1982). Cerebelo y psiquiatria. *Salud Mental, 5,* 25–29.

Dimond, S. (1979). Symmetry and asymmetry in the vertebrate brain. In D. Oakley & H. Plotkin (Eds.), *Brain, behaviour and evolution.* London: Methuen.

Dimond, S., & Beaumont, J. (Eds.). (1974). *Hemispheric function of the human brain.* London: Elek Science.

Dimond, S., & Blizard, D. (Eds.). (1977). *Annals of the New York Academy of Science: Vol. 229. Evolution and laterization of the brain.* New York: New York Academy of Science.

Dinnerstein, A. et al. (1962). Delayed feedback as a possible mechanism in Parkinsonism. *Perceptual and Motor Skills, 15,* 667–680.

Dixon, N. (1971). *Subliminal perception.* London: McGraw-Hill.

Dixon, N. (1972). Who believes in subliminal perception? *New Scientist, 53,* 252–255.

Domzal, T., et al. (1973). Sleep deprivation in healthy subjects and epileptics. In W. Koella & P. Levin (Eds.), *Sleep. Proceedings of the first European congress on sleep researcher.* Basel: Karger.

Douglas, R. (1967). The hippocampus and behaviour. *Psychological Bulletin, 67,* 416–442.

Douglas, R., & Pribram, K. (1966). Learning and limbic lesions. *Neuropsychologia, 4,* 197–220.

Dow, R. (1942). The evolution and anatomy of the cerebellum. *Biol. Review, 14,* 179–220.

Dow, R. (1970). Historical review of cerebellar investigation. In W. Fields & W. Willis (Eds.), *The cerebellum in health and disease.* St. Louis: Green.

Dow, R. (1978). Summary and evaluation of chronic cerebellar stimulation in man. In I. Cooper (Ed.), *Cerebellar stimulation in man.* New York: Raven.

Dow, R., et al. (1962). The influence of the cerebellum on experimental epilepsy. *Electroencephalography and Clinical Neurophysiology, 14,* 383–398.

Dreistadt, R. (1968). An analysis of the use of analogies and metaphors in science. *Journal of Psychology, 68,* 97–116.

Dretske, F. (1986). Aspects of cognitive representation. In M. Brand & R. Harnish (Eds.), *The representation of knowledge and belief.* Tucson: University of Arizona Press.

Dreyfus-Brisac, C., & Monod, N. (1964). Electroclinical studies of status epilepticus and convulsions in the newborn. In P. Kellaway & L. Petersen (Eds.), *Neurological and electroencephalographic correlative studies in infancy.* New York: Grune & Stratton.

Dunlap, K. (1914). *Images and ideas.* Johns Hopkins University Circular No. 3 25–41.

Dunlap, K. (1927). The short circuiting of conscious responses. *Journal of Philosophy, Psychology and Scientific Method, 24,* 263–267.

Eccles, J. (Ed.). (1966). *Brain and conscious experience.* Berlin: Springer.

Eccles, J. (1967). Circuits in the cerebellar control of movement. *Proceedings of the National Academy of Science.* (Washington, DC), *58,* 336–343.

Eccles, J. (1973). The cerebellum as a computer. *Journal of Physiology* (London), *229,* 1–32.

Eccles, J. (1977). *The understanding of the brain.* London: Blackiston.

Ellis, A. (1979). Toward a new theory of personality. In A. Ellis & J. Whiteley (Eds.), *Theoretical and empirical foundations of rational emotive therapy.* Monterey, CA: Brookes/Cole.

Ellis, R. (1920). Norms for some structural changes in the human cerebellum from birth to old age. *Journal of Comparative Neurology, 32,* 1–35.

Ellison, G. (1979). Chemical systems of the brain and evolution. In D. Oakley & H. Plotkin (Eds.), *Brain, behaviour and evolution.* London: Methuen.

Erickson, M. (1941). On the possible occurrence of a dream in an eight-month-old infant. *Psychoanalytic Quarterly, 10,* 382–384.

Essman, W. (1978). Anti depressant action of electroconvulsive therapy. *Lancet, 1,* 933.

Estes, W. (1964). Probability learning. In A. Melton (Ed.), *Categories of human learning.* New York: Academic.

Evans, C., & Newman, E. (1964). Dreaming. *New Scientist, 24,* 577–579.

Evans, T. (1968). A program for the solution of geometric-analogy intelligence test questions. In M. Minsky (Ed.), *Semantic information processing.* Cambridge MA: MIT Press.

Fadiga, E., & Pupilli, G. (1964). Teleceptive components of cerebellar function. *Physiological Review, 44,* 432–486.

Fanardjian, V. (1965). Recruiting response in the cerebral cortex to cerebellar stimulation: Abstract. *Electroenchepalography and Clinical Neurophysiology, 18,* 313.

Faraday, A. (1975). *The dream game.* London: Temple Smith.

Fernandez-Guardiola, A., et al. (1962). Microelectrode recording of cerebellar and cerebral unit activity during convulsive after discharge. *Experimental Neurology, 6,* 48–69.

Fernandez-Guardiola, A., et al. (1974). Changes in spontaneous neuronal firing in cerebellum red nucleus and raphe nuclear complex during convulsive activity. In I. Cooper et al. (Eds.), *The cerebellum, epilepsy and behavior.* New York: Plenum.

Ferrier, D. (1876). *The functions of the brain* (Repr. 1966). London: Dawsons.

Fields, W., & Abbot, S. (Eds.). (1963). *Information storage and neural control.* Springfield IL: C. C. Thomas.

Fields, W., & Willis, W. (Eds.). (1970). *The cerebellum in health and disease.* St. Louis: Green.

Fillion, G., & Fillion, M. (1981). Modulation of affinity of postsynaptic serotonin receptors by antidepressant drugs. *Nature, 292,* 349–351.

Fischer-Williams M. (1961). Cerebellar corticogram in extra cerebellar astrocytoma. *Electroencephalography and Clinical Neurophysiology, 13,* 627–630.

Fish, F. (1961). A neurophysiological theory of schizophrenia. *Journal of Mental Science., 107,* 828–838.

Fisher, C. (1970). Some psychoanalytic implications of recent research on sleep and dreaming. In L. Madow & L. Snow (Eds.), *The psychodynamic implications of the physiological study of dreams.* Springfield, IL: C. C. Thomas.

Fisher, R. (1975). *The chemistry of consciousness.* London: Barrie & Jenkins.

Flohr-Henry, P. (1976). Epilepsy and psychopathology. In K. Grossman (Ed.), *Recent advances in clinical psychiatry* (Vol. 2). Edinburgh: Churchill-Livingstone.

Flohr-Henry, P. (1983). Commentary and synthesis. In P. Flohr-Henry & J. Gruzellier (Eds.), *Laterality and psychopathology.* Amsterdam: Elsevier.

Flohr-Henry, P., & Gruzellier, J. (Eds.). (1983). *Laterality and psychopathology.* Amsterdam: Elsevier.

Foisoreanu, V., et al. (1980). Electrographical and thermographical researches in normal subjects while resting, during some mental processes and in different sleep stages. In L. Popoviciu et al. (Eds.), *Sleep. Proceedings of the fourth international congress on sleep research.* Basel: Karger.

Foulds, G. (1973). The relationship between the depressive illnesses. *British Journal of Psychiatry, 123,* 531–533.

Foulds, G., & Bedford, A. (1975). Hierarchy of classes of personal illness. *Psychological Medicine, 5,* 181–192.

Foulds, G., & Bedford, A. (1976). Classification of depressive illness—a reevaluation. *Psychological Medicine, 6,* 15–19.

Foulkes, D. (1967). Non rapid eye movement mentation. *Experimental Neurology Supplement, 4,* 28–38.

Fox, C., et al. (1967). Mechanism for limbic modification of cerebellar and cerebral afferent information. In W. Adey & T. Tokizane (Eds.), *Progress in brain research: Vol. 27. Structure and function of the limbic system.* Amsterdam: Elsevier.

Fox, C., & Snider, R. (Eds.). (1967). *Progress in brain research: Vol. 25. The cerebellum.* Amsterdam: Elsevier.

Fram, D., et al. (1970). L-Dopa and sleep in depressed patients. *Psychophysiology, 7,* 316–317.

Freedman, R. (1977). Interactions of antipsychotic drugs with norepinephrine and cerebellar neuronal circuitry. *Biological Psychiatry, 12,* 181–197.

Freeman, J. (1970). Responses of cat cerebellar Purkinje cells to convergent inputs from cerebral cortex and periphery sensory systems. *Journal of Neurophysiology, 33,* 697–712.

French, J. (1957). The reticular formation. *Scientific American, 196,* 54–60.

French, T. (1954). *The integration of behavior.* Chicago: Univ. Chicago Press.

French, T., & Fromm, E. (1964). *Dream interpretation.* New York: Basic.

Freud, S. (1900). *The interpretation of dreams.* In J. Strachey (Ed., Trans.), the standard edition of the *Complete psychological works of Sigmund Freud* (Vols. 4 & 5). London: Hogarth.

Freud, S. (1910). *Five lectures in psychoanalysis.* In the standard edition of the *Complete psychological works of Sigmund Freud.* (Vol 11). London: Hogarth.

Freud, S. (1915). *The unconscious.* In the standard edition of the *Complete psychological works of Sigmund Freud* (Vols. 4 & 5). London: Hogarth.

Freudenberg, R. (1979). Mental health education. In I. Sutherland (Ed.), *Health education.* London: Unwin.

Frick, R. (1982). The ego and the vestibulocerebellar system. *Psychoanalytic Quarterly, 51,* 93–122.

Friedman, A., & Polson, M. (1981). Hemispheres as independent resource systems. *Journal of Experimental Psychology: Human Perception and Performance, 7,* 1031–1058.

Fulton, J. (1936). The interrelation of the cerebrum and cerebellum in the regulation of somatic and autonomic functions. *Medicine, 15,* 247–306.

Fuxe, K. (1971). Presentation on: The neuronal circuitry of sleep. In M. Chase, (Ed.), *The sleeping brain.* Los Angeles: Brain Information Service, 1972.

Fuxe, K., et al. (1968). Localisation of indoleakylamines in CNS. *Advances in Pharmacology, 6A,* 235–251.

Gaarder, K. (1965). *Towards a conceptual model of sleep.* Paper presented to the Association for the Psychophysiological Study of Sleep, Washington, DC.

Gadea-Cirea, M. (1976). Cerebellar control of activity of the feline oculomotor system during paradoxical sleep. *Experimental Neurology, 51,* 263-265.

Gadea-Cirea, M., & Fuentes, J. (1976). Analysis of phasic activities in the lateral rectus muscle of the eyes (PALRE) during paradoxical sleep in chronic cerebellectomised cats. *Brain Research, 111,* 416-421.

Galin, D. (1974). Implications for psychiatry of left and right cerebral specialisation. *Archives of General Psychiatry, 31,* 572-583.

Galin, D. (1977). Lateral specialization and psychiatric issues. *Annals of the New York Academy of Sciences, 299,* 397-411.

Gallagher, J. (1977). Piaget's concept of equilibration. In M. Appell & L. Goldberg (Eds.), *Topics in cognitive development* (Vol. 1). London: Plenum.

Gallagher, J. (1978). The future of formal thought research: The study of analogy and metaphor. In B. Presseisan & D. Goldstein (Eds.), *Topics in cognitive development* (Vol. 2). London: Plenum.

Garcia Uria, J., et al. (1980). Modification of the sleep-wakefulness cycle after surgical removal of the cerebellar cortex. In L. Popoviciu et al. (Eds.), *Sleep. Proceedings of the fourth international congress on sleep research.* Basel: Karger.

Garfield, M. (1983). Piaget. In S. Modgil et al. (Eds.), *Jean Piaget.* London: Routledge & Kegan Paul.

Garma, A. (1966). *The psychoanalysis of dreams.* New York: Dell.

Gassel, M., et al. (1965). Activity of the red nucleus during deep, desynchronised sleep in unrestrained cats. *Archives Italiennes de Biologie, 103,* 369-396.

Gastaut, H. (1954). The brain stem and cerebral electrogenesis in relation to consciousness. In J. Delafresnaye (Ed.), *Brain mechanisms and consciousness.* Oxford: Blackwell Scientific.

Gastaut, H., et al. (1958). Clinical, electrographical and anatomical study of epilepsy induced in dogs by the ingestion of agenised proteins. In M. Baldwin & P. Bailey (Eds.), *Temporal lobe epilepsy.* Springfield, IL: C. C. Thomas.

Geffan, G. (1976). Development of hemisphere specialisation for speech perception. *Cortex, 12,* 337-346.

Gellman, R., & Miles, F. (1985). A new role for the cerebellum in conditioning? *Trends in Neuroscience, 5,* 181-182.

Geschwind, W., & Levitsky, W. (1968). Human brain: Left-right asymmetries in temporal speech region. *Science, 161,* 186-187.

Getner, D. (1982). Are scientific analogies metaphors? In D. Miall (Ed.), *Metaphor.* Sussex, England: Harvester.

Giannazzo, E., et al. (1969). Effects of chronic fastigial lesions on the sleep wakefulness rhythm of the cat. *Archives of Italian Biology, 107,* 1-18.

Gibbs, F., & Knott, A. (1949). Growth of electrical activity of the cortex. *Electroencephalography and Clinical Neurophysiology, 1,* 223-229.

Gibson, J. (1979). *The ecological approach to visual perception.* Boston: Houghton Mifflin.

Gick, M., & Holyoak, K. (1983). Schema induction and analogical transfer. *Cognitive Psychology, 15,* 1-28.

Gilbert, P. (1984). *Depression.* London: Erlbaum.

Gilbert, P. F. (1974). A theory of memory that explains the function and structure of the cerebellum. *Brain Research, 70,* 1-18.

Gillin, J., et al. (1973). REM-inhibitory effect of L-dopa infusion during human sleep. *Electroencephalography and Clinical Neurophysiology, 35,* 181-186.

Gillin, J., et al. (1974). Partial REM sleep deprivation, schizophrenia and field articulation. *Archives of General Psychiatry, 30,* 653–662.

Giora, Z. (1972). The function of the dream. *American Journal of Psychiatry, 128,* 1067–1073.

Glick, S., et al. (1977). Behaviour and neuropharmacological correlates of nigrostriatal asymmetry in rats. In S. Harnad et al. (Eds.), *Lateralization in the nervous system.* New York: Academic.

Godel, K. (1931). Cited in M. Kac & S. Ullam, *Mathematics and logic.* New York: Praeger.

Godwin-Austen, R., et al. (1969). Effects of L-dopa in Parkinson's disease. *Lancet, 2,* 165–168.

Goldberger, M., & Growden, J. (1971). Tremor at rest following cerebellar lesions in monkey: Effect of L-dopa administration. *Brain Research, 27,* 183–187.

Goldman, A. (1986). Constraints on representation. In M. Brand & R. Harnish (Eds.), *The representation of knowledge and belief.* Tucson: University of Arizona Press.

Goldstein, L., et al. (1972). Changes in interhemispheric amplitude relationships in the EEG during sleep. *Physiology and Behavior, 8,* 811–815.

Gott, P. (1973). Language after dominant hemispherectomy. *Journal of Neurology, Neurosurgery and Psychiatry, 36,* 1082–1083.

Grant, L., & Jarrard, L. (1968). Functional dissociation within hippocampus. *Brain Research, 10,* 392–401.

Gray, J. (1970). Sodium amobarbital, the hippocampal theta rhythm and the partial reinforcement extinction effect. *Psychological Review, 77,* 465–480.

Green, J., & Arduini, A. (1954). Hippocampal electrical activity in arousal. *Journal of Neurophysiology, 17,* 219–224.

Green, P., et al. (1983). Abnormal interhemispheric integration and hemispheric specialisation in schizophrenia and high-risk children. In P. Flohr-Henry & J. Gruzellier (Eds.), *Laterality and psychopathology.* Amsterdam: Elsevier.

Green, P., & Preston, M. (1981). Reinforcement of vocal correlates of auditory hallucinations by auditory feedback. *British Journal of Psychiatry, 139,* 204–208.

Green, W. (1969). LSD and the sleep dream cycle. *Experimental Med. Surgery, 27,* 138–144.

Greenberg, R., & Dewan, E. (1969). Aphasia and rapid eye movement in sleep. *Nature, 223,* 183–184.

Greenberg, R., & Pearlman, C. (1972, December). *REM sleep and the analytic process.* Report to the American Psychoanalytic Association, New York.

Greeno, J. (1980). Trends in the theory of knowledge for problem solving. In D. Tuma & F. Reif (Eds.), *Problem solving and education.* Hillsdale, NJ: Erlbaum.

Gregg, L. (1974). Perceptual structures and semantic relations. In L. Gregg (Ed.), *Knowledge and cognition.* New York: Wiley.

Gregory, W., et al. (1982). Self-relevant scenarios as mediators of likelihood estimates and compliance. *Journal of Personality and Social Psychology, 43,* 89–99.

Grey-Walter, W. (1950). In D. Hill & G. Parr (Eds.), *Electroencephalography.* London: Macdonald.

Grey-Walter, W. (1953). *The living brain.* London: Duckworth.

Grey-Walter, W. (1954). Theoretical properties of diffuse projection systems in relation to behaviour and consciousness. In J. Delafresnaye (Ed.), *Brain mechanisms and consciousness.* Oxford: Blackwell Scientific.

Gross, C., et al. (1974). Inferotemporal cortex. In F. Schmitt & F. Worden (Eds.), *The neurosciences third study program.* Cambridge, MA: MIT Press.

Grosser, G., & Siegal, A. (1971). Emergence of a tonic-phasic model for sleep and dreaming. *Psychological Bulletin, 75,* 60–72.

Growdon, J., & Wurtman, R. (1979). Dietary influences on the synthesis of neurotransmitters in brain. *Nutrition Reviews, 37,* 129–136.

Gugliemino, S., & Strata, P. (1971). Cerebellum and atonia of the desynchronised phase of sleep. *Archives of Italian Biology, 109,* 210–217.

Gutzmann, H., & Kuhl, K-P. (1987). Emotion control and cerebellar atrophy in senile dementia. *Archives of Gerontology and Geriatrics, 6,* 61–71.

Hadfield, J. (1954). *Dreams and nightmares.* Harmondsworth, UK: Penguin.

Hagbarth, K., & Finer, B. (1961). The plasticity of human withdrawal reflexes to noxious skin stimuli in lower limbs. In G. Moruzzi et al. (Eds.), *Progress in brain research: Vol. 1. Brain mechanisms.* Amsterdam: Elsevier.

Haines, D., et al. (1984). Hypothalamo-cerebellar and cerebello-hypothalamic pathways. *Brain, Behavior and Evolution, 24,* 198–220.

Hamilton, N., et al. (1983). Psychiatric symptoms and cerebellar pathology. *American Journal of Psychiatry, 140,* 1322–1326.

Hamlyn, D. (1970). *The theory of knowledge.* London: Macmillan.

Harlay, F., et al. (1974). Activite unitaire cortico-cerebelleuse et mouvements oculaires. *Physiological Behavior, 12,* 939–949.

Harnad, S., et al. (Eds.). (1977). *Lateralization in the nervous system.* New York: Academic.

Harper, R. (1973). Relationship of neuronal activity to EEG waves during sleep and wakefulness. In M. Phillips (Ed.), *Brain unit activity during behavior.* Springfield IL: C. C. Thomas.

Hartmann, E. (1967). *The biology of dreaming.* Springfield, IL: C. C. Thomas.

Hartmann, E. (1969). The biochemistry and pharmacology of the D-state. *Experimental Medicine and Surgery, 27,* 120–150.

Hartmann, E. (Ed.). (1970). *Sleep and dreaming.* Boston: Little Brown.

Hartmann, E. (1973). *The functions of sleep.* London: Yale University Press.

Hartmann, E., & Bridwell, T. (1970). Effects of AMPT, L-Dopa, and L-tryptophane on sleep in the rat. *Psychophysiology, 7,* 313.

Hasher, L., & Zacks, R. (1979). Automatic and effortful processes in memory. *Journal of Experimental Psychology: General, 108,* 356–388.

Hasse, H., & Jansen, P. (1965). *The action of neuroleptic drugs yearbook.* Chicago: Medical Publisher.

Hawkins, D., et al. (1967). The psychophysiology of sleep in psychotic depression. *Psychosomatic Medicine, 29,* 329–344.

Hayes-Roth, F. (1978). The role of partial and best matches in knowledge systems. In D. Waterman & F. Hayes-Roth (Eds.), *Pattern directed interference systems.* New York: Academic.

Heath, R. (1962). Common characteristics of epilepsy and schizophrenia. *American Journal of Psychiatry, 119,* 1013–1026.

Heath, R. (1975). Brain function and behaviour. *Journal of Nervous and Mental Disorders, 160,* 159–175.

Heath, R. (1976). Correlation of brain function with emotional behaviour. *Biological Psychiatry, 11,* 463–480.

Heath, R. (1977). Modulation of emotion with a brain pacemaker. *Journal of Nervous and Mental Disorders, 165,* 300–317.

Heath, R., et al. (1979). Gross pathology of the cerebellum in patients diagnosed and treated as functional psychiatric disorders. *Journal of Nervous and Mental Disorders, 167,* 585–592.

Hempel, C. (1965). *Aspects of scientific explanation.* New York: Free Press.

Henn, F., & Nasrallah, H. (Eds.). (1982). *Schizophrenia as a brain disease.* Oxford: Oxford University Press.

Hennevin, E., & Leconte, P. (1971). La fonction du sommeil paradoxal. *L'Ann Psychologique, 2,* 489–496.

Hernandez-Peon, R. (1965). A neurophysiological model of dreams and hallucinations. *Journal of Nervous and Mental Disorders, 141,* 623–650.

Herrick, C. (1956). *The evolution of human nature.* New York: Harper & Row.

Herriot, P. (1974). *Attributes of memory.* London: Methuen.

Hilgard, E. (1973). A neodissociation interpretation of pain reduction in hypnosis. *Psychological Review, 80,* 396–411.

Hilgard, E. (1977). *Divided consciousness.* London: Wiley.

Hilgard, E., & Bower, G. (1975). *Theories of Learning.* Englewood Cliffs, NJ: Prentice-Hall.

Hill, D. (1955). Electroencephalographic evidence of cerebral maturation. In H. Waelsch (Ed.), *Biochemistry of the developing nervous system.* New York: Academic.

Himwich, W. (1964). Summary in W. Himwich & H. Himwich (Eds.), *Progress in brain research: Vol. 6. The developing brain.* Amsterdam: Elsevier.

Himwich, W., & Himwich, H. (Eds.). (1964). *Progress in brain research: Vol. 9. The developing brain.* Amsterdam: Elsevier.

Hinde, R. (1970). *Animal behaviour.* New York: McGraw-Hill.

Hobson, J. (1965). The effects of chronic brain-stem lesions on cortical and muscular activity during sleep and waking in the cat. *Electroencephalography and Clinical Neurophysiology, 19,* 41–52.

Hobson, J., et al. (1974a). The course of discharge rate changes by cat pontine brain stem neurons during the sleep cycle. *Journal of Neurophysiology, 37,* 1297–1309.

Hobson, J., et al. (1974b). Selective firing by cat pontine brain stem neurons in desynchronised sleep. *Journal of Neurophysiology, 37,* 497–511

Hobson, J., & McCarley, R. (1970). Spontaneous unit activity of cat cerebellar Purkinje cells in sleep and waking. *Psychophysiology, 7,* 311–320

Hobson, J., & McCarley, R. (1972). Spontaneous discharge rates of cat cerebellar Purkinje cells in sleep and waking. *Electroencephalography and Clinical Neurophysiology, 33,* 457–469.

Hodes, R., & Suzuki, J. (1965). Comparative thresholds of cortex, vestibular system and reticular formation in wakefulness, sleep and rapid eye movement periods. *Electroencephalography and Clinical Neurophysiology, 18,* 238–248.

Hoffer, B., et al. (1971). Spontaneous discharge of Purkinje neurons after destruction of catecholamine-containing afferents by 6-hydroxydopamine. *Brain Research, 30,* 425–430.

Hoffer, B., et al. (1973). Activation of the pathway from locus coeruleus to rat cerebellar Purkinje neurons. *Journal of Pharmacology and Experimental Therapeutics, 184,* 553–569.

Hofstadter, D. (1981). Metamagical themas. *Scientific American, 245,* 18–27.

Hogarty, G. (1984). Depot neuroleptics. *Journal of Clinical Psychiatry, 45,* 36–42.

Hogarty, G., et al. (1974). Drug and sociotherapy in the aftercare of schizophrenic patients. *Archives of General Psychiatry, 31,* 603–608.

Holland, J., et al. (1986). *Induction.* Cambridge, MA: MIT Press.

Holyoak, K. (1984). Analogical thinking and human intelligence. In R. Sternberg (Ed.), *Advances in the psychology of human intelligence* (Vol. 2). Hillsdale, NJ: Erlbaum.

Hoppe, K. (1977). Split brains and psychoanalysis. *Psychoanalytic Quarterly, 46,* 220–244.

Horel, J. (1978). The neuroanatomy of amnesia. *Brain, 101,* 403–445.

Hornykiewicz, O. (1975). Parkinsonism induced by dopaminergic antagonists. In D. Calne et al. (Eds.), *Advances in neurology: Vol. 3. Dopaminergic mechanisms.* New York: Raven.

Horowitz, M. (1972a). Image formation. In P. Sheehan (Ed.), *The function and nature of imagery.* New York: Academic.

Horowitz, M. (1972b). Modes of representation and thought. *Journal of American Psychological Association, 20,* 793–819.

Horowitz, M. (1975). Hallucinations; an information processing approach. In R. Siegal & L. West (Eds.), *Hallucinations.* New York: Wiley.

Horowitz, M. (1983). *Image formation and psychotherapy.* New York: Aronson.

Hull, C. (1943). Principles of behavior. New York: Appleton-Century-Crofts.

Humphrey, M., & Zangwill, O. (1951). Cessation of dreaming after brain injury. *Journal of Neurology, Neurosurgery and Psychiatry, 14,* 322–325.

Hunt, E. (1973). The memory we must have. In R. Shank & M. Colby (Eds.), *Computer models of thought and language.* London: Freeman.

Hunter, I. (1964). *Memory.* Harmondsworth, England: Penguin.

Hurlock, E. (1950). *Child development.* New York: McGraw-Hill.

Huttenlocher, P. (1961). Evoked and spontaneous activity in single units of medial brain stem during natural sleep and waking. *Journal of Neurophysiology, 24,* 451–468.

Ingle, D. (1973). Evolutionary perspectives on the function of the optic tectum. *Brain Behavior and Evolution, 8,* 211–237.

Inhelder, B. (1965). Operational thought and symbolic imagery. In P. Mussen (Ed.), *European research in cognitive development* (Monographs of the Society for Research in Child Development Vol. 30).

Inhelder, B., & Piaget, J. (1958). *The growth of logical thinking from childhood to adolescence.* New York: Basic Books.

Itil, T. (1969). Changes in digital computer analysed EEG during dreams and experimentally induced hallucinations. In W. Keup (Ed.), *Origin and mechanisms of hallucinations.* London: Plenum.

Ito, M. (1967). Neuronal circuitry in the cerebellar efferent system. In M. Yahr & D. Purpura (Eds.), *Neurophysiological basis of normal and abnormal motor activities.* New York: Raven.

Jacobi, J. (1974). *C. G. Jung.* London: Routledge & Kegan Paul.

Jacobowitz, H. (1963). *Electronic computers.* New York: Doubleday.

Jahoda, M. (1958). *Current concepts on mental illness and health.* New York: Basic Books.

James, W. (1890). *The principles of psychology.* New York: Holt.

Janov, A. (1978). *The anatomy of mental illness.* London: Sphere.

Jasper, H. (1949). Diffuse projection systems. *Electroencephalography and Clinical Neurophysiology, 1,* 405–419.

Jasper, H. (1958). Recent advances in our understanding of ascending activities of the reticular formation. In H. Jasper et al. (Eds.), *Reticular formation of the brain.* Boston: Little Brown.

Jasper, H., et al. (Eds.). (1958). *Reticular formation of the brain.* Boston: Little Brown.

Jasper, H., et al. (Eds.). (1969). *Basic mechanisms of the epilepsies.* Boston: Little Brown.

Jasper, H., et al. (1972). The effect of cooling the motor cortex upon experimental Parkinsonian-like tremor, shivering, voluntary movements, and thalamic unit activity in the monkey. In T. Frigyesi et al. (Eds.), *Corticothalamic projections and sensori motor activities.* New York: Raven.

Jenkins, R., & Groh, R. (1970). Psychic effects of patients treated with Levodopa. *Journal of the American Medical Association, 212,* 2265.

Jerison, J. (1973). *Evolution of the brain and intelligence.* New York: Academic.

John, E. (1967). *Mechanisms of memory.* London: Academic.

Jones, R. (1962). *Ego synthesis in dreams.* Cambridge MA: Schenkmann.

Jones, R. (1970). *The new psychology of dreaming.* London: Grune & Stratton.

Jouvet, M. (1961). Telencephalic and rhombencephalic sleep in the cat. In G. Wolstenholme & M. O'Connor (Eds.), *The nature of sleep.* Boston: Little Brown.

Jouvet, M. (1962). Recherches sur les structures nerveuses et les mechanisme responsables des differentes phases du sommeil physiologique. *Archives of Italian Biology, 100,* 125–206.

Jouvet, M. (1965). Etude de la dualite des etats de sommeil et des mechanismes de la phase paradoxale. In M. Jouvet (Ed.), *Aspects anatomo-fonctionnels de la physiologie du sommeil* (pp. 397–499). Paris. Ed. du. C.N.R.S.

Jouvet, M. (1969). Biogenetic amines and the states of sleep. *Science, 163,* 32–41.

Jouvet, M. (1974). The role of monoaminergic neurons in the regulation and function of sleep. In O. Petre-Quadens & J. Schlag (Eds.), *Brain sleep mechanisms.* New York: Academic.

Jouvet, M., & Mounier, D. (1962). Neurophysiological mechanisms of dreaming. *Electroencephalography and Clinical Neurophysiology, 14,* 424–439.

Jouvet, M., et al. (1965). Supression elective du sommeil paradoxal chez le chat par les inhibiteurs de la monoaminoxydase. *Comptes Rendus de Seances, Societie de Biologie et des Ses Filiales* (Paris), *159,* 1595–1599.

Jovanovic, U. (Ed.). (1973). *The nature of sleep.* Stuttgart: Fischer.

Jung, C. (1933). *Modern man in search of a soul.* London: Routledge & Kegan Paul.

Kagan, A. (1975). Epidemiology, disease and emotion. In L. Levi (Ed.), *Emotions: Their parameters and measurement.* New York: Raven.

Kagan, J. (1967). Biological aspects of inhibition systems. *American Journal of Diseases of Children, 114,* 507–512.

Kales, A. (Ed). (1969). *Sleep. A symposium.* Philadelphia: Lippincott.

Karamjan, A. (1962). *Evolution of the function of the cerebellum and cerebral hemispheres.* Jerusalem: Israel program for scientific translations.

Karamjan, A., et al. (1969). The functional and morphological evolution of the cerebellum and its role in behaviour. In R. Llinas (Ed.), *Neurobiology of cerebellar evolution and development.* Chicago: American Medical Association.

Katan, M. (1960). Dream and psychosis. *International Journal of Psychoanalysis, 41,* 341–351.

Kaufman, G. (1984). Mental imagery in problem solving. In A. Sheikh (Ed.), *International review of imagery* (Vol. 1). New York: Human Sciences Press.

Kellaway, P., & Petersen, I. (Eds.). (1964). *Neurological and electroencephalographic correlative studies in infancy.* New York: Grune & Stratton.

Kendel, K., et al. (1972). Der einfluss von L-dopa auf den nachtschlaf bei patienten mit Parkinsonsyndrom. *Archiv fuer Psychiatrie und Nervenkrankheiten, 216,* 82–100.

Kendell, R. (1974). The stability of psychiatric diagnoses. *British Journal of Psychiatry, 124,* 352–356.

Kepecs, J. (1954). Observations on screens and barriers in the mind. *Psychoanalytic Quarterly, 23,* 62–77.

Kimura, D. (1967). Functional asymmetry of the brain in dichotic listening. *Cortex, 3,* 163–178.

Kintsch, W. (1974). *The representation of meaning in memory.* Hillsdale, NJ: Erlbaum.

Kirvel, R. (1974). Multimodal sensory neglect in rats with radical unilateral posterior isocortical and superior collicular ablations. *Journal of Comparative Physiological Psychology, 87,* 156–162.

Kish, S., et al. (1988). Cognitive deficits in olivoponto-cerebellar atrophy. *Annals of Neurology, 24,* 200–206.

Klahr, D., & Wallace, J. (1976). *Cognitive development.* Hillsdale, NJ: Erlbaum.

Klinger, E. (1971). *Structure and functions of fantasy.* New York: Wiley.

Kluver, H., & Bucy, P. (1939). Preliminary analysis of functions of temporal lobes in monkeys. *Archives of Neurology and Psychiatry, 42,* 979.

Koella, W., & Ferry, A. (1963). Cortico-subcortical homeostasis in the cat's brain. *Science, 142,* 586–589.

Koella, W., & Levin, P. (Eds.). (1973). *Sleep. Proceedings of the first European congress on sleep research.* Basel: Karger.

Koella, W., & Levin, P. (Eds.). (1977). *Sleep. Proceedings of the third European congress on sleep research.* Basel: Karger.

Koridze, M. (1980). Effect of petit-mal and generalised seizures on the sleep-wakefulness cycle. In L. Popoviciu et al. (Eds.), *Sleep. Proceedings of the fourth international congress on sleep research.* Basel: Karger.

Kornetsky, C., & Mirsky, A. (1966). On certain psychopharmacological and physiological differences between schizophrenia and normal persons. *Psychopharmacologia, 8,* 309–318.

Kosslyn, S. (1975). Information representation in visual images. *Cognitive Psychology, 7,* 341–370.

Kosslyn, S. (1980). *Image and the mind.* Cambridge, MA: Harvard University Press.

Kosslyn, S. (1981). The medium and the message in mental imagery. *Psychological Review, 88,* 46–66.

Kosslyn, S., & Pomerantz, J. (1977). Imagery, propositions, and forms of internal representation. *Cognitive Psychology, 9,* 52–76.

Kovacs, M., & Beck, A. (1978). Maladaptive cognitive structures in depression. *American Journal of Psychiatry, 135,* 525–533.

Krames, L., & McDonald, M. (1985). Distraction and depressive cognition. *Cognitive Therapy and Research, 9,* 561–573.

Kreindler, A. (1965). *Experimental epilepsy.* Amsterdam: Elsevier.

Kremyanskiy, V. (1960). Certain peculiarities of organisms as a "system" from the point of view of physics, cybernetics and biology. *Social and General Systems Research, 5,* 221–230.

Kubie, L. (1954). Psychiatric and psychoanalytic considerations of the problem of consciousness. In J. Delafresnaye (Ed.), *Brain mechanisms and consciousness.* Oxford: Blackwell Scientific.

Kubie, L. (1966). A reconsideration of thinking, the dream process, and the dream. *Psychoanalytic Quarterly, 35,* 191–198.

Kutty, I., & Prendes, J. (1981). Psychosis and cerebellar degeneration. *Journal of Nervous and Mental Disorders, 169,* 390–393.

Laidlaw, J., & Richens, A. (1976). *A textbook of epilepsy.* Edinburgh: Churchill-Livingstone.

Landau, R., & Godfried, M. (1981). The assessment of schemata. In P. Kendall & S. Hollon (Eds.), *Assessment strategies for cognitive-behavioral interventions.* New York: Academic.

Lang, P. (1985). The cognitove psychophysiology of emotion. In A. Tuma & J. Maser (Eds.), *Anxiety and the anxiety disorders.* Hillsdale, NJ: Erlbaum.

Langworthy, O. (1933). Development of behaviour patterns and myelinisation of the nervous system in the human foetus and infant. *Contributions to Embryology, Carnegie Institute, 139,* 1–57.

Larsell, O., & Jansen, J. (1972). *The comparative anatomy and histology of the cerebellum.* Minneapolis: University of Minnesota Press.

Lashley, K. (1951). The problem, of serial order and behaviour. In L. Jeffress (Ed.), *Cerebral mechanisms and behaviour.* London: Wiley.

Lashley, K. (1954). Dynamic processes in perception. In J. Delafresnaye (Ed.), *Brain mechanisms and consciousness.* Oxford: Blackwell Scientific.

Laurent, J., et al. (1973). Topographical organisation of the PGO activity in the cat. In W. Koella & P. Levin (Eds.), *Sleep. Proceedings of the third European congress on sleep research.* Basel: Karger.

Lazarus, R., et al. (1980). Emotions. In R. Plutchik & H. Kellerman (Eds.), *Emotion: Vol. 1. Theories of emotion.* New York: Academic.

Leaton, R., & Supple, W. (1986). Cerebellar vermis. *Science, 232,* 513–515.

Legge, D., & Barber, P. (1976). *Information and skill.* London: Methuen.

Leigh, D., et al. (1977). *A concise encyclopedia of psychiatry.* Lancaster, UK: MTP Press.

Leighton, A., et al. (1957). *Explorations in social psychiatry.* London: Tavistock.

Leiner, A., et al. (1986). Does the cerebellum contribute to mental skills? *Behavioral Neuroscience, 100,* 443–454.

Lennenberg, E. (1967). *The biological foundations of language.* New York: Wiley.

Leussonhop, A., et al. (1970). Surgical disconnection of the cerebral hemispheres for intractible seizures. *Journal of the American Medical Association, 213,* 1630–1636.

Leventhal, H. (1982). Integration of emotion and cognition. In M. Clark & S. Fiske (Eds.), *Affect and cognition.* Hillsdale, NJ: Erlbaum.

Leventhal, H., & Scherer, K. (1987). The relationship of emotion to cognition. *Cognition and Emotion, 1,* 3–28.

Leventhal, M., et al. (1973). Nitrogen constituents in brain regions of paradoxical sleep-deprived rats. In W. Koella & P. Levin (Eds.), *Sleep. Proceedings of the first European congress on sleep research.* Basel: Karger.

Levi, L. (Ed.). (1975). *Emotions: Their parameters and measurement.* New York: Raven.

Levin, P., & Koella, W. (Eds.). (1975). *Sleep. Proceedings of the second European congress on sleep research.* Basel: Karger.

Levinson, H. (1980). *A solution to the riddle of dyslexia.* New York: Springer-Verlag.

Levy, J. (1969). Possible basis for the evolution of lateral specialisation of the human brain. *Nature, 224,* 614–615.

Levy, J. (1974). Psychological implications of bilateral assymetry. In S. Dimond & J. Beaumont (Eds.), *Hemispheric function of the human brain.* London: Ekek Science.

Lewin, R. (1974). The poverty of undernourished brains. *New Science, 64,* 268–271.

Lin, T., et al. (1961). Observations on the rhythm of Parkinsonian tremor. *Electroencephalography Clinical Neurophysiology, 13,* 631–634.

Lindsley, D. (1939). A longitudinal study of the occipital alpha rhythm in normal children. *Journal of Genetic Psychology, 55,* 197–213.

Lindsley, D. (1959). Attention, consciousness, sleep and wakefulness. In J. Fields (Ed.), *Handbook of physiology.* Baltimore: William Wilkins (p. 1553).

Lindsley, D. (1964). Ontogeny of pleasure. In R. Heath (Ed.), *The role of pleasure in behavior.* New York: Harper & Row.

Lippman, S., et al. (1982). Cerebellar vermis dimensions on computerised tomographic scans of schizophrenic and bipolar patients. *American Journal of Psychiatry. 139,* 667–668.

Lipsitt, L., & Kaye, H. (1964). Conditioned sucking in the human newborn. *Psychonomic Science, 1,* 29.

Livingston, R. (1958). Cerebral control of afferent activity. In H. Jasper et al. (Eds.), *Reticular formation of the brain.* Boston: Little, Brown

Livingstone, W., et al. (1954). Functional organisation of the central nervous system. *Neurology, 4,* 485–496.

Ljungberg, T., & Ungerstedt, U. (1976). Sensory inattention produced by 6-hydroxydopamine induced degeneration of ascending dopamine neurons in the brain. *Experimental Neurology, 53,* 585–600.

Llinas, R. (1969a). Functional aspects of interneuronal evolution in the cerebellar cortex. In M. Brazier (Ed.), *The interneuron.* Los Angeles: University of California Press.

Llinas, R. (Ed.). (1969b). *Neurobiology of cerebellar evolution and development.* Chicago IL: American Medical Association.

Llinas, R., & Hillman, D. (1969). Physiological and morphological organisation of the cerebellar circuits in various vertebrates. In R. Llinas (Ed.), *Neurobiology of cerebellar evolution and development.* Chicago: American Medical Association.

Loranger, A., et al. (1972). Levodopa treatment of Parkinson's syndrome. *Archives of General Psychiatry, 26,* 163–168.

Lorenz, K. (1966). *On aggression.* London: Methuen.

Lowy, S. (1942). *Foundations of dream interpretation.* London: Kegan Paul.

Luchins, D., et al. (1981). Cerebral asymmetry and cerebellar atrophy in schizophrenia. *American Journal of Psychiatry, 138,* 1501–1503.

Lunzer, E. (1965). Problems of formal reasoning in test situations. In P. Mussen (Ed.), *European research in cognitive development.* (Monographs of the Society for Research in Child Development, Vol. 30).

Luria, A. (1973). *The working brain.* Harmondsworth, England: Penguin.

Maas, J. (1975). Biogenetic amines and depression. *Archives of General Psychiarty, 32,* 1357–1361.

Maas, J. (1979). Neurotransmitters and depression. *Trends in Neuroscience, 2,* 306–308.

MacFarlane, A. (1975). Olfaction in the development of social preferences in the human neonate. In *The human neonate in parent-infant interaction.* Ciba Foundation Symposium 33.

Mackay, D. (1949). On the combination of digital and analogue computing techniques in the design of analytical engines. Reprinted in National Physics Laboratory Symposium, *Mechanisms of thought processes* (Vol. 1, National Physics Laboratory Symposium No. 10). London: H.M.S.O., 1959.

Mackay, D. (1955). Cerebral activity. *Nature, 4482,* 576–5798.

Mackay, D. (1956a). The epistemological problem for automata. In C. Shannon & J. McCarthy (Eds.), *Automata studies.* Princeton, NJ: Princeton University Press.

Mackay, D. (1956b). Towards an information-flow model of human behaviour. *British Journal of Psychology, 47,* 30–43.

Mackay, D. (1958). Operational aspects of the intellect. In National Physics Laboratory Symposium, *Mechanisms of thought processes* (Vol. 1, National Physics Laboratory Symposium No. 10). London: H.M.S.O., 1959.

Mackay, D. (1965). From mechanism to mind. In J. Smythies (Ed.), *Brain and mind.* London: Routledge & Kegan Paul.

Mackay, D. (1966). Cerebral organisation and the conscious control of action. In J. Eccles (Ed.), *Brain and conscious experience.* Berlin: Springer.

Mackay, D. (1980). *Brains, machines and persons.* Glasgow: Collins.

MacLean, P. (1958). Contrasting functions of the limbic and neocortical systems of the brain and their relevance to psychophysiological aspects of medicine. *American Journal of Medicine, 25,* 611–626.

MacLean, P. (1973). *A triune concept of brain and behaviour.* Toronto: University of Toronto Press.

MacLean, P. (1975). Sensory and perceptive factors in emotional functions of the triune brain. In L. Levi (Ed.), *Emotions: Their parameters and measurement.* New York: Raven.

Madow, L., & Snow, L. (Eds.). (1970). *The psychodynamic implications of the physiological study of dreams.* Springfield IL: C. C. Thomas.

Mandler, G. (1975). Consciousness. In R. Solso (Ed.), *Information processing and cognition.* Hillsdale, NJ: Erlbaum.

Mandler, G. (1982). The structure of value. In M. Clark & S. Fiske (Eds.), *Affect and cognition.* Hillsdale, NJ: Erlbaum.

Mano, N. (1970). Changes of simple and complex spike activity of cerebellar Purkinje cells with sleep and waking. *Science, 170,* 1325–1327.

Manzoni, T., et al. (1968). EEG and behavioural sleep-like effects induced by the fastigial nucleus in unrestrained, unanestatised cats. *Archives of Italian Biology, 106,* 61–72.

Marcel, A. (1980). Conscious and preconscious recognition of polysemous words. In R. Nickerson (Ed.), *Attention and performance.* Hillsdale, NJ: Erlbaum.

Marcel, A. (1983). Conscious and unconscious perception. *Cognitive Psychology, 15,* 238–300.

Marchesi, G., & Strata, P. (1970). Climbing fibres in the cat cerebellum: modulation of activity during sleep. *Brain Research, 17,* 145–148

Marchesi, G., & Strata, P. (1971). Mossy and climbing fiber activity during phasic and tonic phenomena of sleep. *Pflugers Archive: European Journal of Physiology, 323,* 219–240.

Marchesi, G., et al. (1970). Modification of the responses evoked in the cerebellar cortex by limb nerve stimulation during wakefulness and sleep. *Brain Research, 18,* 557–559.

Marchiafava, P., & Pompeiano, O. (1964). Pyramidal influences on spinal cord during desynchronised sleep. *Archives of Italian Biology, 102,* 500–529.

Margo, A., et al. (1981). The effects of varying auditory input on schizophrenic hallucinations. *British Journal of Psychiatry, 139,* 122–127.

Markand, O., & Dyken, M. (1976). Sleep abnormalities in patients with brain stem lesions. *Neurology, 26,* 769–776.

Marr, D. (1969). A theory of cerebellar cortex. *Journal of Physiology, 202,* 437–470.

Marr, D. (1970). A theory for cerebral neocortex. *Proceedings of the Royal Society B, 176,* 161–234.

Marshall, W. (1968). *Development of the brain.* Edinburgh: Oliver & Boyd.

Martin, J. (1971). Sensory disorder in the autistic child and its implications for treatment. In M. Rutter (Ed.), *Infantile autism.* London: Churchill-Livingstone.

Maslow, A. (1970). *Motivation and personality.* New York: Harper and Row.

Mathers, L. (1971). Tectal projection to the posterior thalamus of the squirrel monkey. *Brain Research, 35,* 295–298.

Mathews, A., & MacLeod, C. (1986). Discrimination of threat cues without awareness in anxiety states. *Journal of Abnormal Psychology, 95,* 131–138.

Matsumo, H. (1961). Cerebellar rhythmic activity induced by arousal stimulation. *Electroencephalography and Clinical Neurophysiology, 13,* 538–552.

Matte-Blanco, I. (1975). *The unconscious as infinite sets.* London: Duckworth.

Mayer-Gross, W., et al. (1969). *Clinical psychiatry.* London: Balliere Tindal.

Mayeux, R., et al. (1984). Depression and Parkinson's disease. In R. Hassler & J. Christ (Eds.), *Advances in neurology (Vol. 40). Parkinson-specific motor and mental disorders.* New York: Raven.

McCaman, R., & Aprison, M. (1964). The synthetic and catabolic enzyme systems for acetylcholine and serotonin in several discrete areas of the developing rabbit brain. In W. Himwich & H. Himwich (Eds.), *Progress in brain research Vol. 9. The developing brain.* Amsterdam: Elsevier.

McCarley, R. (1982). REM sleep and depression. *American Journal of Psychiatry, 139,* 565–570.

McCleary, R., & Moore, R. (1965). *Subcortical mechanisms of behavior.* New York: Basic Books.

McClelland, J., & Rumelhart, D. (1986). A distributed model of human learning and memory. In J. McClelland & D. Rumelhart et al. (Eds.), *Parallel distributed processing: Vol. 2. Psychological and biological models.* London: MIT Press.

McClelland, J., & Rumelhart, D., et al. (Eds.). (1986). *Parallel distributed processing: Vol. 2. Psychological and biological models.* London: MIT Press.

McDonald, J. (1953). Responses following electrical stimulation of the anterior lobe of cerebellum in cat. *Journal of Neurophysiology, 16,* 69–84.

McDougall, W. (1926). *An outline of abnormal psychology.* London: Methuen.

McDowell, F., & Barbeau, A. (Eds.). (1974). *Advances in neurology: Vol. 5. Second Canadian-Amerian conference on Parkinson's Disease.* New York: Raven.

McFie, J. (1961). The effects of hemispherectomy in intellectual functioning cases of infantile hemiplegia. *Journal of Neurology, Neurosurgery and Psychiatry, 24,* 240–249.

McGhie, A., & Chapman, J. (1961). Disorders of attention and perception in early schizophrenia. *British Journal of Medical Psychology, 34,* 103–116.

McGinty, D., et al. (1973). 5-HT-containing neurons. In J. Barchas & E. Usdin (Eds.), *Serotonin and behaviour.* New York: Academic.

McGuigan, F. (1966). Covert oral behaviour in auditory hallucinations. *Psychophysiology, 3,* 73–80.

McIntyre, A. (1941). Physiology of the cerebellum. *Medical Journal of Australia, 28,* 167–172.

McKellar, P. (1979). *Mindsplit.* London: Dent.

McMaster, R., & Russell, G. (1958). Efferent pathways from the deep cerebellar nuclei of the cat. *Journal of Comparative Neurology, 110,* 205–219.

Melton, A., & Martin, E. (Eds.). (1972). *Coding processes in human memory.* Washington, DC: Winston.

Mendelson, E. (1964). *Introduction to mathematical logic.* London: Van Nostrand.

Menninger, K. (1963). *The vital balance.* New York: Viking.

Metcalf, D. (1974). In discussion: Significance of sleep parameters in early behavioural development. In O. Petre-Quadens & J. Schlag (Eds.), *Brain sleep mechanisms.* New York: Academic.

Mettler, F. (1967). Cortical and subcortical relations in abnormal motor functions. In M. Yahr & D. Purpura (Eds.), *Neurophysiological basis of normal and abnormal motor activities.* New York: Raven.

Michel, F., et al. (1964). Sur les mechanismes de l'activite de pointes au niveau du systeme visual au cours de la phase paradoxal su sommeil. *Comptes Rendus de Seances, Societie de Biologie et des Ses Filiales, 158,* 103–106.

Milechnin, A. (1967). *Hypnosis.* Bristol, UK: John Wright & Sons.

Miller, G., et al. (1960). *Plans and the structure of behaviour.* London: Holt.

Mills, C., & Weisenberg, T. (1914). Cerebellar symptoms and cerebellar localization. *Journal of the American Medical Association, 63,* 1813

Milner, B. (1970). Memory and the medial temporal regions of the brain. In K. Pribram & D. Broadbent (Eds.), *Biology of memory.* New York: Academic.

Milner, B. (1972). Disorders of learning and memory after temporal lesions in man. *Clinical Neurosurgery, 19,* 421–446.

Minsky, M. (1958). Some methods of artificial intelligence and heuristic programming. In National Physics Laboratory Symposium, *Mechanisms of thought processes.* (Vol. 1, National Physics Laboratory Symposium No. 10). London: H.M.S.O., 1959.

Mintz, S., & Alpert, M. (1972). Imagery vividness, reality testing and schizophrenic hallucinations. *Journal of Abnormal Psychology, 79,* 310–316.

Mishkin, M. (1972). Cortical visual areas and their interactions. In A. Karczmar & J. Eccles (Eds)., *Brain and human behaviour.* Berlin: Springer.

Mittelstaedt, H. (1968). Discussion. In D. Kimble (Ed.), *Experience and capacity.* New York: New York Academy of Sciences.

Mizuno, S., & Snider, R. (1961). Cerebellar influences on the evoked cerebral response. *Federation Proceedings, 20,* 348.

Modgil, S., et al. (Eds.). (1983). *Jean Piaget.* London: Routledge & Kegan Paul.

Moeser, S., & Bregman, A. (1972). The role of reference in the acquisition of a miniature artificial language. *Journal of Verbal Learning and Verbal Behavior, 11,* 759–769.

Moeser, S., & Bergman, A. (1973). Imagery and language acquisition. *Journal of Verbal Learning and Verbal Behavior, 12,* 91–98.

Molfese, D. (1977). Infant cerebral assymetry. In S. Segalowitz & F. Gruber (Eds.), *Language development and neurological theory.* New York: Academic.

Molinari, S., & Foulkes, D. (1969). Tonic and phasic events during sleep. *Perceptual and Motor Skills, 29,* 343–368.

Morgane, P. (1972). Presentation on: The neuronal circuitry of sleep. In M. Chase (Ed.), *The sleeping brain.* Los Angeles: Brain Information Service.

Morrison, A., & Bowker, R. (1973). Cerebellar and spinal contributions to the regulation of muscle tone and movement during sleep. In U. Jovanovic (Ed.), *The nature of sleep.* Stuttgart: Fischer.

Morrison, A., & Bowker, R. (1975). The biological significance of PGO spikes in the sleeping cat. *Acta Neurobiolgiae Expermentalis, 35,* 821–840.

Mortimer, J. (1975). Cerebellar responses to teleceptive stimuli in alert monkey. *Brain Research, 83,* 369–390.

Moruzzi, G. (1963). Active processes in the brain stem during sleep. *Harvey Lecture, 58,* 233–297. New York: Academic.

Moruzzi, G. (1964). Reticular influences on the EEG. *Electroencephalography and Clinical Neurophysiology, 16,* 2–17.

Moruzzi, G., et al. (Eds.). (1963). *Progress in brain research: Vol. 1. Brain mechanisms.* Amsterdam: Elsevier.

Mountcastle, V. (1975). The view from within: Pathways to the study of perception. *Johns Hopkins Medical Journal, 136,* 109–131.

Mulholland, T., et al. (1980). Components of geometric analogy solution. *Cognitive Psychology, 12,* 252–284.

Munson, J. (1974). Eye movement potentials following visual deafferentation. *Brain Research, 66,* 435–442.

Munson, J., & Hurd, R. (1973). Lateral geniculate spikes and eye movements in sleeping and awake cats following uni- and bilateral labyrinthectomy and cerebellar lesion. *Behavioral Biology, 8,* 39–45.

Murphy, D., et al. (1974). Catecholamine receptor function and depressed patients. *American Journal of Psychiatry, 131,* 1389–1391.

Murphy, D., & Henry, G. (1972). Catecholamines and memory. *Psychopharmalogia, 27,* 319–326.

Murray, E. (1959). Conflict and repression during sleep deprivation. *Journal of Abnormal and Social Psychology, 59,* 95–101.

Murray, H. (1938). *Explorations in personality.* Oxford: Oxford University Press.

Murri, L., et al. (1976). Natural secretion of growth hormone and cortisol in Parkinson's disease. In W. Koella & P. Levin (Eds.), *Sleep. Proceedings of the third European congress on sleep research.* Basel: Karger.

Mussen, P. (Ed.). (1965). *European research in cognitive development* (Monographs of the Society for Research in Child Development Vol 30).

Myslobodsky, M., et al. (1976). Hemispheric asymmetry of EEG and averaged visual evoked potentials during non-REM sleep. In W. Koella & P. Levin (Eds.), *Sleep. Proceedings of the third European congress on sleep research.* Basel: Karger.

Nakamura, S., & Iwama, K. (1975). Antidromic activation of the rat locus coruleus neurons from hippocampus, cerebral, and cerebellar cortices. *Brain Research, 99,* 372–376.

Narabayashi, H. et al. (1974). Importance of the cerebellar hemisphere in the production of tremulous movement or choreodystonic movement in monkeys. *Acta Neurochir.* (Wein), *Suppl. 21,* 35–38.

Narismhan, R. (1970). Computer simulation of natural language behaviour. In S. Kaneff (Ed.), *Picture language machines.* New York: Academic.

Nasrallah, H. (1982). Laterality and hemispheric dysfunction in schizophrenia. In F. Henn & H. Nasrallah (Eds.), *Schizophrenia as a brain disease.* Oxford: Oxford University Press.

Nasrallah, H. (1985). The unintegrated right cerebral hemispheric consciousness as an alien intruder. *Comparative Psychiatry, 26,* 273–282.

National Physics Laboratory Symposium (1959). Mechanisms of thought processes (Vol. 1. National Physics Laboratory Symposium No. 10). London: H.M.S.O.

Natsoulas, T. (1982). Conscious perception and the paradox of "blind-sight." In G. Underwood (Ed.), *Aspects of consciousness* (Vol. 3). London: Academic.

Neisser, U. (1967). *Cognitive psychology.* New York: Appleton-Century-Crofts.

Neisser, U. (1972). Changing conceptions of imagery. In P. Sheehan (Ed.), *The function and nature of imagery.* New York: Academic.

Neisser, U. (1976). *Cognition and reality.* San Francisco: Freeman.

Nelson, J., & Mazure, C. (1985). Ruminative thinking. *Journal of Affective Disorders, 9,* 41–46.

Newell, A., & Simon, H. (1959). *The simulation of human thought.* Santa Monica: Rand.

Newell, A., & Simon, H. (1972). *Human problem solving.* Englewood Cliffs, NJ: Prentice-Hall.

Niell, D., et al. (1972). Selective potentiation of locomotor effects of amphetamine by midbrain raphe lesions. *Physiological Behavior, 9,* 665–657.

Nieoullon, A., et al. (1977a). Interdependence of the nigrostriatal dopaminergic systems of the two sides of the brain in the cat. *Science, 198,* 416–418.

Nieoullon, A., et al. (1977b). Nigral and striatal dopamine release under sensory stimuli. *Nature, 269,* 340–342.

Nieoullon, A., et al. (1978). Release of dopamine in both caudate nuclei and both substantia nigrae in response to unilateral stimulation of cerebellar nuclei in the cat. *Brain Research, 148,* 143–152.

Noback, C., & Demarest, R. (1975). *The human nervous system.* New York: McGraw-Hill.

Norman, D. (1981). Twelve issues for cognitive science. In D. Norman (Ed.), *Perspectives on cognitive science.* Hillsdale, NJ: Erlbaum.

Norman, D. (1986). Reflections on cognition and parallel distributed processing. In J. McClelland & R. Rumelhart et al. (Eds.), *Parallel distributed processing: Vol. 2. Psychological and biological models.* London: MIT Press.

Oakley, D., & Plotkin, H. (Eds.). (1979). *Brain, behaviour and evolution.* London: Methuen.

Oatley, K., & Johnson-Laird, P. (1987). Towards a cognitive theory of emotions. *Cognition and Emotion, 1,* 29–50.

Ojeman, G. (1977). Asymmetric function of the thalamus in man. In S. Dimond & D. Blizard (Eds.), *Annals of the New York Academy of Science: Vol. 229. Evolution and lateralization of the brain.*

Okuma, T., & Akimoto, H. (1966). Fundamental and clinical studies on the neural mechanism of sleep. In T. Tokizane & J. Schade (Eds.), *Progress in brain research: Vol. 21B. Correlative neurosciences.* Amsterdam: Elsevier

Oldfield, R., & Marshall, J. (Eds.). (1968). *Language.* Harmondsworth, England: Penguin.

O'Leary, D. (1980). A developmental study of interhemispheric transfer in children aged 5 to 10. *Child Development, 51,* 743–750.

Olson, L., & Fuxe, K. (1971). On the projections from the locus coeruleus noradrenaline neurons. *Brain Research, 28,* 165–171.

Ornitz, E. (1970). REM sleep and the autisic child. In E. Hartmann (Ed.), *Sleep and dreaming.* Boston: Little Brown.

Oswald, I. (1974). *Sleep.* Harmondsworth, England: Penguin.

Owen, F., et al. (1978). Increased dopamine receptor sensitivity in schizophrenia. *Lancet, 2,* 223–225.

Pagano, G. (1902). Etudes sur la function du cervelet. *Archives of Italian Biology, 38,* 299–308.

Pagano, G. (1905). Essai de localisations cerebelleuses. *Archives of Italian Biology, 43,* 139–159.

Paivio, A. (1969). Mental imagery in associative learning and memory. *Psychological Review, 76,* 241-263.

Paivio, A. (1971). Imagery and language. In S. Segal (Ed.), *Imagery: Current cognitive approaches.* New York: Academic.

Paivio, A. (1974). Language and knowledge of the world. *Educational Research, 3,* 5–12.

Paivio, A. (1975). Imagery and synchronic thinking. *Canadian Psychological Review, 16,* 147-161.

Paivio, A. (1977). Images, propositions, and knowledge. In J. Nicholas (Ed.), *Images, perception and knowledge.* Dordrecht: Reidel.

Paivio, A. (1986). *Mental representations.* Oxford: Clarendon Press.

Palay, S., & Chan-Palay, V. (1973). *Cerebellar cortex.* Berlin: Springer.

Palmer, S. (1975). The nature of perceptual representation. In R. Schank & B. Nash-Weber (Eds.), *Theoretical issues in natural language processing.* Cambridge, MA: Bolt Beranek and Newman, Inc.

Papousek, H. (1965). The development of higher nervous activity in children in the first half year of life. In P. Mussen (Ed.), *European research in cognitive development* (Monographs of the Society for Research in Child Development, Vol. 30).

Parkins, E. (1986). *The cerebellum: A cognitive role?* Paper presented at the annual conference of the British Psychological Society.

Parkins, E. (1988). Equilibration and cognition. *Genetic, Social, and General Psychology Monographs, 114,* 77–96.

Parmelee, A., et al. (1967). Sleep states in premature infants. *Developmental Medicine and Child Neurology, 9,* 70–77.

Passouant, P. (1976). Chairman's introduction to session on "Sleep and epilepsy." In W. Koella & P. Levin (Eds.), *Sleep. Proceedings of the third European congress on sleep research.* Basel: Karger.

Passouant, P., et al. (1974). Night sleep and generalised epilepsies. In P. Levin & W. Koella (Eds.), *Sleep. Proceedings of the second European congress on sleep research.* Basel: Karger.

Pavlov, I. (1958). *Experimental psychology and other essays.* London: Owen.

Payne, L. (1958). In discussion of Minsky (1958), p. 32.

Pearson, R., & Pearson, L. (1976). *The vertebrate brain.* London: Academic.

Pecharde, J., et al. (1976). Parkinsonian akinesia, rigidity and tremor in the monkey. *Journal of Neurological Sciences, 28,* 147–157.

Peiper, A. (1961). *Cerebral function in childhood and infancy.* New York: Consultants Bureau.

Pellegrino, J. (1987). Measuring versus understanding individual differences in cognitive abilities. In S. Modgil & C. Modgil (Eds.), *Arthur Jensen.* London: Falmer.

Pellet, J. (1967). L'ectrocerebellogramme vermien au cours des etats de vielle et de sommeil. *Brain Research, 5,* 266–270.

Pellet, J. (1973). *Contribution a l'etude de l'ectrogenese spontanee du cortex cerebelleux vermien au cours des etats de vielle et de sommeil.* Thesis, Marseille University.

Pellet, J. (1976). Transitory muscle tone suppressions and phasic cerebellar activity during slow wave sleep in the cat. In W. Koella & P. Levin (Eds.), *Sleep. Proceedings of the third European congress on sleep research.* Basel: Karger.

Pellet, J., & Dermonville, D. (1971). Effets eveillants de la stimulation electrique repetitive du vermis au cours du sommeil avec activite coticale lent. *Psychological Behavior, 6,* 165–171.

Pellet, J., & Harlay, F. (1977). Relations entre l'activite unitaire du vermis et les ondes phasiques de l'ectrocerebellogramme au cours du sommeil chez le chat chronique. *Archives of Italian Biology, 115,* 108–135.

Penfield, W. (1954). Studies of the cerebral cortex of man. In J. Delafresnaye (Ed.), *Brain mechanisms and consciousness.* Oxford: Blackwell Scientific.

Penfield, W. (1965). Conditioning the uncommited cortex for language learning. *Brain, 88,* 787–798.

Penfield, W. (1966). Speech, perception, and the uncommitted cortex. In J. Eccles (Ed.), *Brain and conscious experience.* Berlin: Springer.

Penfield, W. (1969). Epilepsy, neurophysiology, and some brain mechanisms related to consciousness. In H. Jasper et al. (Eds.), *Basic mechanisms of the epilepsies.* Boston: Little Brown.

Penfield, W. (1975a). Introduction to the physiology of epilepsy. In D. Purpura et al. (Eds.), *Neurosurgical management of the epilepsies.* New York: Raven.

Penfield, W. (1975b). *The mystery of the mind.* Princeton: Princeton University Press.

Penfield, W., & Jasper, H. (1954). *Epilepsy and the functional anatomy of the human brain.* London: Churchill.

Penfield, W., & Mathieson, G. (1974). Memory. *Archives of Neurology, 31,* 145–154.

Penfield, W., & Perot, P. (1963). The brain's record of auditory and visual experience. *Brain, 86,* 595–696.

Perecman, E. (Ed.). (1983). *Cognitive processing in the right hemisphere.* New York: Academic.

Peters, M., & Monjan, A. (1971). Behaviour after cerebellar lesions in cats and monkeys. *Physiological Behavior, 6,* 205–206.

Petre-Quadens, O. (1974). Sleep in the human newborn. In O. Petre-Quadens & J. Schlag (Eds.), *Brain sleep mechanisms.* New York: Academic.

Petre-Quadens, O. (1980). The logic of sleep and brain-dysfunction. In L. Popoviciu et al. (Eds.), *Sleep. Proceedings of the fourth international congress on sleep research.* Basel: Karger.

Petre-Quadens, O., & Schlag, J. (Eds.). (1974). *Brain sleep mechanisms.* New York: Academic.

Piaget, J. (1927). *The child's concept of time* (repr. 1969). London: Routledge & Kegan Paul.

Piaget, J. (1936). *The origin of intelligence in the child.* London: Routledge & Kegan Paul.

Piaget, J. (1947). *The psychology of intelligence.* London: Routledge & Kegan Paul.

Piaget, J. (1958). Equilibration processes in the psychological development of the child. In H. Gruber & J. Voneche (Eds.), *The essential Piaget.* London: Routledge & Kegan Paul.

Piaget, J. (1959). *The language and thought of the child.* London: Routledge & Kegan Paul.

Piaget, J. (1967). *Biology and knowledge.* Chicago: University of Chicago Press.

Piaget, J. (1974). *Adaptation and intelligence.* Chicago: University of Chicago Press.

Piaget, J. (1975). *The development of thought.* Oxford: Blackwell.

Piaget, J. (1977a). Problems of equilibration. In M. Appell & L. Goldberg (Eds.), *Topics in cognitive development* (Vol. 1). London: Plenum.

Piaget, J. (1977b). *Understanding causality.* New York: Norton.

Piaget, J., & Inhelder, B. (1971). *Mental imagery in the child.* London: Routledge & Kegan Paul.

Piaget, J., & Inhelder, B. (1973). *Memory and intelligence.* London: Routledge & Kegan Paul.

Pickard, P. (1970). *Psychology of developing children.* London: Longmans.

Pierce, C., et al. (1965). Dream patterns in narcoleptic and hydranencephalic patients. *American Journal of Psychiatry, 122,* 402–403.

Poirier, L. (1975). Dopaminergic agonists in animal models of Parkinsonism. In D. Calne et al. (Eds.), *Advances in neurology: Vol. 9. Dopaminergic mechanisms.* New York: Raven.

Poirier, L., et al. (1974). Dopaminergic and cholinergic mechanisms in relation to postural tremor in the monkey and circling movements in the cat. In F. McDowell & A. Barbeau (Eds.), *Advances in neurology: Vol. 5. Second Canadian-American conference on Parkinson's Disease.* New York: Raven.

Polanyi, M. (1957). *Personal knowledge.* London: Routledge & Kegan Paul.

Polanyi, M. (1962). Tacit knowing. *Review of Modern Physics, 34,* 601–606.

Polc, P., et al. (1976). Effects of tricyclic and tetracyclic antidepressants on the sleep wakefulness cycle of cats. In W. Koella & P. Levin (Eds.), *Sleep. Proceedings of the third European congress on sleep research.* Basel: Karger.

Pompeiano, O. (1967a). Functional organisation of the cerebellar projections to the spinal cord. In C. Fox & R. Snider (Eds.), *Progress in brain research: Vol. 25. The cerebellum.* Amsterdam: Elsevier.

Pompeiano, O. (1967b). Sensory inhibition during motor activity in sleep. In M. Yahr & D. Purpura (Eds.), *Neurophysiological basis of normal and abnormal motor activities.* New York: Raven.

Pompeiano, O. (1969). Sleep mechanisms. In H. Jasper et al. (Eds.), *Basic mechanisms of the epilepsies.* Boston: Little Brown.

Pompeiano, O. (1970). Mechanisms of sensorimotor integration during sleep. In E. Stellar & J. Sprague (Eds.), *Progress in physiological psychology* (Vol. 3). New York: Academic.

Pompeiano, O. (1972). Cerebellar control of the vestibular pathways to spinal motoneurons and primary afferents. In A. Brodal & O. Pompeiano (Eds.), *Progress in brain research: Vol. 37. Basic aspects of central vestibular mechanisms.* Amsterdam: Elsevier.

Pompeiano, O. (1973). A neuronal model of REM sleep. In W. Koella & P. Levin (Eds.), *Sleep. Proceedings of the first European conference on sleep research.* Basel: Karger.

Pompeiano, O., & Morrison, A. (1966). Vestibular origin of the rapid eye movements during desynchronised sleep. *Experientia, 22,* 60–61.

Popoviciu, L., et al. (Eds.). (1980). *Sleep. Proceedings of the fourth international conference on sleep research.* Basel: Karger.

Popper, K. (1959). *The logic of scientific discovery.* London: Hutchinson.

Popper, K. (1963). *Conjectures and refutations.* London: Routledge & Kegan Paul.

Popper, K., & Eccles, J. (1977). *The self and its brain.* Berlin: Springer.

Posner, M., et al. (1973). On the selection of signals. *Memory and Cognition, 1,* 2–12.

Postman, L. (1968). Association and performance in the analysis of verbal learning. In T. Dixon & D. Horton (Eds.), *Verbal behavior and general behaviour theory.* Englewood Cliffs, NJ: Prentice-Hall.

Power, M., & Champion, L. (1986). Cognitive approaches to depression. *British Journal of Clinical Psychology, 25,* 201–212.

Powers, W. (1974). *Behaviour.* London: Wildwood House.

Pribram, K. (1960). The amnesic syndromes. In G. Talland & N. Waugh (Eds.), *The pathology of memory.* New York: Academic, 1969.

Pribram, K. (1963). Reinforcement revisited. In M. Jones (Ed.), *Nebraska symposium on motivation.* Nebraska: University of Nebraska Press.

Pribram, K. (1967). The new neurology and the biology of emotion. *American Psychologist, 22,* 830–838.

Pribram, K. (1969). The amnesic syndromes; disturbances in coding? In C. Talland & N. Waugh (Eds.), *The pathology of memory.* New York: Academic.

Pribram, K. (1971). *Languages of the brain.* Englewood Cliffs, NJ: Prentice-Hall.

Pribram, K., & Broadbent, D. (Eds.). (1970). *Biology of memory.* New York: Academic.

Prichard, J. (1964). The character and significance of epileptic seizures in infancy. In P. Kellaway & L. Peterson (Eds.), *Neurological and electroencephalographic correlative studies in infancy.* New York: Grune & Stratton.

Psatta, D., & Constantinescu, C. (1980). In L. Popoviciu et al. (Eds.), *Sleep. Proceedings of the fourth international congress on sleep research.* Basel: Karger.

Puca, F. et al. (1976). REM sleep and total sleep deprivation in humans. In W. Koella & P. Levin (Eds.), *Sleep. Proceedings of the third European congress on sleep research.* Basel: Karger.

Pugh, G. (1978). *The biological origin of human values.* London: Routledge & Kegan Paul.

Purpura, D., et al. (Eds.). (1975). *Neurosurgical management of the epilepsies.* New York: Raven.

Pylyshyn, Z. (1973–74). What the mind's eye tells the mind's brain. *Psychological Bulletin, 80,* 1–24.

Pylyshyn, Z. (1984). *Computation and cognition.* Cambridge, MA: MIT Press.

Quine, W. (1972). Epistemology naturalised. In J. Royce & W. Rozeboom (Eds.), *The psychology of knowing.* New York: Gordon & Breech.

Raaheim, K. (1965). Problem solving and past experience. In P. Mussen (Ed.), *European research in cognitive development* (Monographs of the Society for Research in Child Development, Vol. 30).

Raffaele, R., et al. (1971). Changes in the sleep-wakefulness rhythm after chronic bilateral interruption of the middle cerebellar peduncle in the cat. *Brain Research, 26,* 195–199.

Randall, P. (1983). Schizophrenia, abnormal connection and brain evolution. *Medical Hypothesis, 10,* 247–280.

Rayner, E. (1971). *Human development.* London: Allen Unwin.

Razran, G. (1965). Evolutionary psychology. In B. Wolman & E. Nagel (Eds.), *Scientific psychology.* New York: Basic Books.

Reichenbach, H. (1947). *Elements of symbolic logic.* New York: Free Press.

Reichenbach, H. (1956). *The direction of time.* Berkeley: University of California Press.

Reider, R., et al. (1983). Computed tomographic scans in patients with schizophrenia, schizoaffective and bipolar affective disorder. *Archives of General Psychiatry, 40,* 735–739.

Reis, D. (1974). Central noradrenergic neurons. In F. McDowell & A. Barbeau (Eds.), *Advances in neurology: Vol. 5. Second Canadian-American conference on Parkinson's Disease.* New York: Raven.

Reitman, W. (1965). *Cognition and thought.* New York: Wiley.

Reivich, M., et al. (1969). The effect of slow wave sleep and REM sleep on regional cerebral blood flow in cats. *Journal of Neurochemistry, 15,* 301–306.

Richards, W. (1971). Motion detection in man and other animals. *Brain, Behavior and Evolution, 4,* 162–181.

Richardson, J. (1972). Encoding and stimulus selection of paired associate verbal learning. In A. Melton & E. Martin (Eds.), *Coding processes in human memory.* Washington, DC: Winston.

Richardson, K., & Brynner, J. (1984). Intelligence. *International Journal of Psychology, 19,* 499–562.

Riklan, M., et al. (1974). Psychological studies of chronic cerebellar stimulation in man. In I. Cooper et al. (Eds.), *The cerebellum, epilepsy and behavior.* New York: Plenum.

Riklan, M., et al. (1978). Behavioural alterations following acute, short-term, and longer-term cerebellar stimulation in humans. In I. Cooper (Ed.), *Cerebellar stimulation in man.* New York: Raven.

Rioch, D. (1954). Psychopathological and neuropathological aspects of consciousness. In J. Delafresnaye (Ed.), *Brain mechanisms and consciousness.* Oxford: Blackwell Scientific.

Rippere, V., & Adams, N. (1982). Clinical ecology and why clinical psychology needs it. *Bulletin of the British Psychological Society, 35,* 151–152.

Risberg, J., & Ingvar, D. (1973). Increase of regional cerebral blood volume during REM-sleep in man. In W. Koella & P. Levin (Eds.), *Sleep. Proceedings of the first European congress on sleep research.* Basel: Karger.

Riss, W., et al. (1972). Levels of function and their representation in the vertebrate thalamus. *Brain, Behavior and Evolution, 6,* 26–41.

Robb, P. (1975). Focal epilepsy. In D. Purpura et al. (Eds.), *Neurosurgical management of the epilepsies.* New York: Raven.

Rock, I. (1975). *An introduction to perception.* New York: Macmillan

Roffwarg, H. et al. (1966). Ontogenetic development of the human sleep-dream cycle. *Science, 152,* 604–619.

Romer, A. (1971). *The vertebrate body.* London: Saunders.

Rorke, L., & Riggs, H. (1969). *Myelination of the brain in the newborn.* Philadelphia: Lippincott.

Rose, G. (1971). Relationship of the electrophysiological and behavioural indices of visual development in mammals. In M. Sterman et al. (Eds.), *Brain development and behavior.* New York: Academic.

Rosenblatt, F. (1958). Two theorems of statistical separability in perception. In National Physics Laboratory Symposium. *Mechanisms of thought processes* (Vol. 1, National Physics Laboratory Symposium No. 10). London: H.M.S.O., 1959.

Rossi, G., & Zanchetti, A. (1957). The brain stem reticular formation. *Archives of Italian Biology, 95,* 199–438.

Rossi, G., et al. (1961). Researches on the nervous mechanisms underlying deep sleep in the cat. *Archives of Italian Biology, 99,* 270–292.

Rossi, G., et al. (1963). An experimental study of the hypnogenic mechanisms of the brainstem. *Archives of Italian Biology, 101,* 470–492.

Rotter, J. (1966). Generalised expectancies of internal versus external control of reinforcement. *Psychological Monographs, 80,* 1–28.

Rozin, P. (1976). The evolution of intelligence and access to the cognitive unconscious. *Progress in Psychological and Physiological Psychology, 6,* 245–280.

Ruch, T. (1951). Motor systems. In S. Stevens (Ed.), *Handbook of experimental psychology.* New York: Wiley.

Rugg, H. (1963). *Imagination.* New York: Harper & Row.

Rumelhart, D. (1986). Schemata and sequential thought processes in PDP models. In J. McClelland & D. Rumelhart et al. (Eds.), *Parallel distributed processing: Vol. 2. Psychological and biological models.* London: MIT Press.

Russell, B. (1950). *An inquiry into meaning and truth.* London: Allen Unwin.

Russell, B. (1961). Introduction, in L. Wittgenstein (Ed.), *Tractatus logico-philosophicus.* London: Routledge & Kegan Paul.

Russell, J. (1894). Experimental researches into the functions of the cerebellum. *Philosophical Transactions of the Royal Society, B, 185,* 819–861.

Russell, M. (1976). Human olfactory communication. *Nature, 260,* 520–522

Sabah, N. (1972). Aspects of cerebellar computation. In *Proceedings of the European meeting in Vienna: Vol. 1. Advances in cybernetics and systems research.* London: Transcripta.

Sagan, C. (1978). *The dragons of Eden: Speculations on the evolution of human intelligence.* London: Hodder & Stoughton.

Salamy, A. (1978). Commissural transmission. *Science, 200,* 1409–1411.

Salmon, W. (1963). *Logic.* Englewood Cliffs, NJ: Prentice-Hall.

Salmon, W. (1970). Statistical explanation. In R. Colodny (Ed.), *The nature and function of scientific theories.* Pittsburgh: University of Pittsburgh Press.

Sampson, H. (1965). Deprivation of dreaming sleep by two methods. *Archives of General Psychiatry, 13,* 79–86.

Sarnat, H., & Netsky, M. (1974). *Evolution of the nervous system.* Oxford: Oxford University Press.

Sasaki, K. (1985). Cerebreo-cerebellar interactions and organisation of a fast and stable hand movement. In J. Bloedel et al. (Eds.), *Cerebellar functions.* Berlin: Springer.

Sauber, S. (1973). *Preventive educational intervention for mental health.* Cambridge, MA: Ballinger.

Sawyer, C., et al. (1961). Autonomic and EEG responses to cerebellar stimulation in rabbits. *American Journal of Physiology, 200,* 405–412.

Sayre, K. (1976). *Cybernetics and the philosophy of mind.* London: Routledge & Kegan Paul.

Schank, R., & Nash-Weber, B. (Eds.). (1975). *Theoretical issues in natural language processing.* Cambridge, MA: Bolt Beranek and Newman Inc.

Schatzman, M. (1980). Evocations of unreality. *New Science, 87,* 935–937.

Scheibel, M., & Scheibel, A. (1958). Structural substrates for integrative patterns in the brainstem reticular core. In H. Jasper et al. (Eds.), *Reticular formation of the brain.* Boston: Little Brown.

Scheibel, M., & Scheibel, A. (1964). Some structural and functional substrates of development in young cats. In W. Himwich & H. Himwich (Eds.), *Progress in brain research: Vol. 9. The developing brain.* Amsterdam: Elsevier.

Scheibel, M., & Scheibel, A. (1971). Selected structural-functional correlations in the postnatal brain. In M. Sterman et al. (Eds.), *Brain development and behavior.* New York: Academic.

Scheier, M., & Carver, C. (1977). Self-focussed attention and the experience of emotion. *Journal of Personality and Social Psychology, 35,* 625–636.
Scherer, K. (1984). On the nature and function of emotion. In K. Scherer & P. Ekman (Eds.), *Approaches to emotion.* Hillsdale, NJ: Erlbaum.
Schilder, P. (1951). *Brain and personality.* New York: International University Press.
Schildkraut, J. (1976). The current status of biological criteria for classifying the depressive disorders and predicting responses to treatment. *Psychopharmacology Bulletin, 10,* 5–25.
Schmitt, F., & Worden, F. (Eds.). (1974). *The neurosciences third study program.* Cambridge, MA: MIT Press.
Schneider, D. (1948). Time-space and the growth of the sense of reality. *Psychoanalytic Review, 35,* 229–252.
Schneider, E., et al. (1980). Sleep EEG alterations in Parkinson's disease after Levodopa long-term treatment. In L. Popoviciu et al. (Eds.), *Sleep. Proceedings of the fourth international congress on sleep research.* Basel: Karger.
Schneider, S. (1976). Selective attention in schizophrenia. *Journal of Abnormal Psychology, 85,* 167–173.
Schneider, W., et al. (1984). Automatic and control processing in attention. In R. Parasuraman & D. Davies (Eds.), *Varieties of attention.* Orlando, FL: Academic.
Schneider, W., & Shiffrin, R. (1977). Controlled and automatic human information processing. *Psychological Review, 84,* 1–66.
Schoolman, A., & Delgado, J. (1958). Cerebro-cerebellar relations in the awake cat. *Journal of Neurophysiology, 21,* 1–16.
Schroder, H., et al. (1967). *Human information processing.* London: Holt Rinehart & Winston.
Schvaneveldt, A. (1980). Comment reported during faculty seminar on the concept of structure in Piaget's genetic epistemology. In H. Silverman (Ed.), *Piaget, philosophy and the human sciences.* Sussex: Harvester.
Schweitzer, L. (1982). Evidence of right cerebral lateralisation among schizophrenic patients with left hemispheric dysfunction. *Biological Psychiatry, 17,* 721–733.
Sechzer, J., et al. (1977). Effects of neonatal hemispheric disconnection in kittens. In S, Harnad et al. (Eds.), *Lateralization in the nervous system.* New York: Academic.
Segalowitz, S., & Gruber, F. (Eds.). (1977). *Language development and neurological theory.* New York: Academic.
Serafetinedes, E., et al. (1965). EEG patterns induced by intercarotid injection of sodium amytal. *Electroencephalography and Clinical Neurophysiology, 18,* 170–175.
Shallice, T. (1972). Dual functions of consciousness. *Psychological Review, 79,* 383–393.
Shannon, C., & McCarthy, J. (Eds.). (1956). *Automata studies.* Princeton, NJ: Princeton University Press.
Shannon, C., & Weaver, W. (1949). *The mathematical theory of communication.* Urbana: University of Illinois Press.
Shapiro, S. (1967). Dreaming and the physiology of sleep. *Experimental Neurology, Suppl. 4,* 56–81.
Sheehan, P. (Ed.). (1972). *The function and nature of imagery.* New York: Academic.
Shephard, R. (1984). Ecological constraints on internal representation. *Psychological Review, 91,* 417–447.
Sherrington, C. (1906). *Integrative action of the nervous system.* New York: Scribner.
Shevrin, H., & Dickman, S. (1980). The psychological unconscious. *American Psychologist, 35,* 421–434.

Shiffrin, R., & Schneider, W. (1977). Controlled and automatic human procesing. *Psychological Review, 84,* 127–190.

Siegal, R., & West, L. (Eds.). (1975). *Hallucinations.* New York: Wiley.

Siggins, G. R., et al. (1971). Activation of a central nor-adrenergic projection of the cerebellum. *Nature, 233,* 481–483.

Sjoquist, O., & Weinstein, E. (1942). The effect of section of the medial lemniscus on proprioceptive functions in chimpanzees and monkeys. *Joural of Neurophysiology, 5,* 67–74.

Skelton, R. (1988). Bilateral cerebellar lesions disrupt conditioned eyelid responses in unrestrained rats. *Behavioral Neuroscience, 102,* 586–590.

Slade, P. (1974). The external control of auditory hallucinations. *British Journal of Social and Clinical Psychology, 13,* 73–79.

Slade, P. (1976). Towards a theory of auditory hallucinations. *British Journal of Social and Clinical Psychology, 15,* 415–423.

Slater, E., et al. (1963). The schizophrenia-like psychoses of epilepsy. *British Journal of Psychiatry, 109,* 95–129.

Sloman, A. (1968). Explaining logical necessity. *Proceedings of the Aristotelian Society, 69,* 33–50.

Sloman, A. (1971). Interactions between philosophy and artificial intelligence. *Artificial Intelligence, 2,* 209–225.

Sloman, A. (1978). *The computer revolution in philosophy.* Sussex, England: Harvester.

Smith, A. (1966). Speech and other functions after left (dominant) hemispherectomy. *Journal of Neurology, Neurosurgery and Psychiatry, 29,* 467–471.

Smith, F., & Miller, G. (Eds.). (1966). *The genesis of language.* Cambridge MA: MIT Press.

Smythies, J. (Ed.). (1965). *Brain and mind.* London: Routledge & Kegan Paul.

Smythies, J. (1970). *Brain mechanisms and behaviour.* Oxford: Blackwell Scientific.

Snider, R. (1950). Recent contributions to the anatomy and physiology of the cerebellum. *Archives of Neurology Psychiatry, 64,* 196–219.

Snider, R. (1967). Functional alterations of cerebral sensory areas of the cerebellum. *Progress in Brain Research, 25,* 322-333.

Snider, R. (1970). *Discussion.* In W. Fields & W. Willis (Eds.), *The cerebellum in health and disease.* St. Louis: Green.

Snider, R. (1974). Cerebellar modifications of abnormal discharges in cerebral sensory and motor areas. In I. Cooper et al. (Eds.), *The cerebellum epilepsy and behavior.* New York: Plenum.

Snider, R. (1975). A cerebellar-ceruleus pathway. *Brain Research, 88,* 59–63.

Snider, R., & Cooke, P. (1955). Electro-anatomical evidences for projections from cerebellum to "reticular activating" system. *Anatomical Record, 121,* 417.

Snider, R., & Eldred, E. (1948). Cerebral projections to the tactile, auditory and visual areas of the cerebellum. *Anatomical Record, 100,* 714.

Snider, R., & Maiti, A. (1976). Cerebellar contributions to the Papez circuit, *Journal of Neural Science Research, 2,* 133–146.

Snider, R., & Mitra, J. (1970). Cerebellar influences on units in sensory areas of cerebral cortex. In W. Fields & W. Willis (Eds.), *The cerebellum in health and disease.* St. Louis: Green.

Snider, R., & Sato, K. (1958). Some cerebellar influences on evoked cerebral auditory response. *Federation Proceedings, 17,* 152.

Snider, R., & Stowell, A. (1944). Receiving areas of the tactile, auditory and visual systems in the cerebellum. *Journal of Neurophysiology, 7,* 331–357.

Snider, R., & Wetzel, N. (1965). Electroencephalographic changes induced by stimulation of the cerebellum in man. *Electroencephalography and Clinical Neurophysiology, 18,* 176–183.

Snider, S. (1982). Cerebellar pathology in schizophrenia—Cause or consequence? *Neuroscience and Behavioral Reviews, 6,* 47–53.

Snider, S., & Snider, R. (1977). Alteration in forebrain catecholamine metabolism produced by cerebellar lesion in the rat. *Journal of Neural Transmission, 40,* 115–128.

Snyder, F. (1963). New biology of dreaming. *Archives of General Psychiatry, 8,* 381–391.

Snyder, F. (1969). The physiology of dreaming. In M. Kramer (Ed.), *Dream psychology and the new biology of dreams.* Springfield, IL: C. C. Thomas.

Snyder, F. (1972). NIH studies of EEG sleep in affective illness. In T. Williams et al. (Eds.), *Recent advances in the psychobiology of depressive illness* (DHEW Publication No. [HSM] 70-9053). Washington, DC: DHEW.

Sperry, R. (1952). Neurology and the mind-brain problem. *American Science, 40,* 291–312.

Sperry, R. (1966). Brain bisection and mechanisms of consciousness. In J. Eccles (Ed.), *Brain and conscious experience.* Berlin: Springer.

Sperry, R. (1974). lateral specialisation in the surgically separated hemispheres. In F. Schmitt & F. Worden (Eds.), *The neurosciences third study program.* Cambridge, MA: MIT Press.

Spinelli, D. (1970). OCCAM: A content addressable memory model for the brain. In K. Pribram & D. Broadbent (Eds.), *Biology of memory.* New York: Academic.

Sprague, J., & Chambers, W. (1957). An analysis of cerebellar function in the cat, as revealed by its partial and complete destruction, and its interaction with the cerebral cortex. *Archives of Italian Biology, 97,* 68–88

Sprague, J., et al. (1961). Attentive, affective, and adaptive behaviour in the cat. *Science, 133,* 165–173.

Stahl, B. (1977). Early and primitive brain forms. In S. Dimond & D. Blizard (Eds.), *Annals of the New York Academy of Science: Vol. 229. Evolution and lateralization of the brain.* New York: New York Academy of Sciences.

Starr, A., & Achor, J. (1975). Auditory brain stem responses in neurological disease. *Archives of Neurology, 32,* 761–768.

Sterman, M., et al. (Eds.). (1971). *Brain development and behavior.* New York: Academic.

Sternberg, R. (1977). Component processes in analogical reasoning. *Psychological Review, 84,* 353–378.

Sternberg, R. (1983). Components of human intelligence. *Cognition, 15,* 1–48.

Sternberg, R. (1984). Toward a triarchic theory of human intelligence. *Behavioral and Brain Sciences, 7,* 269–315.

Stevens, J. (1973). Psychomotor epilepsy and schizophrenia: A common anatomy. In M. Brazier (Ed.), *Epilepsy.* New York: Academic.

Stevens, J., et al. (1971). Ultradian characteristics of spontaneous seizure discharges recorded by radio telemetry in man. *Electroencephalography and Clinical Neurophysiology, 31,* 313–325.

Suinn, R. (1983). Imagery and sports. In A. Sheikh (Ed.), *Imagery.* New York: Wiley.

Swank, R., & Brendler, S. (1951). The cerebellar electrogram. *Electroencephalography and Clinical Neurophysiology, 3,* 207–212.

Talland, G., & Waugh, N. (Eds.). (1969). *The pathology of memory.* New York: Academic.

Tarski, A. (1951). *Logic, semantics and mathematics.* Oxford: Clarendon Press.

Tarski, A. (1969). Truth and proof. *Scientific American, 220,* 63–77.

Taylor, J. (Ed.). (1932). *Selected writings of John Hughlings Jackson.* Kent, England: Hodder & Stoughton.

Thagard, P. (1978). The best explanation. *Journal of Philosophy, 75,* 76-92.

Theobald, D. (1968). *An introduction to the philosophy of science.* London: Methuen.

Thierry, A., et al. (1976). Selective activation of the mesocortical DA system by stress. *Nature, 263,* 242-244.

Thomas, A. (1912). *Cerebellar functions* (Nervous and Mental Disorders Monographs No. 12).

Thompson, D., & Tulving, E. (1970). Associative encoding and retrieval. *Journal of Experimental Psychology, 86,* 255-262.

Thompson, R. (1967). *Foundations of physiological psychology.* New York: Harper & Row.

Thompson, R. F., et al. (1984). Neuronal substrates of learning and memory: a multiple-trace view. In G. Lynch et al. (Eds.), *Neurobiology of learning and memory.* New York: Guilford Press.

Thorndyke, P., & Hayes-Roth, B. (1979). The use of schemata in the acquisition and transfer of knowledge. *Cognitive Psychology, 11,* 82-106

Tinbergen, N. (1951). *A study of instinct.* Oxford: Oxford University Press.

Tomkins, S. (1962). *Affect, imagery, consciousness* (Vol. 1). Berlin: Springer.

Torda, C. (1968). Observations on a physiological process related to dreams. *Communications in Behavioral Biology, 2,* 39-45.

Torre, A., et al. (1980). Relationships between reverie, induced verbal behaviour and some polygraphic sleep parameters. In L. Popoviciu et al. (Eds.), *Sleep. Proceedings of the fourth international conference on sleep research.* Basel: Karger.

Traill, R. (1976). Acquisition of knowledge without transcendental assistance. *Kybernetes, 5,* 73-82.

Travis, A. (1955). Neurological deficiencies after ablation of the precentral motor area in Macaca mulatta. *Brain, 78,* 155.

Treisman, A. (1964). Selective attention in man. *British Medical Bulletin, 20,* 12-16.

Trevarthen, C., & Sperry, R. (1973). Perceptual unity of the ambient visual field in human commissurotomy patients. *Brain, 96,* 547-570.

Trulson, M., & Jacobs, B. (1975). Raphe neurons. *Brain Research, 97,* 350-355.

Turner, J. (1975). *Cognitive development.* London: Methuen.

Tzeng, O., et al. (1979). Visual lateralization effect in reading Chinese characters. *Nature, 282,* 499-501.

Ullmann, L., & Kranser, L. (1975). *A psychological approach to abnormal behavior.* New Jersey: Prentice-Hall.

Ullmann, M. (1958). The dream process. *American Journal of Psychotherapy, 12,* 671-690.

Ullmann, M., & Krippner, S. (1970). An experimental approach to dreams and telepathy. *American Journal of Psychiatry, 126,* 1282-1289.

Ungerstedt, U. (1971). *Acta Physiologica Scandinavica, 82,* 1-93.

Ungerstedt, U., & Arbuthnott, G. (1970). Quantitative recording of rotational behaviour in rats after 6-hydroxy-dopamine lesions of the nigrostriatal dopamine system. *Brain Research, 24,* 485-493.

Ungerstedt, U., et al. (1973). Animal models of Parkinsonism. In D. Calne (Ed.), *Advances in neurology: Vol. 3. Progress in the treatment of Parkinsonism.* New York: Raven.

Upton, A., & Cooper, I. (1976). Some neurophysiological effects of cerebellar stimulation in man. *Canadian Journal of Neurological Science, 3,* 237-254.

Uttley, A. (1956a). Conditional probability machines and conditioned reflexes. In C. Shannon & J. McCarthy (Eds.), *Automa studies*. Princeton, NJ: Princeton University Press.

Uttley, A. (1956b). Temporal and spatial patterns in a conditional probability machine. In C. Shannon & J. McCarthy (Eds.), *Automa studies*. Princeton, NJ: Princeton University Press.

Uttley, A. (1956c). A theory of the mechanism of learning based on the computation of conditional probabilities. *Proceedings of the first international congress on cybernetics*, Namur, Belgium.

Valtax, J. (1973). Possible functional roles of paradoxical sleep. In W. Koella & P. Levin (Eds.), *Sleep. Proceedings of the first European congress on sleep research*. Basel: Karger.

Van Den Burg, W., et al. (1980). Sleep disturbances in serious depression. In L. Popoviciu et al. (Eds.), *Sleep. Proceedings of the fourth international congress on sleep research*. Basel: Karger.

Van Heerden, J. (1968). *The foundation of empirical knowledge*. Wassenaar N.V. Uitgeverij: Netherlands: Wistik.

Van Heerden, J. (1970). Models for the brain. *Nature, 227*, 410–411.

Van Heerden, P. (1963). Theory of optical information storage in solids. *Applied Optics, 2*, 393–407.

Vein, A., et al. (1980). Peculiarities of night sleep in temporal epilepsy with different distribution of generalised epileptic seizures in cycle of sleep-wakefulness. In Popoviciu, L. et al. (Eds). *Sleep. Proceedings of the fourth international congress on sleep research*. Basel: Karger.

Venables, P. (1982). *Cerebral mechanisms, autonomic responsivity and attention in schizophrenia*. Paper presented at the Nebraska Symposium on Motivation, University of Nebraska, Lincoln.

Vernon, M. (1962). *The psychology of perception*. Harmondsworth, England: Penguin.

Vogel, G., et al. (1973). The effect of REM deprivation on depression. In W. Koella & P. Levin (Eds.), *Sleep. Proceedings of the first European congress on sleep research*. Basel: Karger.

Von Baumgarten, R., & Mollica, A. (1954). Der einfluss sensibiler reizung auf die entlandungsfrequenz kleinhirnabhangiger reticularizellen. *Pflugers Archive: European Journal of Physiology, 259*, 79–96.

Voneche, J., & Bovet, M. (1982). Training, research and cognitive development. In S. Modgil & C. Modgil (Eds.), *Piaget*. London: Holt Rinehart & Winston.

Vygotsky, L. (1962). *Thought and language*. Cambridge MA: MIT Press.

Wada, J. (1977). Pre-language and fundamental asymmetry of the infant brain. In S. Diamond & D. Blizard (Eds.), *Evolution and lateralization of the brain*. New York: New York Academy of Sciences.

Wada, J., et al. (1975). Cerebral hemispheric asymmetry in humans. *Archives of Neurology, 32*, 239–246.

Waldhorn, H. (1967). The place of the dream in clinical psychoanalysis. In E. Joseph (Ed.), *Monograph 2: Monograph series of the Kris study group of the New York Psychoanalytic Institute*. New York: International University Press.

Walsh, L. (1973). Surgical treatment of Parkinsonism. In D. Calne (Ed.), *Advances in neurology: Vol 3. Progress in the treatment of Parkinsonism*. New York: Raven.

Ward, J. (1970). In Discussion. In W. Fields & W. Willis (Eds.), *The cerebellum in health and disease*. St. Louis: Green.

Waterman, D., & Hayes-Roth, F. (1978a). An overview of pattern directed inference systems. In D. Waterman & F. Hayes-Roth (Eds.), *Pattern directed inference systems*. New York: Academic.

Waterman, D., & Hayes-Roth, F. (Eds.). (1978b). *Pattern directed inference systems*. New York: Academic.

Watson, J. (1925). *Behaviourism*. London: Kegan Paul, Trench & Trubner.

Watson, P. (1978). Nonmotor functions of the cerebellum. *Psychological Bulletin, 85*, 944–967.

Watson, R., et al. (1974). Neglect after mesencephalic reticular formation lesions. *Neurology* (Minneapolis), *24*, 294–298.

Watts, F., & Sharrock, R. (1985). Description and measurement of concentration problems in depressed patients. *Psychological Medicine, 15*, 317–326.

Webster, W. (1977). Hemispheric asymmetry in cats. In S. Harnad et al. (Eds.), *Lateralization in the nervous system*. New York: Academic.

Weckowicz, T., & Blewett, T. (1959). Size constancy and abstract thinking in schizophrenics. *Journal of Mental Science, 105*, 909–934.

Weinberger, D., et al. (1980). Cerebellar pathology in schizophrenia. *American Journal of Psychiatry, 137*, 359–361.

Weiskrantz, L. (1974). The interaction between the occipital and temporal cortex in vision. In F. Schmitt & F. Worden (Eds.), *The neurosciences third study program*. Cambridge, MA: MIT Press.

Weller, M., & Montagu, J. (1979). Electroencephalographic coherence in schizophrenia. In J. Gruzelier & P. Flohr-Henry (Eds.), *Hemispheric asymmetries of function in functional pathology*. Amsterdam: Elsevier.

West, L. (1962). A general theory of hallucinations and dreams. In L. West (Ed.), *Hallucinations*. New York: Grune & Stratton.

West, L., et al. (1962). The psychosis of sleep deprivation. *Annals of New York Academy of Sciences, 96*, 66–70.

Whyte, L. (1954). A hypothesis regarding brain modifications underlying memory. *Brain, 77*, 158–165.

Wiederholt, W., & Iragui-Madoz, V. (1977). Far field somatosensory projections in the rat. *Electroencephalography and Clinical Neurophysiology, 42*, 456–465.

William, M., et al. (1988). *Cognitive psychology and emotional disorders*. New York: Wiley.

Winston, P. (1978). Learning and reasoning by analogy. *Communications of Association for Computing Machinery, 23*, 689–703.

Wishner, J. (1955). A concept of efficiency in psychological health and psychopathology. *Psychology Review, 62*, 69.

Witelson, S. (1977). Early hemisphere specialisation and interhemispheric plasticity. In S. Segalowitz & F. Gruber (Eds.), *Language development and neurological theory*. New York: Academic.

Witkin, H. (1959). Perception of the upright. *Scientific American, 200*, 50–56.

Witkin, H. (1975). Some implications of research on cognitive style for problems in education. In J. Whitehead (Ed.), *Personality and learning* (Vol. 1). London: Hodder & Stoughton.

Wittgenstein, L. (1961). Tractatus logico-philosophicus (trans. D. F. Pears and B. F. McGuiness). London: Routledge & Kegan Paul.

Wolfe, B., et al. (1978). Presynaptic modulation of beta adrenergic receptors in the rat cerebral cortex after treatment with anti depressants. *Journal of Pharmacology Experimental Therapeutics, 207,* 446–457.

Wyler, A. (1974). Epileptic neurons during sleep and wakefulness. *Experimental Neurology, 42,* 593–608.

Yadalam, G., et al. (1985). Mania in two sisters with similar cerebellar disturbance. *American Journal of Psychiatry, 142,* 1067–1069.

Yahr, M., & Purpura, D. (Eds.). (1967). *Neurophysiological basis of normal and abnormal motor activities.* New York: Raven Press.

Yakolev, P., & Lecours, A. (1967). The myelogenetic cycles of regional maturation of the brain. In A. Minkowski (Ed.), *Regional development of the brain in early life.* Oxford: Blackwell Scientific Publications.

Yamaguchi, Y., et al. (1967). A study of the invasive hippocampal theta-waves to the cortex. In W. Adey & T. Tokizane (Eds.), *Progress in brain research: Vol. 27. Structure and function of the limbic system.* Amsterdam: Elsevier.

Yang, R., et al. (1976). Stimulation of pontine reticular formation supresses firing of serotonergic neurones in the dorsal raphe. *Nature, 264,* 365–368.

Yeo, C. (1979). The anatomy of the vertebrate nervous system. In D. Oakley & H. Plotkin (Eds.), *Brain, behaviour and evolution.* London: Methuen.

Yeo, C., et al. (1985). Classical conditioning of the nictitating membrane response of the rabbit. *Experimental Brain Research, 60,* 99–113.

Yoshii, N., & Ogura, H. (1960). Studies on the unit discharge of the brain stem reticular formation in the cat. *Medical Journal of Osaka University, 11,* 1–13.

Young, J. (1962). Why do we have two brains? In V. Mountcasle (Ed.), *Interhemispheric relations and cerebral dominance.* Baltimore: Johns Hopkins.

Young, J. (1964). *A model of the brain.* Oxford: Clarendon.

Young, J. (1971). *An introduction to the study of man.* Oxford: Oxford University Press.

Yukawa, H. (1973). *Creativity and intuition.* Tokyo: Kodansha International.

Zaidel, E. (1976). Unilateral auditory language comprehension on the token test following cerebral commissurotomy and hemispherectomy. *Neuropsychologia, 15,* 1–17.

Zaidel, E. (1985). Language in the right hemisphere. In D. Benson & E. Zaidel (Eds.), *The dual brain.* New York: Guilford.

Zajonc, R. (1980). Feeling and thinking. *American Psychologist, 35,* 151–175.

Zajonc, R. (1984). On the primacy of affect. *American Psychologist, 39,* 117–123.

Zangwill, O. (1974). Consciousness and the cerebral hemispheres. In S. Dimond & J. Beaumont (Eds.), *Hemispheric function of the human brain.* London: Methuen.

Zarcone, V., & Dement, W. (1969). Sleep disturbances in schizophrenia. In A. Kales (Ed.), *Sleep. A symposium.* Philadelphia: Lippincott.

Zarcone, V., et al. (1970). The effect of L-Dopa on the sleep of two depressed patients. *Psychophysiology, 7,* 314–315.

Zimkina, A. (1946). The cerebellum and sleep. *Fiziologicheski Zhurnal SSSR, 32,* 207–212.

Zucker, S. (1978). Production systems with feedback. In D. Waterman & F. Hayes-Roth (Eds.), *Pattern directed inference systems.* New York: Academic.

Index

ABOUT THE AUTHOR

E. J. PARKINS is a lecturer in the School of Education, University of Nottingham, England. Previous work includes employment as an educational psychologist in Local Education Authorities, and employment in a number of psychiatric units.

Born in Blackburn in 1951, he studied engineering at Imperial College, London from 1969–1975 and obtained the degrees of B.S. and Ph.D. After completing a postgraduate course at Oxford University, he worked for a number of years as a teacher. Subsequently, he studied psychology at Manchester University, where he was awarded the degrees of M.Ed. and M.S.

A chartered psychologist and associate fellow of the British Psychological Society, he has contributed a number of articles to various psychology journals and has presented papers at national and international conferences.

www.ingramcontent.com/pod-product-compliance
Ingram Content Group UK Ltd.
Pitfield, Milton Keynes, MK11 3LW, UK
UKHW020813290926
15470UKWH00003B/1137

9 780275 93609